HISPANIC AMERICANS:
ISSUES AND BIBLIOGRAPHY

HISPANIC AMERICANS: ISSUES AND BIBLIOGRAPHY

KARL A. LAWRENCE (EDITOR)

Nova Science Publishers, Inc.
New York

Senior Editors: Susan Boriotti and Donna Dennis
Coordinating Editor: Tatiana Shohov
Office Manager: Annette Hellinger
Graphics: Wanda Serrano
Editorial Production: Jennifer Vogt, Matthew Kozlowski and Maya Columbus
Circulation: Ave Maria Gonzalez, Indah Becker, Raymond Davis and Vladimir Klestov
Communications and Acquisitions: Serge P. Shohov
Marketing: Cathy DeGregory

Library of Congress Cataloging-in-Publication Data
Available Upon Request

ISBN: 1-59033-227-X.

Copyright © 2002 by Nova Science Publishers, Inc.
          400 Oser Ave, Suite 1600
          Hauppauge, New York 11788-3619
          Tele. 631-231-7269   Fax 631-231-8175
          e-mail: Novascience@earthlink.net
          Web Site: http://www.novapublishers.com

Printed in the United States of America

CONTENTS

PREFACE

About one out of eight people in the United States is of Hispanic origin. The Hispanic population traces its roots to Mexico, Puerto Rico, Cuba, Central and South America, and other places. This group is expected to become the largest ethnic group in the U.S. during the 21st century. This book presents issues crucial to Hispanic Americans, as well as a selective bibliography of important sources. In the bibliography section, access is provided by subject, title, and author indexes.

Chapter 1

Latino[1] Electoral Participation and Representation

Kevin Coleman

Abstract

Of all the colonizing nations of Europe, Spain alone sought to claim most of North and South America as its empire. Spain's colonial domain in North America preceded the formation of the United States by nearly 250 years, encompassing at least half of what is now the lower 48 states. Vestiges of the Spanish empire are still visible in St. Augustine (the oldest city in North America), and Santa Fe and villages across the Southwest, but the enduring legacy of Spanish colonialism is the Latino people and culture that developed from the blending of native Indian, African, and Spanish influences.

Until the 1950s, the Latino population was found mostly in the Southwest, in New York's Puerto Rican enclave, and Florida's Cuban community. In the past four decades, the Latino population of the United States has grown from four million people to a population of over 22 million. Latinos are the fastest-growing segment of the population in numerical terms (the Asian population is growing faster on a percentage basis). They are the nation's second largest minority group and are projected to become the leading minority population within the next 25 years.

Because the Latino population is geographically concentrated, the potential for exerting political leverage and power has grown along with the rapid rise in population. In California and Texas, where the Latino share is now more than 25% of the population and growing rapidly, at least two of every ten eligible voters is Latino. Political power has remained elusive, however, due to their relatively low levels of voter turnout. This report surveys the past record of Latino electoral activity and explores issues surrounding participation now and in the future.

---

[1] The term *Latino*, rather than *Hispanic*, is used in this report. Observers have long debated which term properly describes this population, and Latino and Hispanic are commonly used interchangeably. However, some observers have argued that *Hispanic* is less desirable, based on the view that the term was imposed on persons of Spanish origin by the U.S. Census Bureau. This issue is discussed in greater detail in (Latinos and Electoral Politics) Section Two of this report.

Section one surveys Latino history in the United States, outlines the rapid growth of the population in recent decades, and provides a demographic portrait of the Latino community based on the 1990 Census. The focus of the second section is Latino political participation, which has yet to reach the levels predicted when the population began to grow rapidly. Voter turnout in the Latino community is consistently lower than the national rate, but it includes nearly as many ineligible as eligible voting age citizens. This factor and others affecting voter turnout are explored in this section, along with information on voting patterns and party identification. Additional data on the Latino voting age population in selected states and congressional districts is presented in tabular form, as well as information on Latino elected officials and the results of public opinion surveys.

Section One: Latino Culture and the United States
I. Historical Overview[2]

Among the European nations that colonized the New World, Spain pursued a singularly expansive effort to claim dominion over vast territories north and south of the equator. Over several centuries of settlement, the Spanish influence in the New World, beginning with Columbus's expeditions for Ferdinand and Isabella, was lasting, widespread, and profound. The 16th century establishment of Spanish colonies in the Caribbean – Hispaniola (the Dominican Republic) in 1496, Puerto Rico in 1508, Jamaica in 1509, and Cuba in 1511 – provided secure posts for launching expeditions into the interior of the Americas. Although Spain eventually focused primarily on Central and South America, the Spanish left an indelible mark on the exploration and settlement of North America.

The founding of Spain's colonial empire, which spanned both continents, preceded French and English attempts in North America by a century, leaving a lasting influence even after Spain's possessions were lost. Spanish exploration of the North American continent produced the first permanent settlements well before Jamestown and Plymouth. By the middle of the 16th century, more than fifty years before a tentative English settlement was founded on the shores of the Chesapeake Bay, the Spanish empire in the New World extended from Cape Horn to Vancouver Island. In a brief half-century, Spain founded and organized an empire on a scale previously unknown: "There has been no other conquest like this in the annals of the human race. In one generation, the Spaniards acquired more new territory than Rome conquered in five centuries."[3] Spanish missions were established quickly behind the explorers who pushed inland, first in Florida (St. Augustine in 1565) and then later in the Southwest – into New Mexico (Santa Fe in 1609), and later in Arizona, and California.

---

[2] Sources for this historical overview include: Weber, David J. *The Spanish Frontier in North America*. New Haven and London, Yale University Press, 1992; Chitwood, Oliver Perry. *A History of Colonial America*, 3rd ed. New York, Evanston, and London, Harper & Row, Publishers, 1961; Morison, Samuel Eliot, Henry Steele Commager, and William E. Leuchtenburg. *The Growth of the American Republic*. New York and Oxford, Oxford University Press, 1980; v. 1; *Encyclopedia of America History*, 6th ed. Richard B. Morris, editor. New York, Harper & Row, 1982; and Acosta-Belén, Edna and Barbara R. Sjostrom. *The Hispanic Experience in the United States: Contemporary Issues and Perspectives*. New York, Praeger, 1988.

[3] Morison, Samuel E., Henry Steele Commager, and William E. Leuchtenburg. *The Growth of the American Republic*. New York, Oxford University Press, 1980. v. 1. p, 29.

Among the most distinctive legacies of Spanish colonization, in contrast to the other European colonizers, was the highly integrated mix of races and cultures that resulted. The conquering Spanish subdued native populations by force, and those who did not perish in this manner were enslaved and many more of these succumbed to diseases for which they had no natural resistance. The decimation of native populations in turn gave rise to the African slave trade, initiated by the Portuguese but predicated on the Spanish policy of extracting natural resources with forced labor.

Yet Spanish colonialism and Catholic missionary work were inseparable, and even in its most extreme form, Spanish colonialism attempted to integrate Indians and Africans into the culture. The Spanish encountered more highly developed cultures in Central and South America than existed among the indigenous populations of North America. A synthesis of the cultures of native Indians, enslaved Africans, and the Spanish colonists and their descendants emerged, the exploitation of the *conquistadors* notwithstanding. The principal link within this heterogeneous culture, forged in the New World, was the use of a common language – Spanish. From these separate elements and forces, some pre-existing and some imposed by the Spanish adventurers, emerged the rich and varied Latino culture that is a distinctive feature of the Americas and of American history.

Spain's pre-eminence as a global power had begun to decline by 1600, when French and English colonization in the New World began in earnest. The defeat of the Spanish Armada, sent to attack the English fleet for an eventual invasion of Britain in 1588, foretold Spain's diminishing strength as a European power. Exhausted by several centuries of hostilities with its enemies on the continent and beset by the demands of administering its far-flung empire and the strain of transformation from feudal society to modern state, Spain was struggling to maintain its colonial empire as the 17th century began.

Over the next two centuries, a general policy of retrenchment, the eventual movement toward independence in the Caribbean, Central and South America, and continued political and armed conflict with the other European powers forced Spain to give up parts of its empire in the Americas. Pressed to defend its possessions from the onslaught of French and British settlement and expansion, Spain first attempted to reorganize its colonial venture in North America, and then to cede territory strategically, in order to gain whatever advantage might exist, as the balance of power on the North American continent began to turn.

For the newly formed United States, the acquisition of the Louisiana territory was vitally important. Spain's claims in North America included much of the interior from the Mississippi River to California, though no large-scale colonization was ever undertaken. The Spanish presence depended largely on missions scattered across the Gulf coast in Louisiana and Texas and the Southwest in Arizona, New Mexico, and California. In 1762, France transferred the Louisiana territory to Spain, which sold the area back to France in 1800. With the purchase of the territory in 1803, the United States nearly doubled its area (from the Mississippi to the Rocky Mountains and from the Gulf of Mexico to the Great Lakes) and secured control of the Mississippi River and its fertile watershed.

The push of westward settlement throughout the 19th century created conflict between American settlers (Anglos) and both the inhabitants of the Mexican territory (established under Mexican independence in 1821) and the new Mexican nation. The result of this conflict was the gradual annexation of the Southwest, California, and parts of the Rocky Mountain and Midwest States in 1845. Following the Mexican-American War, the United States acquired lands north of the Rio Grande – California, Nevada, and Utah, and parts of New

Mexico, Arizona, Colorado, Kansas, Wyoming, and Oklahoma – under the terms of the Treaty of Guadalupe Hidalgo (1848), and the subsequent Gadsden Purchase (1853). Fifty years later, the Treaty of Paris (1898), which ended the Spanish-American War, stripped Spain of all remaining New World possessions: Cuba, Puerto Rico, and the Philippines.

20th Century Developments

Until immigration laws were reformed in the mid-20th century, the sparse Latino population of the United States was concentrated mainly in the Southwest. New York contained a significant Puerto Rican community, and a Cuban presence in Florida, New Orleans, and New York dated to the 1860s, yet most Latinos in the United States in the 1950s were of Mexican descent.

Some Mexican Americans could trace their family history to the Spanish colonial period; others were more recent arrivals who fell into two groups: those intending to remain in the United States permanently and those, such as migrant workers, who met the intermittent demand for labor but were expected or forced to return to Mexico once their labor was no longer needed. Itinerant workers might have possessed work documents or not, but they were customarily treated the same regardless. An estimated 4 million Mexicans had been deported by the 1950s, including some who were U.S. citizens.[4]

Immigration from Cuba and Puerto Rico rose sharply in the decades following the Second World War. The small but steady in – and out – migration of Puerto Ricans, a pattern established after Puerto Rico became a United States possession in 1898, changed after World War II. The Puerto Rican population grew rapidly to over 1.4 million by 1970, and Cuban immigration to the United States surged following Fidel Castro's rise to power.[5] Political unrest in South and Central America in the 1970s and 1980s stimulated immigration from these areas, contributing to the diversification of the Latino population in America. Predominantly Mexican, Puerto Rican, and Cuban until mid-century, the composition of the Latino population has been transformed in the last three decades as immigrants from El Salvador, Guatemala, Honduras, Costa Rica, Panama, and countries in South America and the Caribbean have arrived in the United States.

II. POPULATION AND SUBGROUPS

Until 1970, Latinos were not counted systematically by the Census Bureau when the nation's population was enumerated every ten years. The Census Bureau had previously gathered information on Latinos by using a question about place of birth and a list of Spanish surnames compiled by the Bureau. This methodology provided some information on the Latino population, but could not provide a complete court or profile of Latinos in the United States. Beginning in 1970, the Census survey included a question allowing respondents to

---

[4] Acosta-Belén, Edna and Barbara R. Sjostrom. *The Hispanic Experience in the United States: Contemporary Issues and Perspectives*. New York, Praeger, 1988. p. 91.
[5] Ibid, p. 94.

self-identify as being of Spanish origin, and information on Latinos since then has been much more complete and consistent.

Latino Population of the United States, 1950-1990

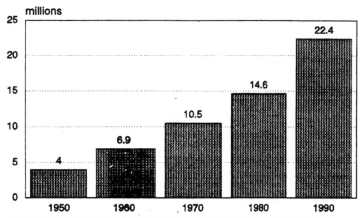

Source: For 1950-1980: Acosta-Belén and Sjostrom. The Hispanic Experience in the United States. Praeger, 1988. p. 11; 1990 figure is from the Census Bureau. General Population Characteristics, p.3.

Census information on Latinos (the Census Bureau uses the terms "Hispanic" and "Hispanic origin") includes people whose backgrounds differ considerably. There are four general categories used by the Census Bureau: Mexican, Cuban, and Puerto Rican, and a category labeled "Other Hispanic," which includes persons who trace their origin to the Spanish-speaking countries of Central and South America or Spain. The overwhelming majority of Latinos in the United States, Nearly 78%, are of Mexican, Cuban, or Puerto Rican ancestry. The common definition of Spanish origin excludes countries in which another language is spoken, Brazil (Portuguese) and Haiti (French), for example. The language distinction refers to the language spoken in the person's country of origin (or the country to which they trace their natural origin), rather than to the language spoken by an individual, because not all Latinos speak Spanish. The common link is historical and derives from the arrival of the Spanish 500 years ago. Consequently, the terms "Latino" or "Hispanic" transcend racial categories. Latinos includes blacks, whites, Asians (Spain colonized the Philippines in the 16th century), Native American Indians, and people of mixed racial background, particularly since intermarriage was a dominant feature of the Spanish Empire in the Americas.

The nation's relatively small Latino population in 1950, estimated to have been less than 3% of the total, swelled rapidly in the post-war boom years and the following decades. The Latino population grew more rapidly during this period than the national population or any subgroup except Asian Americans. As the second-largest minority group, Latinos currently comprise 9% of all Americans (blacks are 12.1% of the total).[6] The Latino population grew by an estimated 265% between 1950 and 1990, whereas the total U.S. population grew by

---

[6] U.S. Department of Commerce. Bureau of the Census. *1990 General Population Characteristics. United States.* 1990. CP-3-6. p. 3.

approximately 50% during these four decades.[7] As of 1990, the minority population included 22.4 million Latinos, 29.9 million blacks, 7.3 million Asian Americans, and 1.9 million people whose ancestry is American Indian, Eskimo, or Aleut, out of a total population of 248.7 million.[8]

High birth and immigration rates largely explain the accelerated growth of the Latino population, which is expected to continue at a fast pace into the next century. According to Census Bureau projections, Latinos will replace blacks as the largest minority group in the nation by2020, when the Latino proportion of the population is estimated to be 15.2%, compared with 14.2% for blacks. The Latino population is expected to account for an increasing percentage of the country's growth in population over the next 55 years, eventually reaching a point when nearly 60% of the nation's population growth is occurring in the Latino community. By 2050, the Latino population is projected to triple.[9]

Aside from the population increase of the last few decades, a change in the composition of the Latino community occurred as the result of immigration. Most Latinos in the United States in 1950 were of Mexican descent, but the influx of immigrants from other places, particularly Central and South America, has altered the composition of both the Latino and the general populations. The arrival of large numbers of immigrants from Spanish-speaking countries is part of a larger trend that began after immigration laws were reformed in the 1960s. Since then, the foreign-born percentage of the population began to climb steadily, partly because of the change in immigration policies and also as the result of armed conflicts and political unrest in Southeast Asia and Central America.

National Origin of the Latino Population, 1980

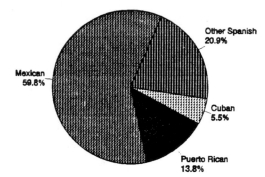

Source: U.S. Census Bureau. Persons of Spanish Origin by State: 1980. p. 2.

---

[7] Acosta-Belén, Edna, and Barbara R. Sjostrom. *The Hispanic Experience in the United States. Contemporary Issues and Perspectives*. New York, Praeger, 1988. p. 10.

[8] U.S. Bureau of the Census. *1990 General Population Characteristics*, p. 3.

Mexicans, Puerto Ricans, and Cubans still comprise nearly 80% of the Latino Population, but members of other groups have steadily increased in number. More than five million Latinos trace their national origin to El Salvador, the Dominican Republic, Colombia, Guatemala, Nicaragua, Ecuador, Peru, Honduras, Panama, or other Central and South American countries, mostly as the result of immigration over the past two decades.[10] Although this "other Hispanic" group is only 2% of the national population, in comparative terms they outnumber Native Americans (about two million people) and the combined Cuban and Puerto Rican populations (slightly less than four million). Though not large enough to rival Asian Americans, who are 2.9% of all Americans and the fastest growing population in the country, the "other Hispanics" are a significant segment of both the Latino and minority populations.

National Origin of the Latino Population, 1990

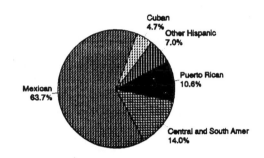

Source: U.S. Bureau of the Census. The Hispanic Population in the United States: March 1992

Geographical Distribution

The newly arrived Latino immigrants are an urban population, a phenomenon which tends to magnify their presence in some cities. Because Cubans and Puerto Ricans are also highly urbanized, the establishment of immigrant communities in some of the nation's largest cities – New York, Los Angeles, Miami, Chicago, San Francisco – has had a twofold effect. The urban Latino population has increased overall, and smaller but significant new communities have taken hold. Los Angeles is home to more than 250,000 El Salvadorans and

---

[9] U.S. Department of Commerce. Bureau of the Census. Current Population Reports. *Population Projections of the United States, by Age, Sex, Race, and Hispanic Origin: 1992 to 2050*. P.25-1092. November, 1992. p. xviii.

[10] U.S. Bureau of the Census. *1990 General Population Characteristics. United States*, p. 3.

133,000 Guatemalans. The Dominican Republican community of New York City numbers 403,000, although Colombians there number 152,000 and Ecuadorans number 115,000. In some cases, the arrival of so many immigrants at a single destination has created communities that rival in size the largest city in the country from which they emigrated: New York's Puerto Rican population exceeds that of San Juan, for example.[11] Even cities that do not have large numbers of residents from any single country may have a large multi-national population. Washington D.C.'s diverse Latino community includes more than 89,000 residents whose nation of origin is either El Salvador, Guatemala, Nicaragua, Ecuador, Peru, or Panama.

Compared with the national population, Latinos are highly concentrated. The combined Latino populations of California and Texas (approximately 12 million) account for 54% of all Latinos living in the United States.[12] The concentration of Latinos in these two states is suggestive or regional population patterns, as 45% of Latinos live in the West, that includes California, and 30% live in the South, which includes Texas. The West also includes the first, fourth, and fifth ranked states in terms of percentage of Latino population – New Mexico (38.2%), Arizona (18.8%), and Colorado (12.9%). The total Latino population living in the West and the Sough is 16.8 million compared with 3.7 million in the Northeast and 1.7 million in the Midwest. Between 1980 and 1990, the Latino population grew substantially according to pre-existing geographic patterns, with the West showing a 61.6% gain and the South registering a 51.3% increase. In the Northeast, the Latino population increase was 44.2% and in the Midwest 35.2%.

Much of the growth in the Hispanic population since 1980 reinforced the existing patterns of geographic concentration described above. California's Hispanic population rose by more than three million during the 1980-1990 period, an increase of nearly 70% (the national increase was 53%). That population gain was the largest in numeric terms, although twelve states and the District of Columbia registered higher increases in percentage terms.[13] Among states with at least 100,000 Hispanic residents, Massachusetts (104%), Florida (84%), and Washington (79%) recorded the highest percentage increases in the Hispanic population. With the exception of Colorado, the ten states with the largest Hispanic populations (California, Texas, New York, Florida, Illinois, New Jersey, Arizona, New Mexico, Colorado, and Massachusetts) were also the ten states in which the Hispanic population increased most during the decade.

Nearly 90% of the nation's Latino population resides in the ten states listed in table 1, although significant increases in states not listed in the table may signal that new patterns are emerging. In New England, the Latino population doubled in New Hampshire and Rhode Island; Connecticut reported a 71% increase. Pennsylvania's Latino population increased by 50% (to 232,262); along with New York and New Jersey, the combined Latino population of

---

[11] Winsberg, Morton. Specific Hispanics. *American Demographics*, v. 16, no. 2, February 1994. p. 52.

[12] All data on state and regional populations is from: U.S. Department of Commerce. Bureau of the Census. *Race and Hispanic Origin*. Number 2, June 1991.

[13] The following states and the District of Columbia registered higher percentage gains in their Hispanic population than did California: New Hampshire (102.8), Massachusetts (103.9), Rhode Island (132.2), Connecticut (71.2), Maryland (93.2), the District of Columbia (85.0), Virginia (100.7), Georgia (77.8), Florida (83.4), Nevada (130.9), Washington (78.8), Oregon (71.2), and Arkansas (87.3). Source: Bureau of the Census. 1990 Census Profile. *Race and Hispanic Origin*. Number 2, June 1991. p. 5.

these three Middle Atlantic states exceeds three million. But because the Latino population is highly concentrated, newly emerging residential trends are not likely to alter the existing patterns in a significant way for some time. On the whole, the 1990 Census documented a rapid increase in the Latino population along well-established patterns and revealed the first signs of new trends emerging.

Table 1. Hispanic Population Gains Since 1980 in the Ten States with the Largest Hispanic Population

State	Hispanic Population Gain from 1980-1990	1980-1990 Percentage Increase in Hispanic Population	Total 1990 Hispanic Population of the State	Percent Hispanic of State's Total Population
California	3,144,000	69.2	7,688,000	25.8
Texas	1,354,000	45.4	4,340,000	25.5
New York	555,000	33.4	2,214,000	12.3
Florida	716,000	83.4	1,574,000	12.2
Illinois	269,000	42.3	904,000	7.9
New Jersey	248,000	50.4	740,000	9.6
Arizona	248,000	56.2	688,000	18.8
New Mexico	102,000	21.4	579,000	38.2
Colorado	84,000	24.9	424,000	12.9
Massachusetts	147,000	103.9	288,000	4.8

Source: U.S. Bureau of the Census. 1990 Census Profile. *Race and Hispanic Origin*, Number 2, June 1991. pps. 5-8.

In addition to being geographically concentrated, Latinos are a highly urbanized population. According to the 1990 Census, fewer than 2 million Latinos are rural residents; more than 18 million live in urban areas. Another 2 million live outside urbanized areas, but not in places categories as "rural."[14] Many of the nation's largest cities – Los Angeles, Miami, Houston, New York, Chicago, and Washington, D.C. – are home to substantial numbers of Latinos, but most of the cities with the largest Latino populations are mid-sized urban centers, and nearly all are in Texas. Of the ten cities with the largest percentage Latino populations (all of which exceed 50% of the total), six are in Texas: Laredo, El Paso, Corpus Cristi, San Antonio, and the urbanized areas of McCallen/Edinburgh/Mission and Brownsville/Harlingen/San Benito. The other four cities are Miami, Las Cruces (NM), Santa Fe, and Yuma (AZ).

Reinforcing this trend is the tendency among many of the newly arrived Latino immigrants to gather in places where they have family or friends, as discussed previously in this section. In the future, a continuation of rapid population growth in combination with a high degree of geographic and urban concentration will have important consequences for both the Latino community and the larger population. One of these effects will almost certainly

---

[14] U.S. Department of Commerce. Bureau of the Census. *1990 Census of Population. Social and Economic Characteristics*: 1990 (p-2-1. November 1993. p. 48.

occur in the sphere of politics, where an ever-increasing percentage of potential voters who are Latino could change the electoral dynamics in local, state, and federal races.

Demographic Characteristics

Income

According to the 1990 Census, family income for Latinos was considerably lower than it was for white and Asian Americans, but slightly higher than for blacks. The Latino median family income of $25,064 was 61% of the median for Asian Americans ($41,251), 67% of the median for non-Hispanic whites ($37,628), and 112% of the median family income for blacks ($22,429).[15] Like Asian Americans, the nation's other diverse and fast-growing group, the Latino population includes a variety of subgroups whose members' economic circumstances are widely divergent. Among Latino subgroups, median family income ranges from $19,726 for Dominicans to $39,044 for Argentineans.[16] Of the sixteen Latino subgroups identified by the Census Bureau, nine have median family incomes that exceed $30,000 (Cubans, Costa Ricans, Panamanians, Argentineans, Chileans, Colombians, Ecuadorians, Peruvians, and Venezuelans); only among Dominicans does the median fall below the $20,000 figure.

Economic security generally depends on such factors as education, skills, work ethic, and the job market, and immigrants often face additional obstacles to finding suitable and stable employment. The vast number of immigrants who arrived from Central and South America in recent decades came from disparate circumstances and arrived here with varied resource levels. As a result, economic well-being differs across the spectrum of Latino groups, particularly among the newly arrived. In a recent article comparing the experiences of Latinos and Asian Americans, a *Washington Post* writer observed that "poverty rates vary widely . . . depending on when, and from what country, members emigrated. In Los Angeles, unemployment is only 4% among Korean Americans, who flocked to the United States in the 1860s, but it is 21% among newly arrived Cambodian refugees. In New York, 32% of Dominican Americans are poor, but only 11% of Colombian Americans are."[17] Family poverty is highest in the Dominican and Puerto Rican communities, where three of every ten families had median incomes below the poverty level in 1989.

Latino workforce participation among males is higher than it is for non-Hispanic white males, based on Census information. Eighty percent of Latino males are in the workforce, compared with 75% of non-Hispanic white males; workforce participation is even higher for some Latino subgroups. An estimated 86% of Central and South American males, a population that includes substantial numbers of immigrants, were in the workforce in march 1992. Workforce participation for Latinas lagged slightly behind that of non-Hispanic women – 52% compared with 58%. In spite of the generally high level of workforce participation for Latinos, the unemployment rate was much higher for Latino men (12.2%) than for non-

---

[15] U.S. Department of Commerce. Bureau of the Census. *1990 Census of Population. Social and Economic Characteristics*: 1990 (p-2-1. November 1993. p. 48.

[16] Ibid., p. 135-36.

[17] Constable, Pamela. A 'Glass Ceiling' of Misperceptions: Hispanics, Asians Fight Stereotypes Both Bad and Good. *Washington Post*, October 10, 1995. A 1.

Hispanic white males (7.5%), and also substantially higher for Latinas (9.8%) than non-Hispanic white women (5.4%).[18]

Education

The percentage of Latinos 25 years of age and older who are college graduates is considerably lower than for whites and Asian Americans and slightly lower than for blacks. Asian Americans lead all groups in educational achievement, as nearly four in ten persons 25 and older (36.6%) possess a bachelor's degree or higher, compared with 22% of whites, 11.4% of blacks and 9.2% of Latinos. With respect to advanced degrees, including master's, professional and doctoral degrees, Asian Americans again lead all other groups by a sizeable margin: 14% of Asian Americans hold advanced degrees, followed by 8% of whites, 4% of blacks, and 3% of Latinos.[19]

But Census data on education in the Latino community also underscore the disparate circumstances that characterize the population in many respects. The proportion of college-educated persons in certain Latino subgroups is much larger than it is for white and blacks and even surpasses that of Asian Americans for one group. Venezuelans claim the highest proportion of persons with bachelor's degrees or higher (37.6%); educational achievement among Argentineans (28.6%) and Chileans (24.7%) is also relatively high. The relationship between education and earnings also seems clear with respect to these specific groups, because median income is highest for Venezuelans, Argentineans, and Chileans among all Latino subgroups, a correlation that holds true as well for the larger population.

Family Characteristics

Latinos have the largest families and the second-lowest divorce rate compared to the nation's three racial groups. Only Asian Americans have a lower divorce rate than Latinos; marriage statistics place Latinos in the middle range (at 50%), between Asians and whites, with the highest marriage rates at 56 and 58%, respectively, and blacks, with the lowest at 34%.[20]

The Census Bureau reported a Latino divorce rate of 7.4%, compared with 3.9% for Asians, but divorce rates for non-Hispanic whites and blacks were 8.5% and 10%, respectively. Family size ranges from a high of 3.9 persons per family for Latinos to a low of 3.1 persons, for white families. Asian American families averaged 3.8 persons, and black families averaged 3.5 persons.[21]

---

[18] All data on workforce participation are from: U.S. Department of Commerce. Bureau of the Census. *The Hispanic Population in the United States: March 1992*. P20-465RV. July 1993. p. 6.

[19] U.S. Department of Commerce. Bureau of the Census. *1990 Census of Population. Social and Economic Characteristics*. 1990 CP-2-1. November 1993. p. 42. U.S. Department of Commerce. Bureau of the Census. *1990 Census of Population. Persons of Hispanic Origin in the United States*. 1990 CP-3-3. August 1993. pps. 77-114.

[20] U.S. Bureau of the Census. *1990 General Population Characteristics*, p. 47.

[21] Ibid, p. 53.

SECTION TWO: LATINOS AND ELECTORAL POLITICS

Studies of group voting behavior are based on the general idea that the electorate can be subdivided according to certain traits – race, gender, age, ethnicity – and that useful comparisons and generalizations about voting patterns can then be made. As noted earlier, the term *"Latino"* is neither a racial nor an ethnic category but encompasses both. As a consequence, broad generalizations about Latino voters as a group are perhaps even less reliable than those made about racial or ethnic groups per se. Whereas the preceding section of this report sought only to describe demographic characteristics (also referring to problems associated with generalizing about Latinos), a political analysis of the Latino community is perhaps even more sensitive because it seeks to describe group behavior.

There are several problems in discussing the Latino population as a single group with regard to electoral behavior. An initial problem is whether Latinos can even be considered a single group politically, since *Latino* or *Hispanic* are umbrella terms that impose a single label on people of different nationalities and cultures, in spite of the dissimilarities among them. What is known as the *Latino community* is comprised of people of different races, several nationalities, and a variety of distinct ethnic or cultural groups: both native and foreign-born, from a broad range of socio-economic groups, and marked by regional differences within the United States. They may be recent immigrants to the United States, second or third generation Americans, or descendants of centuries-long inhabitants of the Southwest. Among Latinos themselves, there has been much debate as to whether *Latino* has any valid meaning as a descriptive term.[22]

In his study of Latino political behavior, Rodney E. Hero notes that "Latinos may be a group in name-a nominal group – but not necessarily a politically identifiable group." Furthermore, discussions of Latino politics necessarily assume "certain similarities within and between groups of Americans of Hispanic descent that have not always been borne out in political action or in research."[23] If ties among the different groups are vague, generalizations about political views and participation rates of Latinos as a whole are less certain.

In spite of these drawbacks, analyzing social, economic, and political trends on the basis of group identifications is a common approach in this pluralistic society. Particularly in the area of politics, comparing voters' candidate choices according the group distinctions, (e.g., the "Catholic vote" or the "black vote") is a widely accepted method of analysis, even if the imposed group labels vary in their accuracy. In some cases, group labels may delineate understandable or obvious differences, but at other times they may suggest a group cohesiveness that is questionable or unclear for certain populations, Latinos and Asian Americans in particular.

---

[22] Rodney E. Hero notes that he used "the term 'Latino,' although it should be noted that 'Hispanic' has become widely and popularly accepted. Considerable, and often heated, debate has taken place over the more correct or appropriate name. Despite precedents for its use, several scholars have criticized 'Hispanic' as a label largely imposed by government agencies, particularly the U.S. Census Bureau, for the sake of convenience and simplicity." Hero, Rodney E. *Latinos and the U.S. Political System: Two-Tiered Pluralism*. Philadelphia, Temple University Press. 1992. pps. 2-3.

[23] Ibid., p. 2.

III. VOTING AGE POPULATION

The Latino electorate has grown at an extraordinary pace in recent decades, from 5.6 million in 1972 to 14.7 million in 1992, an increase of 162% and a rate of growth unmatched by any other segment of the electorate. In comparison, the national electorate grew 36% during these two decades; the black electorate grew 56% and white voters increased 30%. (Figures for Asian American voters are not available prior to 1990.) As a proportion of the electorate, the number of eligible Latino voters increased from 4.1% in 1972 to 7.9% by 1992. In comparison, whites are 78% of eligible voters nationwide, blacks comprise 10.7% of the voting age population, and Asian Americans are 2.7%.[24]

States with the Highest Latino Voting Age Population

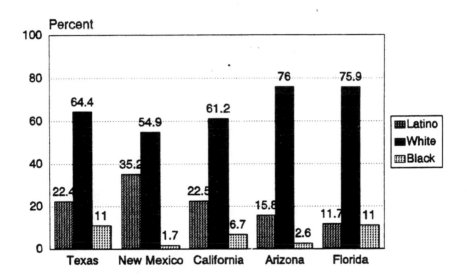

Source: Brace, Kimball W. and Election Data Services, Inc. The Election Data Book, 1992. Lanham, MD, Bernan Press. 1993. various pages.

Among the states, New Mexico has the highest proportion of Latinos in the electorate – 35%. But more important in terms of national politics is the significant number of eligible Latino voters in the four largest states in the nation: California, New York, Texas, and Florida (in rank order). In both California and Texas, Latinos are the largest minority group by far, and nearly one of every four eligible voters is Latino. In New York and Florida, Latino voters comprise more than 10% of the electorate. The presence of such large numbers of eligible Latino voters in these four states demonstrates a vast potential for affecting national politics: California, New York, Texas, and Florida account for 27% of the electoral votes needed to

---

[24] All historical data on the electorate is from: U.S. Department of Commerce. Bureau of the Census. *Current Population Reports. Voting and Registration in the Election of November 1992.* P20-466. April-1993. Appendix A. Historical Tables.

elect the President and 25% of the seats in the U.S. House of Representatives (these states accounted for 28% of the popular vote in the 1992 presidential election). In addition, Latinos comprises more than one of every ten eligible voters in Illinois and New Jersey, ranked sixth and ninth in total population among the states.[25]

The ten states with the highest proportion of Latinos among the voting age population are, in descending order, New Mexico (35.2%), California (22.5%), Texas (22.4%), Arizona (15.8%), Florida (11.7%), Colorado (11.2%), New York (11.2%), Nevada (9.2%), New Jersey (8.7%), and Illinois (6.8%). Census Bureau projections suggest that recent Latino population trends will continue into the next century, particularly in several of the states listed above. The Latino population in California, for example, is projected to more than double between 1993 and 2020, growing from 8.5 million to more than 17 million.

While most of the nation's Latino population is found in the states listed above, increasingly there are scattered concentrations of Latinos in other states as well. As the Latino population gradually disperses, small communities have been established beyond those areas traditionally populated by Latinos. In Washington's adjoining Adams and Franklin counties, for example, Latinos represent 25% or more of eligible voters, and in six Idaho counties, Latinos comprise at least 10% of the voting age population. In political terms, the high concentration of the nation's Latino population in such states as California and Texas creates the potential to affect the outcome of state-wide elections; scattered Latino communities in other states may have an effect at the local level, if not yet in state-wide elections.

At the congressional district level, a notable increase in the number of districts with substantial numbers of Latinos has accompanied the rapid growth of the overall population in the past decade. Latinos were 20% or more of the voting age population in 35 congressional districts after the 1980 Census.[26] Since the 1990 Census, there have been 44 such districts, a significant increase from 1980. These are listed in Table 2. But a more revealing statistic, given the geographic concentration of the Latino population, is the number of districts wherein Latinos constitute at least half of the eligible voters. After 1980, there were six congressional districts with a Latino majority; now there are 17. Table 2 lists congressional districts in which the Latino percentage of the voting age population is 20% or more.

Sixteen of the 44 congressional districts listed in Table 2 are represented by Latino members of Congress (of whom there are 18; one represents Puerto Rico and the other was elected from the Illinois 20th congressional district, which has a Latino VAP of 0.65). Latino members represent thirteen of the sixteen Latino-majority districts.

---

[25] Information on voting age population in the states is from: Brace, Kimball vs. and Election Data Services, Inc. *The Election Data Book: A Statistical Portrait of Voting in America, 1992*. Lanham, MD, Bernan Press. 1993. various pages.

[26] U.S. Department of Commerce. Bureau of the Census. *1980 Census of Population. Congressional District Profiles, 98th Congress*. PC80-S1-00, September 1983. pps. 9-18.

Table 2. Congressional Districts with at Least 20% Latino Eligible Voters

State	District	Voting Age Population (VAP)	Latino Voting Age Population	Percent of VAP that is Latino (%)
Arizona	2	414,281	185,598	44.8
California	16	409,054	136,624	33.4
	17	419,952	112,547	26.8
	18	391,176	87,623	22.4
	19	404.642	82,952	20.5
	20	373,560	189,395	50.7
	23	412,637	109,349	26.5
	26	410,112	192,343	46.9
	28	423,910	90,293	21.3
	30	415,463	237,229	47.1
	31	403,689	217,185	43.8
	32	435,038	114,850	26.4
	33	384,158	305,406	79.5
	34	402,266	233,717	58.1
	35	389,470	149,946	38.5
California	37	375,216	153,088	40.8
	38	435,049	95,276	21.9
	39	430,089	87,308	20.3
	41	400,070	114,020	28.5
	42	381,173	116,639	30.6
	43	401,020	88,224	22.0
	44	417,411	97,257	23.3
	46	405,602	183,738	45.3
	50	398,704	145,128	36.4
Florida	17	391,015	94,235	24.1
	18	450,048	303,782	67.5
	21	424,355	299,595	70.6
Illinois	4	383,497	227,030	59.2
New Jersey	13	454,356	176,744	38.9
New Mexico	1	371,875	129,041	34.7
	2	350,557	131,809	37.6
	3	345,896	114,837	33.2
New York	12	417,930	226,936	54.3
	15	437,484	190,743	53.6
	16	385,188	226,105	58.7
	17	438,290	114,394	26.1
Texas	14	407,375	83,105	20.4
	15	369,299	257,032	59.6
	16	382,985	254,302	66.4
	20	398,984	223,830	56.1
	23	374,947	328,594	58.3
	27	390,622	233,702	61.4
	28	382,636	216,189	56.5
	29	377,455	209,110	55.4

Source: Brace, *The Election Data Book*, various pages.

IV. ATTITUDES TOWARD PUBLIC ISSUES: SURVEY RESEARCH FINDINGS

A composite profile of Latino attitudes, like a composite national profile, will show the broad outlines of beliefs and opinions but does not reveal more complex and subtle variations of opinion. Detailed polling information on the Latino community is limited. Furthermore, both the size and diverse character of the Latino population allow for describing their political and social views in general terms only, using existing public opinion polls.

Ideally, periodic and detailed polls that compared views among Latino subgroups and also provided comparisons between Latinos and the larger population would have allowed for drawing firm conclusions about the differences and similarities between Latinos and the majority population. Although extensive, time-series polls of this kind have not been done, several polls taken over the past five years were intended to reveal some of the subtle variations in Latino views and also compare their views with those of the larger population. A search of standard sources for public opinion polls and the surveys collection of the Congressional Research Service found several surveys that permit making some observations about Latino attitudes on social and political issues. In some cases, comparative data for the general population or for blacks and whites is included. This section presents survey data for Latinos on selected issues and makes comparisons with the general public or other groups whenever possible.[27]

According to the polls included herein, Latinos' views on a number of broad public issues resemble closely the views of the general population. But on issues of particular concern to Latinos, such as the movement to declare English the official language or bilingual education, opinions within the Latino community may differ from those of the population at large. At times, Latino respondents may also hold opinions that appear to contradict the notion that they depart from the majority opinion only in ways that can be attributed to cultural differences.

Efforts to designate English as the country's official language and the ensuing debate provide an example of the divergence of opinion between Latinos and the population at large: fewer than half the Latino respondents to the Latino National Political Survey (LNPS), cited below, supported recognizing English as the nation's "official" language, but nearly 80% of Anglos did. On the related topic of bilingual education, an overwhelming majority of Mexican – Puerto Rican – and Cuban-Americans registered their support for it (see Table 3a. below). Moreover, nearly 80% of Mexican and Puerto Rican respondents and 54% of Cubans reported that they were willing to pay more taxes to fund bilingual education (the poll did not provide comparative data for Anglos on either question concerning bilingual education).

---

[27] The beliefs and opinions of Latino respondents in the polls included here are subject to the possible limitations of survey design and the representativeness of the population samples. Also, it should be noted that opinions may have already shifted since these polls were taken and that they are subject to further change for a variety of reasons. This section is intended as a general guide only.

Table 3a. Latino Attitudes on Language Issues

Laws should be passed making English the official language of this country?				
	Mexican	Puerto Rican	Cuban	Anglo
Strongly Agree	13.7%	12.1%	10.7%	45.6%
Agree	30.7%	36.8%	29.3%	33.7%
Disagree	39.2%	41.2%	47.5%	17.3%
Strongly Disagree	16.4%	10.0%	12.4%	3.4%
How strongly do you support or oppose bilingual education?				
	Mexican	Puerto Rican		Cuban
Strongly Support	37.1%	39.7%		32.3%
Support	42.5%	47.5%		56.1%
Feel Uncertain	13.0%	7.2%		6.1%
Oppose	5.3%	3.9%		1.9%
Strongly Oppose	2.1%	1.7%		3.5%

Source: "Latino National Political Survey in:" de la Garza, Rodolfo et al. *Latino Voices*. pps. 97, 99.

But generalizing about the distinct cultural identity of Latinos and its effect on opinion formation can be misleading. For example, although most of the current immigrants to the United States are from Central and South America, a solid majority of Latinos in the LNPS agreed with the statement, "There are too many immigrants coming to this country."[28] Most Anglos (73.8%) agreed with the statement as well, but the percentage of Mexicans (75.2) and Puerto Ricans (79.4) was even higher. A slightly smaller proportion of Cubans, but still a solid majority (65%), agreed that immigration rates are too high. The slight drop-off among Cuban respondents can most likely be attributed to concerns about the specific issues surrounding immigration from Cuba to the United States for political reasons.

In a heterogeneous society like the United States, perceptions which group members have about themselves and about how they are viewed y others can often provide a useful context for interpreting attitudes and beliefs. The *Los Angeles Times* conducted a poll in August and September of 1995 that asked a series of questions about the reasons for "the economic and social problems that some Hispanics and Asian Americans face today." It provided the responses of Latinos and also of three other racial groups – whites, blacks and Asians.

On questions concerning perceptions about Latinos, a majority of respondents from all four groups believed that "language difficulties" were a primary factor in explaining economic and social problems. Majorities or ncar-majorities also cited a "lack of jobs" and a "lack of educational opportunities" as causes for the problems encountered by Latinos.

Slightly less than a majority of Latinos agreed that "the breakup of the Hispanic family," "past and present discrimination," and a "lack of motivation and an unwillingness to work hard" contributed to socio-economic difficulties, but whites, Asians, and blacks (except on discrimination as a factor) gave substantially less weight to these factors as a cause.

---

[28] de la Garza, *Latino Voices*, p. 101.

Table 3b. Major Reasons for Hispanic Problems

	Hispanics who said "yes"	Whites who said "yes"	Blacks who said "yes"	Asians who said "yes"
Is this a major reason for Hispanic problems?				
Lack of jobs	68%	42%	74%	53%
Language difficulties	66%	56%	59%	59%
Lack of educational opportunities	51%	46%	63%	53%
Breakup of the Hispanic family	45%	28%	38%	22%
Past and present discrimination	43%	31%	58%	29%
Lack of motivation and an unwillingness to work hard	41%	25%	19%	32%

Source: Los Angeles Times poll, October 10, 1995. A1.

Latino respondents indicated more overall acceptance of the given explanations for problems or difficulties than did members of other groups in the *L.A. Times* poll. On most of the factors listed, higher percentages of Latinos agreed that it was a major reason for problems (the significance of disintegrating families, for example) and appeared to be self-critical in comparison with the more "generous" attitudes of others. Forty-one percent of the Latinos polled believed that the break-up of the family was a valid explanation for the difficulties experienced in some parts of their community, whereas only about one-third or less of whites, blacks, and Asians thought so. And 41% of Latinos agreed that a lack of motivation and hard work was a major reason for their problems, but others polled had lower negative judgements of Latinos in this regard (between 19 and 32%). In analyzing the findings of the survey, the accompanying article observed that Latinos "tended to be more pessimistic and to believe others' critical views of them," and noted with respect to a work ethic, Latinos in face "have an unusually high level of participation in the work force."[29]

A poll comparing views among Latinos, blacks and whites on questions about abortion, capital punishment, prayer in schools, welfare, crime and law enforcement, and other issues was commissioned by the Christian Coalition in 1993. The polling organization, Fabrizio, McLaughlin and Associates, interviewed 500 whites, 500 Latinos, and 500 blacks and found general agreement among the three groups on these issues.[30] The survey contributed to the Coalition's broader strategy of recruiting minorities, and the results were cited as evidence of the compatibility of views between whites and minorities. Results are listed in Tables 3c and 3d.[31]

---

[29] Sun, Lena H. Cultural Differences Set Asian Americans Apart: Where Latinos Have Common Threads, They Have None. *Los Angeles Times*, October 10, 1995. A1.

[30] It should be noted that some of these results are at variance with those in other surveys. For example, the 63% figure for Hispanic support of English as the official language of the U.S. (Table 3d) is notably higher than the 40-50% support levels found among subgroups in the survey cited in Table 3a.

[31] Hallow, Ralph Z. Christian Coalition to Court Minorities: Blacks, Hispanics Back Key Stands. *Washington Times*, September 10, 1993. A5. At the news conference called for releasing the survey

The poll relied on a series of statements concerning issues in the news, and respondents were asked to indicate their approval or disapproval. Latino and white respondents were generally in agreement on questions concerning school choice, establishing free enterprise zones, voluntary prayer in schools, "requiring that school age children be taught homosexuality is a normal and acceptable lifestyle," and "allowing taxpayer funding of elective abortions as part of a government-run national health care plan." The majority response (either approving or disapproving) for Latinos was within 5 percentage points of the majority white responses on these issues. Black and Latino majority responses were within a five-point range on these dame issues as well, with the exception of school prayer.

Latino and white majority opinions were separated by more than five percentage points on questions regarding the death penalty, making English the official language, requiring welfare recipients to work, affirmative action, the government's role in "strengthening traditional values," and the relationship between the nation's economic and social problems and the deterioration of the family. Latino and black majority responses were similar on most issues (within six percentage points), except two: making English the nation's official language and attributing economic and social problems to the disintegration of families. The largest gap in the responses of whites and those of Latinos and blacks occurred on the issue of affirmative action. An overwhelming majority of white (84%) disagreed with the statement, "African-Americans and Hispanics and other minorities should receive special preferences in hiring to make up for past inequalities," while considerably smaller majorities of Latinos (57%) and blacks (53%) disagreed.

Latino and white majority opinions were separated by more than five percentage points on questions regarding the death penalty, making English the official language, requiring welfare recipients to work, affirmative action, the government's role in "strengthening traditional values," and the relationship between the nation's economic and social problems and the deterioration of the family. Latino and black majority responses were similar on most issues (within six percentage points), except two: making English the nation's official language and attributing economic and social problems to the disintegration of families. The largest gap in the responses of whites and those of Latinos and blacks occurred on the issue of affirmative action. An overwhelming majority of whites (84%) disagreed with the statement, "African-Americans and Hispanics and other minorities should received special preferences in hiring to make up for past inequalities," while considerably smaller majorities of Latinos (57%) and blacks (53%) disagreed.

Latino views on the selected sample of issues included here place them squarely in the national mainstream. Like whites and blacks, Latinos may feel more or less strongly on a particular issue in comparison with other groups, and opinions within the Latino community may vary according to age, gender, socio-economic status, and other factors.

---

results, Coalition Executive Director Ralph Reed announced, "We are not going to concede the minority community to the political left anymore" and outlined plans to recruit new members through churches in minority communities.

Table 3c. Public Attitudes Concerning Schools and Enterprise Zones

Here is a list of items recently prominent in the news. **Would you tell me whether you approve or disapprove of each of the following:**
Allowing parents to choose the schools their children attend.

	Hispanic	White	Black
Approve	84%	82%	82%
Disapprove	12%	13%	15%

Allowing voluntary prayer in school.

	Hispanic	White	Black
Approve	83%	85%	89%
Disapprove	14%	12%	09%

Establishing free enterprise zones where new businesses would be provided tax breaks and other incentives to create jobs and economic opportunity.

	Hispanic	White	Black
Approve	88%	85%	85%
Disapprove	07%	07%	11%

Source: Fabrizio, McLaughlin & Associates, Inc. poll for the Christian Coalition, September 8, 1993.

Table 3d. Public Attitudes on Selected Social Issues

Here is a list of items recently prominent in the news. **Would you tell me whether you approve or disapprove of the following?**
Imposing the death penalty for convicted murderers.

	Hispanic	White	Black
Approve	63%	74%	58%
Disapprove	28%	17%	30%

Requiring able-bodies welfare recipients to work for their benefits.

	Hispanic	White	Black
Approve	86%	95%	91%
Disapprove	11%	03%	06%

Making English the official language of the United States.

	Hispanic	White	Black
Approve	63%	82%	76%
Disapprove	34%	11%	19%

Many of our country's economic and social problems are as a result of the deterioration of the American family.

	Hispanic	White	Black
Approve	60%	75%	70%
Disapprove	32%	22%	22%

Source: Fabrizio, McLaughlin & Associates, Inc. poll for the Christian Coalition, September 8, 1993.

V. VOTING PARTICIPATION

Despite the sharp increase in the number of eligible Latino voters in the past two decades, the challenge of translating potential strength into political power remains largely unfulfilled. Latinos have been the fastest growing population in the country for some time, but their voting participation consistently lags behind that of blacks and whites and surpassed the rate for Asian Americans only slightly in 1992. In presidential elections between 1976 and 1992, the rate of participation for Latinos never exceeded 33%, although it never fell below 59% for whites and 50% for blacks.

Contrary to widely-held expectations, Latino voting participation did not increase along with the rise in population that began in the 1970s. Following the 1980 census, it was expected that the number of Latino voters would climb rapidly, and long-awaited political power would follow as a result. A 1982 article noted that increasing Latino political activism was a phenomenon "that both political parties recognize is crucial to national politics in the rest of the 1980's."[32] Heightened expectations about Latino turnout had an unfortunate effect, because each time participation failed to meet the initial predictions, expectations were raised even higher for the next election: "The assertion was that with increased numbers, Latino political clout would influence the outcome of the presidential election of 1980; when that did not materialize, they made a stronger claim for the 1984 election, and then the 1988 election."[33] Following a modest increase in turnout in both the 1982 congressional election (from 23.5% in 1978 to 25.3%) and the 1984 presidential (see Table 4. below), voting participation among Latinos leveled off just below the 30% mark; it has not exceeded that threshold since.

Table 4. Latino Voting Participation in Presidential Elections, 1976-1992

	1976	1980	1984	1988	1992
Latino	31.8	29.9	32.6	28.8	28.9
White	60.9	60.9	61.4	59.1	63.6
Black	48.7	50.5	55.8	51.5	54.0
Asian	NA	NA	NA	NA	27.3

Source: U.S. Census Bureau. *Voting and Registration in the Election of November 1992.* Current Population Reports. P20-466. p. v.

Observers cite a variety of factors to explain the relatively low levels of voting participation among Latinos. The high proportion of immigrants and youth among the Latino population suppresses turnout numbers, it is argued, since both groups traditionally include large numbers of non-participants. The median age for Latinos is 25.6, compared with a median age of 34.4 for whites, 28.3 for blacks, and 30.1 for Asian Americans. For some Latino groups, the median age is even lower than for Latinos as a whole. The median age for

---

[32] Gurwitt, Rob. Widespread Political Efforts Open New Era for Hispanics. *Congressional Quarterly Weekly Report*, v. 40, no. 43. October 23, 1992. pps. 2707-2709.

[33] De la Garza, Rodolpho O. and Louis DeSipio, F. Chris Garcia, John Garcia, and Angelo Falcon. *Latino Voices: Mexican, Puerto Rican, & Cuban Perspectives on American Politics.* Westview Press, 1992. p. 2.

Mexican Americans, for example, the largest Latino subgroup by far, is 23.8. But immigration is likely the single most important factor for understanding low turnout. While immigration increased the Latino population, it probably delayed a rise in political participation, because immigrants must first complete the citizenship process before undertaking the steps to become eligible voters.

Immigration

The political potential that exists because of the surge in the number of voting age Latinos is constrained by the large number of ineligible voters this group includes. Like the Asian Americans, the Latino population includes many recent immigrants who are not citizens and, therefore, are ineligible to vote. Naturalization can begin only after a five-year residency, meaning that legal immigrants swell the Latino voting age population used to calculate turnout, even though they are ineligible to vote. In fact, the number of noncitizens who are ineligible to vote in any given year may exceed the total number of eligible voters.[34] According to 1990 Census Bureau figures, of the 13.8 million Latino adults in the United States, 37.7% were not citizens, a higher proportion of the Latino population than who claimed to be registered to vote (35.0%) in the 1992 election.[35]

The National Association of Latino Elected and Appointed Officials (NALEO) issued a report in 1992 that cited non-citizenship as a crucial factor when comparing turnout of Latinos with that of other groups; it suggested that including non-citizens when calculating turnout seriously reduces actual turnout figures for eligible Latinos. After adjusting turnout figures to exclude non-citizens, the authors of the report found that Latino participation was still lower than, but much closer to, the national rate. As further evidence that those who are not naturalized suppress Latino turnout, the NALEO study reported that ineligible non-citizens account for 48% of Latino non-voters, but only 9% of white and 6% of black non-participants.

The challenge for Latino political groups, such as NALEO and the Southwest Voter Registration Project, extends beyond voter registration to encouraging and facilitating naturalization, since most legal immigrants are eligible for citizenship. But Latinos are comparatively slow to naturalize: only 13% of Mexican immigrants who arrived here in the 1970s had become citizens by 1989 (Mexican-Americans comprise the largest share of the Latino population.)[36] By comparison, the naturalization rate of Asians who emigrated to the U.S. during the same period was 55.4%.[37]

---

[34] U.S. Census Bureau. Current Population Reports. *Voting and Registration in the Election of November 1992.* April, 1993. p. vi.

[35] National Association of Latino Elected and Appointed Officials. *The Latino Vote in 1992.* NALEO Background Paper #19, by Harry P. Pachon, Louis DeSipio, Juan-Carlos Alegre, and Mark Magana. Washington, 1992. p. 5.

[36] Stanfield, Rochelle L. Cracking el Sistema. *National Journal*, v. 23, no. 22, June 1, 1991. p. 1284.

[37] Barringer, Herbert R., Robert W. Gardner, and Michael J. Levin. *Asians and Pacific Islanders in the United States.* New York, Russell Sage Foundation, 1993. p. 46.

Language Difficulties and Bilingual Ballots

Even for those who have become citizens, language difficulties may discourage some immigrants from participating in elections. The language provisions of the Voting Rights Act (PL 94-73) were adopted to eliminate language barriers to voting, and the 1992 extension of the Act increased the number of jurisdictions in which bilingual ballots are available by changing the formula. Under the earlier version of the law, election officials were required to make bilingual ballots available if a language minority comprised 5% of the population of a country. The Voting Rights Language Assistance Act of 1992 (PL 102-344) requires that states or jurisdictions print ballots in a language other than English if (1) a language minority in the jurisdiction equals 5% or more or the population; (2) the language minority exceeds 10,000 people; or (3) the illiteracy rate of the group is greater than the national illiteracy rate.

The long-term effect of expanding bilingual ballot requirements will not be known for some time, but its immediate effect is that it removes an obstacle to voting for a number of Latino immigrants (at least those who live in places with a significant Spanish-speaking population). The success of the law will ultimately depend on vote requests for the bilingual materials. In some jurisdictions, relatively few voters have taken advantage of the program in the recent past. Los Angeles county officials spent more than $125,000 on multilingual voting materials in 1992, but handled only 3,264 requests on election day. In Long Beach, voting officials prepared multilingual voter information pamphlets explaining ballot initiatives at a cost of $6,200 and had 22 requests for them.[38] the use of bilingual voting materials should increase as more voters become aware of the program, but its potential in the Latino community is tied in large part to the success of naturalization efforts.

Other Factors Affecting Turnout

Studies have demonstrated that education and income are also factors that affect turnout, and the Latino population includes a sizeable number of persons whose income and educational background is comparatively low. Slightly fewer than 10% of Latinos are college graduates (9.2%), a lower level of educational achievement than for whites, blacks, or Asian Americans. And median family income is also lower for Latinos than whites or Asian Americans, but it is slightly higher than for blacks. Latinos have the lowest per capita income, compared to whites, blacks, or Asian Americans (demographic characteristics are discussed in greater detail in Chapter II).

And while the political parties reportedly are making efforts to recruit voters among the fast-growing Latino and Asian populations, low participation rates have a stifling effect on large-scale recruitment. Parties and candidates must budget resources to meet a variety of tasks, and campaign strategists are unlikely to target groups of voters whose participation remains consistently low compared with other groups. In California, where Latinos and Asians are potential "swing voters" with sufficient numbers to decide elections, "neither party is ready to mount an all-out effort to court these new voters."[39]

---

[38] Gurwitt, Rob. How Do You Say 'Party Ticket' in Tagalog? *Governing*, April 1993. p. 26.

[39] Kirschten, Dick. Building Blocs. *National Journal*, v. 24, no. 39, September 26, 1992. pps. 2173-2177.

For now, the sharp increase in the Latino population has not resulted in a corresponding increase in political strength. But the largely untapped pool of potential Latino voters, especially the large number of unnaturalized residents, could assume greater significance in electoral politics in the future. Efforts by the parties and voter registration groups to mount naturalization campaigns as the first step to voter registration might be worthwhile, since "NALEO studies show that naturalized citizens have higher voter participation rates than native-born citizens."[40] And the rapid growth of the Latino population is expected to continue unabated for some time, according to Census projections. Midway through a third decade of extraordinary population growth, Latinos remain poised to wield the political power that has remained elusive thus far.

VI. VOTING PATTERNS AND POLITICAL PARTY IDENTIFICATION

Latino voting patterns over the past two decades illustrate a strong tendency to support Democratic Party candidates. In both presidential and U.S. House elections, Latino voters have generally supported Democratic candidates by a ratio of 2 to 1 over their Republican opponents, a degree of voter loyalty among major racial and ethnic groups that is surpassed only by black support for Democratic candidates.

Latino voters registered their strongest support for Democratic candidates in House races, rather than for Democratic presidential candidates. Since the 1980 election, the level of support for Democratic House candidates among Latino voters was nearly always above the 70% mark. Only in 1984, the year of Ronald Reagan's landslide victory, did Latino support for Democratic House candidates fall below the 70% threshold, when 79% voted for Democrats (presidential candidate Walter Mondale received 62% of the Latino vote that year). Support for Democratic presidential candidates in the last five elections was usually in the range of 70-75%. Among Democratic presidential candidates, Jimmy Carter received both the highest and lowest share of the Latino vote, winning 76% of the Latino vote in 1976 and 59% in 1980.

The conventional wisdom about political party preference among Latinos has long suggested that the Democratic Party receives the support of the majority, although that perception may be based more on voting behavior than on opinion polls.[41] A combined series of polls conducted by the *Gallup News Service* and *CNN/USA Today* from 1991 and 1992 found solid, but less than majority support for the Democratic party among Latino respondents: 44% identified themselves as Democrats, 29% as Republicans, and 27% as Independents.[42]

---

[40] Stanfield, Cracking el Sistema, p. 1287.

[41] Opinion polls probably understate Democratic and Republican voting preference, as compared with party preference, because a sizeable number of respondents to any given poll identify themselves as Independents, and the number of Independent candidates on the elections ballot is usually small. Public opinion polls provide the means for tracking party identification, but tend to provide only a limited understanding of what voters will do in the voting booth.

[42] Benson, John, and Marc Maynard. A Party Whose Allegiances Continue to Shift. *Christian Science Monitor*, July 10, 1992. p. 19.

Table 5. Group Voting Percentage in Presidential Elections, 1976-1992

		National vote	Latino	Black	White	Asian
1976	Carter	50%	76%	83%	47%	na
	Ford	48	24	18	52	na
1980	Reagan	51	33	11	56	na
	Carter	41	59	85	36	na
	Anderson	7	6	3	7	na
1984	Reagan	59	37	9	64	na
	Mondale	40	62	90	35	na
1988	Bush	53	30	12	59	na
	Dukakis	45	69	86	40	na
1992	Clinton	43	62	82	39	29
	Bush	38	25	11	41	55
	Perot	19	14	7	20	16

Source: 1992 data are from a Voter Research and Surveys poll; 1980-1988 data are from *New York Times* and CBS News election day polls; and 1976 data are from a CBS News election day poll. See the *New York Times*, November 5, 1992, p. B9.

An earlier, extensive survey of nearly 5,000 Latino respondents in 1990 found a slightly lower preference for the Democratic Party and provided additional insight into Latino party identification by examining party preferences according to a series of factors.[43] The survey by City University of New York Professors Barry A. Kosmin and Ariela Keysar examined party identification according to income, state of residence, religious affiliation, age, and other variables. The authors found that "in 1990 two-thirds of US Hispanics identified with the two major parties and favored the Democrats in a ratio of just under 2:1," with 41% identifying as Democrats, 24% as Republicans, and 27% as Independents (the remaining 8% preferred some other party, answered "don't know," or declined to answer).

Most of the Latino population (84%) is concentrated in 5 states (California, Florida, Illinois, New York, and Texas), and state patterns emerged as the strongest variable for predicting party preference. In California, Texas, New York, and Illinois, Democratic party preference ranged from 44 to 51%, and Republican allegiance ranged from 17 to 28%. The pattern was reversed for Florida, where 46% favored the Republican Party and 25% identified as Democrats. This reversal in party identification cannot be entirely attributed to the high concentration of Cubans in Florida, who comprised about 30% of the Latino population at the time of the study, but points to what the authors call a "specific local political culture."[44] As further evidence of this distinct political environment, the authors note that religious identification does not correlate with party affiliation in Florida, as it does in other states (25% of Catholics and 24% of Protestants in Florida identify themselves as Democrats). In all five states, approximately 30% of respondents identified themselves as Independents. The

---

[43] Kosmin, Barry A., and Ariela Keysar. Party Political Preferences of US Hispanics: The Varying Impact of Religion, Social Class and Demographic Factors. *Ethic and Racial Studies*, April 2, 1994. pps 336-347.

[44] Ibid.

second most important variable was age, with majorities of older Latinos favoring the Democrats and considerably lower Democratic identification among 18-34 year olds.

The correlation between religious affiliation and party choice in the Latino community is similar to what is found among the population at large, according to this study. Most Latino Catholics are Democrats (48% compared with 24% Republicans); Latino Protestants also favored the Democratic party, but to a lesser degree (31% Republican compared with 40% for the Democrats), a pattern that mirrors the non-Hispanic white population. Gender, income and education also appear to have a similar significance regarding party affiliation among Latinos, as they do for the larger population. Women tend to support the Democratic Party more than men; Republican support grows as education levels rise, but falls off among those with graduate degrees. Democratic support is highest among those with low household incomes and falls off considerably at levels above $40,000.

The authors of the CUNY study offered several predictions about Latino party identification in the future. As the Latino population ages and the number of college graduates and household incomes increases, "Hispanic support for the two main parties will slowly become more balanced and [that] the pattern of Hispanic political preferences will increasingly reflect that of the majority of Americans."[45] These trends would be reinforced if immigration from South and Central America continues to rise, further altering the demographic profile of the population in favor of the Republicans.

VII. LATINO ELECTED OFFICIALS

In the ten years between 1984 and 1994, the total number of Latino elected officials nation-wide increased by nearly 50% (see figure below). Most observers attribute this growth to three factors: the adoption of bilingual ballot laws; a surge in Latino political activism; and an increase in the number of Latino candidates competing in local, state, and federal elections. Even with these gains, the number of Latinos holding elective office remains low in proportion to the size of the Latino population in the country. Latinos are nearly 9% of U.S. citizens, but the total number of Latino officeholders nation-wide is less than 1% (0.9%) of the country's estimated 511,039 elected officials.[46]

The greatest proportion of Latino elected officials is in municipal and school board positions. Within the universe of Latino elected officials, nearly 98% serve as local officials, slightly more than 3% hold state elective positions, (most in the state legislatures), and less than one-half of 1% are federal officeholders.[47] Presently there are no governors who are Latino, but eight Latinos serve as state elected officials and 176 are state legislators.

The first Latino Member of Congress, Joseph Marion Hernandez of the Territory of Florida, was sworn in more than 170 years ago in 1822. For the remaining years of the 19th century and into the early part of the 20th century, Congress sporadically included one or two

---

[45] Ibid, p. 346.

[46] The total number of elected officials is from: the U.S. Department of Commerce. Bureau of the Census. *1992 Census of Governments: Popularly Elected Officials in 1992.* Preliminary report. GC92-2(P). Washington, U.S. Govt. Print. Off. October 1994. p. 1.

[47] National Association of Latino Elected Officials Education Fund. *Hispanic Elected Officials, 1994, Statistics* (factsheet). Revised December 1994. p. 2.

Latino Members, representing Puerto Rico or the Territory of New Mexico (New Mexico was admitted to the Union in 1912). Since 1905, Congress has always included at least one Latino Member. The total number of Latino Members climbed slowly and steadily throughout the century, and, beginning with the 88th Congress (1963-65), has never fallen below five. The 103rd Congress, with 21 Latino members, was the high mark.

Latino Elected Officials, 1984-1994

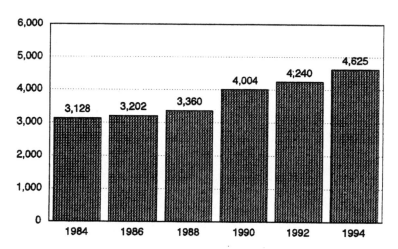

Source: the National Association of Latino Elected Officials

Twenty-eight of the 31 Latino members elected from the states have served in the House of Representatives. Three have served in the Senate, but there have been no Latino Senators in nearly twenty years.[48] The last was Senator Joseph M. Montoya of New Mexico who was defeated in his re-election bid in 1976, having been first elected to the Senate in 1964.

In addition to Latino Members elected from the states, others have served in Congress as resident commissioners from Puerto Rico, nonvoting delegates from Guam and the Virgin Islands, and as territorial delegates prior to their state's admission to the Union. Latino Members who have served in Congress in these positions include 10 territorial delegates, 14 resident commissioners of Puerto Rico, and two nonvoting delegates from Guam and one from the Virgin Islands. The 104th Congress includes 17 Latino Members, all of whom serve in the House of Representatives.

Although Latinos have served in the U.S. Congress since the 1820s, some political milestones are only now being reached. Ileana Ros-Lehtinen's election to Congress in 1988 was a first for Latinas and Cuban-Americans both; in 1992, Nydia Velázquez was the first

---

[48] Of the 31 Latino Members of Congress elected from the states, 29 served in the House only, one served in both the Senate and House, and one served in the Senate only. Congressional Quarterly's *Guide to Congress, 4th Edition*, Washington, Congressional Quarterly Press, Inc., 1991, p. 108-A.

Puerto Rican woman and Lucille Roybal-Allard the first Mexican American woman elected to Congress.

Table 6. Latino Members of 104th Congress

Name (Party)	State or Territory, District	Chamber	Years of Service
Xavier Becerra, (D)	California, 30	House	1992-present
Henry Bonilla, (R)	Texas, 23	House	1992-present
Lincoln Diaz-Balart, (R)	Florida, 21	House	1992-present
E. (Kika) de la Garza, (D)	Texas, 15	House	1964-present
Henry B. Gonzalez, (D)	Texas, 20	House	1961-present
Luis V. Gutierrez, (D)	Illinois, 4	House	1992-present
Matthew G. Martinez, (D)	California, 31	House	1982-present
Robert Menéndez, (D)	New Jersey, 13	House	1992-present
Solomon P. Ortiz, (D)	Texas, 27	House	1982-present
Ed Pastor, (D)	Arizona, 2	House	1991-present
Bill Richardson, (D)	New Mexico, 3	House	1982-present
Carlos Romero-Barceló, (D)	Puerto Rico	House	1992-present
Ileana Ros-Lehtinen, (R)	Florida, 18	House	1989-present
Lucille Roybal-Allard, (D)	California, 33	House	1992-present
José E. Serrano, (D)	New York, 16	House	1990-present
Frank Tejeda, (D)	Texas, 28	House	1992-present
Esteban E. Torres, (D)	California, 34	House	1982-present
Robert A. Underwood, (D)	Guam	House	1992-present
Nydia Velázquez, (D)	New York 12	House	1992-present

Sources: Congressional Hispanic Caucus; and Duncan, Philip D., and Christine C. Lawrence. *Politics in America, 1996.* Washington, Congressional Quarterly, Inc., 1995.

Chapter 2

HISPANICS IN THE LABOR FORCE:
A BRIEF STATISTICAL PORTRAIT

Gail McCallion

ABSTRACT

Hispanics are projected to represent an increasing share of our future population and labor force. Yet, Hispanics continue to experience serious labor market problems. These include generally high levels of unemployment, employment in lower-paying occupations, and low average wages. This short report provides a statistical summary of the labor force experience of Hispanics.[1]

LABOR MARKET EXPERIENCE

In 1993, Hispanics, 16 and over, made up 8.1 percent of the U.S. civilian labor force. (See table 1.) By the year 2000, Hispanics are projected to represent 11.4 percent of the labor force, and, in 2005, Hispanics are projected to represent 11.0 percent of the labor force. (In most Bureau of Labor Statistics (BLS) published data, because Hispanic is not a racial category, Hispanics are under the white category.) Whites, 16 and over, are projected to decrease as a share of the labor force, from 85.4 percent in 1993 to 84.4 percent in 2000, and further to 83.0 percent by 2005. Blacks, 16 and over, are projected to increase from 10.9 percent of the labor force in 1993 to 11.4 percent in 2000, and to 11.6 percent, by 2005. Asians and others, 16 and over, are projected to increase from 3.7 percent of the labor force in 1993 to 4.9 percent in 2000, and increase further to 5.5 percent by 2005.[2]

---

[1] This short report is excerpted from a longer report – U.S. Library of Congress. Congressional Research Service. *Hispanics in the Labor Force*, by Gail McCallion. CRS Report No. 94-552E. Wash., July 7, 1994. 19 p.

[2] These data are from the Current Population Survey (CPS), which is conducted by the Bureau of the Census for the Bureau of Labor Statistics (BLS). Data are collected monthly from a sample of 60,000 households. These data are then multiplied by census weights in order to generalize from the

Hispanics of Mexican extraction make up the largest share of the U.S. Hispanic workforce, 63 percent in 1992. The most rapid growth among Hispanic workers in the last few years has been among Central and South Americans, and among Mexican workers, with growth rates of 61 percent and 28 percent, respectively, between 1986 and 1992.[3]

Hispanic workers are younger than either white or black workers. The median age of the Hispanic labor force in 1992 was 33.9 years. For whites, blacks, and Asian and other races, the median age was 37.5, 35.6 and 30.5 years, respectively. Hispanic workers currently are younger than any other ethnic or racial group except Asians and others; and, by 2005, they are projected to be the youngest group in the labor force with a median age of 35.8 years. In 2005, for whites, blacks, and Asian and other races, the median age is projected to equal 40.9, 38.8, and 38.3 years, respectively.[4] Hispanics' lower median age is due to high immigration and fertility rates. Immigrants lower median age through two mechanisms. First, they tend to be young, and second, because of their youth, they are more likely to have children.[5]

OCCUPATIONAL DISTRIBUTION

Compared to whites, Hispanics are more likely to be employed in blue collar, service, and agricultural occupations. In 1993, 19.9 percent of Hispanics were employed in service occupations; 13.2 percent in precision, production, draft and repair occupations; 22.2 percent as operators, fabricators and laborers; and, 5.8 percent in farming, forestry, and fishing. Compared to whites, Hispanics were much less likely to be employed in the relatively well-paid executive, administrative and managerial occupations, and in professional specialty occupations. (See table 2.)

Hispanics are not a homogenous population. There are significant differences in the distribution of occupations among Hispanics. A special Current Population Survey tabulation for the first quarter of 1994 allows us to examine how the occupational distribution among Hispanics differs by detailed ethnic origin. Compared to other Hispanics, Mexicans are more likely to be employed in: precision, production, craft and repair occupations; or as operators, fabricators and laborers; or in farming, forestry, and fishing. Compared to other Hispanics, Cubans and Puerto Ricans are more likely to be employed in administrative support occupations; executive, administrative and managerial occupations; or in professional

sample to the entire U.S. labor force. Prior to January 1994, CPS data reflected weights based on 1980 Census figures. Beginning with January 1994, Current Population Survey data reflected new weights based on the 1990 Census. These new weights reflect a higher level of Hispanic immigration (particularly of young Hispanic males) and a faster rate of growth of the Hispanic population. Thus, 1994 CPS data, reflecting these new weights, show higher levels of Hispanic population, labor force, and unemployment. BLS data are generally not available by the same racial and ethnic detail as Census data. Whenever available, data be detailed racial and ethnic origin are used in this report.

[3] Cattan, Peter. The Diversity of Hispanics in the U.S. workforce. *Monthly Labor Review*, August 1993. p. 1.

[4] Fullerton, Howard. Another Look at the Labor Force. *Monthly Labor Review*, November 1992. p. 38.

[5] See: U.S. Library of Congress. Congressional Research Service. *U.S. Hispanics: A Demographic Profile*. Report No. 89-469 GOV, by Jennifer Williams. Washington, D.C., 1989. p. 1-7.

specialty occupations. When viewed across all occupations, Cubans have the occupational distribution most closely resembling that of non-Hispanics. (This data series combines blacks and whites in the non-Hispanic category.) Finally, compared to other Hispanics, Central Americans are more likely to be employed in service occupations, and as operators, fabricators, and laborers. (See table 3.)

EDUCATIONAL ATTAINMENT

Hispanics, on average have less formal education than other ethnic and racial groups. Recent data indicate that 53.1 percent of Hispanics 25 years and older had completed four years of high school or more, compared to 82.4 percent of the non-Hispanic population 25 years and older. Hispanics also have the highest high school dropout rates of any ethnic or racial group.[6] In addition, only 9.0 percent of Hispanics had completed four years of college or more compared to 22.9 percent of the non-Hispanic population. Although all groups in the labor force have experienced an increase in their levels of educational attainment over time, Hispanics continue to lag in overall years of schooling.

Some Hispanics, however, have fared much better than others. Rivera-Batiz found evidence of convergence between 1970 and 1987 in high school completion rates for both Cubans and Puerto Ricans compared to non-Hispanic whites. However, high school completion rates for Mexicans compared to non-Hispanic whites fell during the same time period.[7]

---

[6] DeFreitas, Gregory. *Inequality at Work*. New York, Oxford University Press, 1991. p. 187.

[7] Rivera-Batiz, Francisco. The Effects of Literacy on the Earnings of Hispanics in the United States. In: Melendez, Edwin, Clara Rodriquez, and Janis Barry Figueroa, ed. *Hispanics in the Labor Force*. New York Plenum Press, 1991. p. 59.

Table 1. Civilian Labor Force and Participation Rates by Age, Race and Hispanic Origin Actual 1993 and Moderate Growth Projections for 2000 and 2005 (Numbers in Thousands)

Race and Age	1993 Labor Force			2000 Labor Force			2005 Labor Force		
	Level	Percent	Participation Rate	Level	Percent	Participation Rate	Level	Percent	Participation Rate
Hispanic									
16+	10,377	8.1	65.9	16,046	11.4	68.0	16,581	11.0	68.4
16-24	2,116	1.7	59.9	1,825	2.0	62.5	3,316	2.2	43.4
25-34	3,365	2.6	77.6	4,077	2.9	80.3	4,266	2.9	81.6
35-44	2,671	2.1	78.9	3,967	2.8	82.8	4,516	3.0	84.4
45-54	1,442	1.1	73.1	2,291	1.6	75.6	3,004	2.0	76.8
44-64	646	0.5	51.6	942	0.7	54.6	1,271	0.8	56.0
65+	137	0.1	10.8	171	0.1	9.3	208	0.1	9.3
White									
16+	109,359	85.4	66.7	118,845	84.4	68.7	124,847	83.0	69.3
16-24	17,191	13.4	69.1	18,293	13.0	69.8	19,926	13.2	70.7
25-34	38,996	22.7	84.6	26,180	18.6	87.2	25,198	16.7	88.7
35-44	29,190	22.8	85.3	32,849	23.3	89.2	31,404	20.9	90.9
45-54	20,407	15.9	82.5	26,051	18.5	85.8	29,825	19.8	87.4
44-64	10,386	8.1	57.2	12,143	8.6	60.2	15,127	10.1	61.7
65+	3,199	2.5	11.5	8,326	2.4	11.3	3,466	2.3	11.4
Black									
16+	13,943	10.9	62.4	16,046	11.4	61.4	17,395	11.6	66.2
16-24	2,467	1.9	53.8	2,703	1.9	54.9	3,019	2.0	56.6
25-34	4,168	3.3	78.4	4,045	2.9	80.6	4,031	2.7	81.2
35-44	3,738	2.9	81.0	4,647	3.3	84.4	4,629	3.1	85.7
45-54	2,213	1.7	74.9	3,131	2.2	80.0	3,890	2.6	81.7
44-64	1,102	0.9	50.5	1,214	0.9	51.9	1,485	1.0	51.5
65+	257	0.2	9.6	304	0.2	10.7	332	0.2	11.1

Table 1. Continued

Race and Age	1993 Labor Force			2000 Labor Force			2005 Labor Force		
	Level	Percent	Participation Rate	Level	Percent	Participation Rate	Level	Percent	Participation Rate
Asian & Other									
16+	4,738	3.7	64.9	6,948	4.9	56.9	8,274	5.5	50.5
16-24	722	0.6	50.5	1,056	0.8	53.1	1,282	0.9	53.9
25-34	1,321	1.0	77.8	1,901	1.4	77.8	2,119	1.4	73.8
35-44	1,336	1.0	77.9	1,955	1.4	83.0	2,254	1.5	84.5
45-54	922	0.7	71.8	1,351	1.0	80.7	1,703	1.1	81.6
44-64	380	0.3	56.9	565	0.4	58.0	762	0.5	58.9
65+	81	0.1	12.4	120	0.1	11.9	152	0.1	11.7

Note: Details do not add to totals. Because Hispanic is not considered a racial category, Hispanics are also included in white or black population groups. All projections are based on the Census Bureau's middle growth path. The middle growth path assumes: (1) a 2.1 total fertility rate; (2) life expectancy of 82.1 years; and (3) annual net immigration of 880,000.

Source: U.S. Bureau of Labor Statistics. Unpublished Current Population Survey data. 1993 Labor Force data are for December 1993, and are from *Employment and Earnings*, January 1994.

Table 2. Employed Civilians by Occupation, Race, and Hispanic Origin 1993 Annual Averages (Percent Distribution)

	Total	Executive, Administrative, and Managerial	Professional Specialty	Technicians and Related Support Occupations	Sales Occupations	Administrative Support Inc. Clerical	Service Occupations	Precision Production, Craft & Repair	Operators, Fabricators & Laborers	Farming, Forestry, & Fishing
Total	100.0	12.9	14.2	3.4	11.9	15.6	13.8	11.2	14.3	2.8
Hispanic	100.0	7.5	6.6	2.2	9.0	13.7	19.9	13.2	22.2	5.8
White	100.0	13.5	14.6	3.3	12.5	15.4	12.6	11.6	13.5	3.0
Black	100.0	7.9	9.7	3.2	7.6	17.1	23.5	8.1	20.9	1.7

Source: U.S. Bureau of Labor Statistics. *Employment and Earnings*, January 1994. p. 230.

Table 3. Experienced Labor Force (Employed and Experienced Unemployed) by Occupation and Origin, 1st Quarter 1994

	Total	Executive, Administrative, and Managerial	Professional Specialty	Technicians and Related Support Occupations	Sales Occupations	Administrative Support Including Clerical	Service Occupations	Precision Production, Craft & Repair	Operators, Fabricators & Laborers	Farming, Forestry, & Fishing
All Hispanics	99.9	6.7	6.3	1.6	9.3	13.2	20.2	13.2	23.7	5.8
Mexicans	99.8	5.9	5.3	1.2	8.4	12.4	19.0	14.0	25.3	8.3
Puerto Ricans	100.1	9.1	9.0	2.8	10.0	18.0	19.6	11.5	18.7	1.2
Cubans	100.0	12.6	7.8	1.7	15.2	17.8	17.1	8.8	17.5	1.4
Central & South Americans	99.9	5.6	6.7	2.0	8.1	11.3	26.7	13.1	24.5	1.9
Other Hispanics	100.1	9.0	9.5	1.8	13.4	15.2	18.4	11.7	19.4	1.7
Non-Hispanics	100.0	13.1	14.7	3.3	12.4	15.4	13.7	10.9	14.0	2.4

Source: U.S. Bureau of Labor Statistics. Unpublished Current Population Survey data.

INCOME

Hispanic men's income and wages relative to white men's income and wages were stagnant in the 1940s, improved in thc 1960s, and then declined in the 1970s and 1980s.[8] This historical overview of income trends was compiled by DeFreitas based on Census data through 1980, and CPS data on median income for 1973 through 1987. An examination of subsequent Bureau of Labor Statistics (BLS) data on median weekly earnings for full-time wage and salary workers does not indicate any significant turnaround in this downward trend. These BLS data show that the Hispanic-white earnings ratio for men declined from 68.0 in 1987 to 66.3 in 1993. There was a slight improvement in 1992 and 1993 compared to earlier years, but that was probably attributable to an improving economy

The Hispanic-white income gap for women improved during the 1950s and 1960s and then worsened during the 1970s. If we look only at wages we see that the Hispanic-white wage gap for women was constant in the 1950s, improved in thc 1960s, and continued to improve at a slower rate in the 1970s. It is interesting to note that while the Hispanic-white income gap for women worsened in the 1970s, the wage gap improved slightly. This counterintuitive result is probably due to reduced labor force participation by Hispanic women in the 1970s, which would inflate their average wage level. DeFreitas did not examine subsequent CPS wage data for women; the earliest comparable data on median weekly earnings begin in 1985. In contrast with the 1960s and 1970s trend, these data indicate a steady decline in the Hispanic-white earnings ratio for women between 1985 and 1993. In 1985, the Hispanic-white earnings ratio for women equaled 81.5, by 1993 it equaled 77.9

UNEMPLOYMENT

Hispanics have historically experienced unemployment rates that are higher than whites, but lower than blacks. In 1993, the unemployment rate for Hispanic workers, 16 and over, equaled 10.6 percent. The unemployment rate for white and black workers, 16 and over, equaled 6.0 and 12.9 percent, respectively. Hispanics and blacks unemployment and labor force participation rates are also more highly correlated with cyclical downturns. During recessions, Hispanics and blacks experience higher increases in unemployment, and greater reductions in labor force participation rates, than whites. Among Hispanics, Cubans experience lower than average jobless rates. In the first quarter of 1994, the unemployment rate for Cubans equaled 7.4 percent compared to 10.5 for all Hispanics.

---

[8]   DeFreitas, *Inequality*, p. 55-59.

Chapter 3

HISPANIC TRADITION AND ACHIEVEMENT IN THE UNITED STATES

Garrine P. Laney

ABSTRACT

This report provides a review of Hispanic heritage in the United States. It includes a retrospective of the history of people of Hispanic origin in the United States, summarizes their achievements in contemporary America, and highlights the contributions of distinguished Hispanic Americans. It is a revision of CRS Report 89-532 and CRS Report 93-906.

PREFACE

The Hispanic tradition in what is now the continental United States began with the first Spanish landing on the coast of Florida in 1513. Beginning in about 1699, Mexicans gradually settled much of the Southwest, establishing an enduring cultural identity. The United States annexed Florida in 1819 and, according to the terms of the Treaty of Guadalupe Hidalgo negotiated after the Mexican War, in 1848 also annexed much of the Southwest.

In the 20th century, the Hispanic population, which once consisted largely of Mexican Americans, has become more numerous and diverse, through a high rate of natural growth, and a continuing inflow of Puerto Ricans, Cubans, Dominicans, and Central and South Americans. Hispanic-Americans have at times been victims of various forms of discrimination. In recent years they have been energized by an enhanced awareness of their cultural vitality and potential for economic and political self-empowerment. They have established many organizations to promote the interests of Hispanic Americans and protect their civil rights, such as the League of United Latin American Citizens, the American G.I. Forum, the Mexican American Legal Defense and Education Fund, and the Puerto Rican Legal Defense and Education Fund among others.

Passage of the Voting Rights Act of 1965, as amended, encouraged many Hispanics to participate in the political arena without fear of negative repercussions. As a consequence, there has been an increase in the number of Hispanics holding public office, elective and appointive,, throughout the United States. There are presently 17 Members of the Congressional Hispanic Caucus.

Hispanics share the common goals with other Americans of freedom, opportunity, and a chance to build a better life. In pursuing these aspirations they have made important contributions to life in the United States in the fields of culture, sports, entertainment, business enterprise, science, politics and others. Hispanic Heritage Month, commemorated annually between September 15 and October 15, seeks to increase national awareness and understanding of and respect for Hispanics and their tradition of achievement in this country.

INTRODUCTION

The growing number of Hispanic Americans, the richness of their cultural experiences, and their increasing political and economic visibility have led to an emerging awareness of not only their presence but their many contributions to our richly pluralistic and diverse national culture.

Hispanics are considered an ethnic group whose members may be of any race. They constitute one of the fastest growing segments of the U.S. population. By the turn of the century, the United States will be second only to Mexico in the number of Spanish speaking residents.

This review of the Hispanic experience in the United States, drawn from the sources cited at the end of this report, provides only selected highlights of Latino tradition and achievement. For every struggle or triumph it recounts, hundreds more remain untold. For every Hispanic it identifies, there are countless others who worked, and continue to work, toward their goals outside the spotlight of national fame.

TRADITION

Discovery

The Hispanic presence in the United States began almost 500 years ago, in 1493, when Christopher Columbus discovered and claimed what are now the U.S. Virgin Islands and the Commonwealth of Puerto Rico. In fact, more than two-thirds of the territory of the 48 contiguous United States was discovered, settled, or governed at some period by Spanish speaking people.

The Hispanic tradition in the United States is as new as the families who every day enter the United States in hope of building a better life, and as old as Easter Sunday, 1513, when

Juan Ponce de León landed on the east coast of the peninsula he named "La Florida" – both for its lush vegetation, and for the liturgical season.[1]

Ponce de León spent little time on the North American mainland during his first expedition, but returned eight years later on a fruitless quest for the legendary Fountain of Youth. He was followed on the mainland by a succession of Spanish explorers whose expeditions traversed what is now the American "Sunbelt" from Florida to New Mexico and California: Alvarez de Pinela, Cabeza de Vaca, Cabrillo, Coronado, and de Soto, whose arrival at the Mississippi in 1541 is commemorated in one of the great historical canvases commissioned for the Capitol Rotunda in Washington.[2]

The conquistadors came for gold, adventure, and a chance to spread the Christian faith, but in the face of incredible hardship none remained. The first permanent European settlement in what is now the United States was established by Pedro Menéndez de Avilés, on August 28, 1565. Menéndez, landing near the spot where Ponce de León had first planted the Spanish flag 52 years before, named his settlement in Florida for Saint Augustine, the saint whose feast day was celebrated when he first touched shore.[3]

Forty-two years would pass before English settlers founded Jamestown, in Virginia, far to the north, and still 14 more before the Pilgrims celebrated the first Thanksgiving at Plymouth in 1621.

Settlement

In 1598, Juan de Onate, under the authority of the Viceroy of New Spain (now Mexico), led the first expedition into what is now the United States. After several unsuccessful tries, Pedro de Peralta founded Santa Fe in 1610 as capital of the Province of New Mexico. Throughout the 17th century, a slow trickle of migration and settlement continued into the new lands. The Hispanic presence suffered a major setback in 1680, when Pueblo Indians rose in revolt against mistreatment, forcing the abandonment of Santa Fe; but the settlers returned, and Santa Fe was restored to Spanish control in 1696 and regained its position as center of the Spanish-Mexican presence in the Southwest. It remains the capital of New Mexico today, three centuries later.[4]

As settlement continued, many of the Pueblo Indians gradually adopted Christianity and Hispanic culture, and intermarried with the Mexican immigrants. The hardy churros, Spanish-bred sheep that thrived in the arid conditions of the Southwest, were raised by Indian and settler alike. Horses that escaped or were taken by Indians, spread throughout the region, changing the life of the Plains Indians forever.[5]

A few years before the end of the century, Alonso Ponce de León led the first expedition east from the Rio Grande, crossing the Nueces, San Antonio, and Guadalupe Rivers. Although Ponce de León's original settlements were temporarily withdrawn, the determined

---

[1] David J. Weber, *The Spanish Frontier in North America*, New Haven, Yale University Press, 1992, pp. 31-33.

[2] *Ibid.*, pp. 34, 40-54.

[3] *Ibid.*, pp. 60-64.

[4] *Ibid.*, pp. 80-86.

[5] *Ibid.*, p. 310.

Mexicans returned to stay in 1716, settling an area that would become the State of Texas. On their return, they were surprised to find herds of wild horses and cattle, abandoned or strayed from the earlier settlements. The cattle, lean and hardy, had adapted to local conditions, evolving into the famous Texas longhorn.[6]

The final thrust of exploration and settlement under the Spanish crown began in what is now California, the richest and most populous of the 50 United States. In April 1769, Juan Peréz led an expedition by sea from Mexico to the lands known as Alta California. In a few months, he was joined by another ship and by two expeditions that had marched overland from Mexico. Given little assistance of protection by the weak and often oppressive Spanish colonial administration, the settlements north of Old Mexico were left largely to their own devices.[7] In Florida, missions were abandoned and only isolated garrisons remained at Pensacola and Saint Augustine, possession of which alternated between Britain and Spain during the colonial wars of the 18th century.[8] Further west, in Texas, New Mexico and California, a new had hardy culture was slowly emerging, although the population remained small – only about 10,000 in New Mexico in 1750, and even less in Texas. But in these two provinces, and later in California, small towns, ranchos and haciendas were gradually being established.

Contact With Anglo-America

Far to the east, on the Atlantic coastline of North America, English speaking and other northern European settlers, in far greater numbers than the Mexican Americans of the Southwest, were involved in a similar process of exploration, settlement, and cultural evolution.

While there was little direct contact between the two peoples, Hispanic America had already made many valuable contributions to the life of the thirteen colonies of British North America. Wild hogs, the descendants of those brought to early Spanish missions and settlements, proved a valuable source of food for English settlers as far north as Jamestown. As early as 1532, a Spanish royal decree required all ships sailing for the New World to transport plants, seeds, and domesticated animals. Spanish settlers and explorers introduced a broad range of agricultural products, such as wheat, barley, figs, oranges, grapes, and ginger to the Americas. The commercial production of sugar and tobacco, staples of Southern plantation agriculture, was pioneered in Hispanic America. The Spanish dollar circulated so widely in North America that the dollar established as the official monetary unit of the United States in 1786 was based on it.[9]

In 1763, the last of the great colonial wars of the 18th century came to an end. France was driven from North America, and her colonies were acquired by Britain (Canada) and Spain (Louisiana). At this moment of triumph, however, Britain reversed its long-standing policy of

---

[6] *Ibid.*, pp. 33-34.

[7] *Ibid.*, pp. 249, 252-53, 264-65.

[8] *Ibid.*, pp. 100-105, 199-200.

[9] Adams, James T., *Dictionary of American History*, New York, Charles Scribner's Sons, 1951, vol. 2, p. 157; *Ibid.*, vol. 5, p. 140.

"benign neglect" of the North American colonies, and sought to strengthen and extend her colonial administration.[10]

After more than a decade of rising tension, hostilities broke out between the American colonists and British authorities. In the ensuing American Revolution, the United States received both financial aid from Span and military assistance in the form of successful expeditions against Mobile and Pensacola led by Spain's capable governor or Louisiana, Bernardo de Galvez. Galvez also promoted the shipment of military supplies up the Mississippi, where they were extremely helpful to the expedition of George Rogers Clark that drove the British from the old Northwest. Galvez' campaign on the Mississippi River in 1779 operated as far north as Saint Louis and resulted in the capture of Baton Rouge and Natchez.[11]

Liberated from the restraints of British rule, and having established a stable, democratic government under the Constitution adopted in 1789, the United States began a relentless process of westward exploration and settlement. With steady natural growth and a continuing flow of immigration, an advantage not enjoyed by the Hispanic peoples of Texas, New Mexico, and California, the population of the United States increased from an estimated 2,200,000 in 1770 to 17,100,000 as measured by the 1840 Census.

In 1803, the United States purchased the vast Louisiana Territory from France (it has been a Spanish possession between 1763 and 1801), and in 1819, annexed Florida.[12] With Mexico's independence from Spain in 1821, the two nations shared a long common border through lands sparsely populated by Native Americans. The westward flow of settlers from the Atlantic seaboard made it inevitable, however, that Hispanic America and Anglo America would soon meet.

American Annexation of the Southwest

Stephen F. Austin and other Anglo "empresarios" were awarded contracts by Mexico to settle lands in Texas in the early 1820s. The trickle of Anglo colonists soon grew to a flood – by 1835, 25,000 U.S. citizens had settled in Texas. At the same time, opposition to the authoritarian rule of President Antonio López de Santa Ana was increasing among both Anglo settlers and Hispanic Texans as the liberal Mexican Constitution of 1824 was discarded. In 1835, the Texans revolted against the central government. Santa Ana, attempting to suppress the revolt, crushed a rebel force at the Alamo, in San Antonio, but was himself decisively defeated at the Battle of San Jacinto. Texans declared their state an independent republic.[13]

The Republic of Texas is viewed in retrospect as basically an Anglo enterprise, but the Texas Revolution of 1836 also owed much to the work of Lorenzo de Zavala. Zavala was a distinguished Mexican political figure who signed the Constitution of 1824 and served both in the Cabinet and as a state governor. Although he was a personal friend of Santa Ana, Zavala

---

[10] *Ibid.*, pp. 198-199.

[11] *Ibid.*, pp. 266-267.

[12] *Ibid.*, p. 291; *Federal Writers' Project, Florida, A Guide to the Southernmost State*, New York, Oxford University Press, 1949, pp. 55-56.

[13] *Federal Writers' Project, Texas, A guide to the Lone Star State*, New York, Hastings House, 1949, pp. 42-46.

refused to bow to his authoritarian rule, resigned his post as ambassador to France in 1835, and sailed for Texas, where he joined the independence movement. Before his untimely death by drowning in 1836, Lorenzo de Zavala served in the Texas Independence Convention and was elected first Vice President of the Republic of Texas.[14]

After a decade of independence, in which Mexico and Texas observed an uneasy truce, Texas was admitted to the United States as the 28th State of the Union in December 1845. Hostilities broke out along the ill-defined border, and on May 11, 1846, President James Polk, strongly influenced by the expansionist views widely held in the United States, asked for a declaration of war against Mexico. Congress voted for war on May 13, and within weeks U.S. forces were engaged in combat against Santa Ana's army. The bulk of U.S. forces were committed first in northern Mexico and, later, at Mexico City from the port of Vera Cruz. Far to the north a small expedition under Colonel Stephen W. Kearney marched overland from Fort Leavenworth, Kansas, to Santa Fe, and on to California, meeting little resistance from Mexican forces, and none from the civilian population.[15]

In California, Kearney's expedition was welcomed by Mariano G. Vallejo (1807-1890). A native Californian, Vallejo had served as an officer in the provincial militia until the Santa Ana government attempted to establish an authoritarian administration in California. In 1836, Vallejo led an open revolt against the Mexican government and proclaimed the "Free State of California". From his home in Sonoma, he and his supporters defeated every Mexican attempt to subdue them, while at the same time welcoming and protecting Anglo settlers who were beginning to arrive in small numbers. With the end of the Mexican War, and annexation, Vallejo strongly supported statehood for California, and served in both the State Constitutional Convention and State Senate. Known as "the Lord of the North" Vallejo remained influential in California politics and became a legend during his long and productive life. In 1966 the United States honored his memory when the Navy commissioned the U.S.S. Mariano G. Vallejo, a nuclear powered fleet ballistic missile submarine.[16]

In the South, U.S. General Winfield Scott fought his way from Vera Cruz to Mexico City in 1847, capturing the capital in a fierce campaign that culminated in the heroic, though unsuccessful defense of Chapultepec. On September 14, the U.S. flag was hoisted over the National Palace, and Mexico sued for peace. Pursuing the policies of "manifest destiny," the United States forced Mexico to cede the huge territories that now comprise the States of California, New Mexico, Arizona, Nevada, and Utah, and parts of Wyoming and Colorado, and recognize U.S. control over Texas, in return for a payment of $15,000,000. The Senate ratified the treaty, negotiated at Guadalupe Hidalgo, on May 10, 1848, and the United States found itself in possession of vast new lands and its first substantial non-English speaking minority population – the Mexican Americans.[17]

---

[14] Lorenzo de Zavala, *Journey to the United States of North America*, Austin, Texas, Shoal Creek Publishers, Inc., 1980, pp. xv-xvi.

[15] *Federal Writers' Project, Texas*, pp. 46-47; *Federal Writers' Project, California, A Guide to the Golden State*, New York, Hastings House, p. 52; Bancroft, Hubert Howe, *History of Arizona and New Mexico, 1530-1888*, Albuquerque, Horn and Wallace, pp. 415-28.

[16] *The Encyclopedia of Americana*, International Edition, Danbury, Connecticut, Grolier, Inc., 1987, vol. 27, p. 864; Malone, Dumas, *Dictionary of American Biography*, New York, Charles Scribner's Sons, vol. 19, pp. 145-46.

[17] Stephan Thernstrom, *Harvard Encyclopedia of American Ethnic Groups*, Cambridge, Massachusetts, Harvard University Press, pp. 701-702.

Anglo Domination

Mexican Americans might have expected "the blessings of liberty" to flow from annexation, but instead, U.S. citizenship brought discrimination and gradual dispossession from lands held for generations in many cases. In California, the tiny population of Californios was overwhelmed by Anglos who were lured by news of the discovery of gold at Sutter's Mill in 1848. With a few exceptions, such as Mariano Vallejo, Hispanics were relegated to the lowest rung of the economic and social ladder. Proud owners of haciendas and ranchos gradually lost control of their land, and Hispanics were largely reduced to peonage.[18]

In Texas, the equally sparse Hispanic population was displaced from the eastern and central parts of the State by the incursion of Anglo ranchers and cotton planters. Only in the valley of the Rio Grande did Mexican culture continue to survive and thrive.[19]

Hispanic society in New Mexico did not suffer the same fate as in California and Texas. Settled earlier, New Mexico had more missions, towns, and ranchos than the other two States combined, and boasted a population of 44,000 as early as 1827, ten times the number of Hispanics in either California or Texas Moreover, New Mexico possessed neither the lure of quick wealth nor the rich range and cotton lands of Texas. U.S. Army garrisons were established, and Anglos began to settle, but they were comparatively few in number. New Mexico retained its traditional language and culture proud and intact. For the first century of U.S. rule, life in New Mexico was little changed from the two previous centuries of Spanish and Mexican domination.[20]

THE TWENTIETH CENTURY: IMMIGRATION AND REVIVAL

Towards the end of the 19th century, political and economic factors combined to generate an influx of Spanish speaking Cubans, Puerto Ricans, Mexicans and other Hispanics into the United States. The Hispanic population continues to grow and has expanded beyond the traditional Southwest region into the Midwest. Census data for 1990 show that Illinois has a larger Hispanic population than the south-western States of Arizona, Colorado, or New Mexico.

Cubans

The Spanish-American War of 1898 led to independence for Cuba. During the long struggle for independence, Cubans had sought refuge from Spanish colonial misrule in Florida, where, in fact, José Martí, the father of Cuban independence, established the Cuban Revolutionary Party in 1892. Although Cubans had first entered the United States with the de

---

[18] Julie Catalano, *The Mexican Americans*, New York, Chelsea House, 1988, pp. 32, 43; Jodine Mayberry, *Mexicans*, New York, Franklin Watts, Inc., 1990, pp. 15-19; Thernstrom, *Harvard Encyclopedia of American Ethnic Groups*, pp. 706-707.

[19] Catalano, *Mexican Americans*, pp. 41-42.

[20] Bancroft, *History of Arizona and New Mexico*, pp. 629-55; Catalano, *Mexican Americans*, p. 43.

Soto expedition in 1539, following the war, a show but steady trickle of Cubans began to arrive as permanent residents in the States, some to New York, but more the cigar factories of Tampa, where a small but stable Cuban American community sprang up.[21]

Table 1. States With Largest Hispanic Population

State	Population	Percent
California	7,687,938	26
Texas	4,339,905	26
New York	2,214,026	12
Florida	1,574,143	12
Illinois	904,446	8
New Jersey	739,861	10
Arizona	688,338	19
New Mexico	579,224	38
Colorado	424,302	13
Massachusetts	287,549	5
Pennsylvania	232,262	2

Source: U.S. Department of Commerce. Bureau of the Census. 1990 CPH-1-49. 1990. *Census of Population and Housing.* Summary, Population and Housing Characteristics. Washington, D.C. Government Printing Office. 1992.

Cuban migration continued at a slow rate until the watershed events that followed Fidel Castro's Cuban revolution of 1959. After 1961, Cubans, many from the professional and middle classes, increasingly fled the Castro regime, settling largely in southern Florida. The Cuban-American population received another large-scale influx of refugees in 1980, when the Castro government encouraged the migration of 125,000 "marielitos" in the Mariel boat lift.[22] According to the Census of 1990, over 1,000,000 people of Cuban origin or descent live in the continental United States.

Puerto Ricans

Puerto Rico, Spain's other remaining colony in the New World, was retained after the Spanish-American War as a U.S. possession. In 1917, citizenship was extended to all inhabitants of the island, but the number of Puerto Ricans who settled in the continental United States remained small until after the Second World War.

After 1945, spurred by economic hardship at home, and drawn by the establishment of cheap air service and the demand for workers in New York's labor intensive industries, Puerto Rican migration to the mainland surged.[23] According to the Census of 1990, 2,727,754

---

[21] Renee Gernand, *The Cuban Americans*, New York, Chelsea House, 1988, pp. 22-27, 43.

[22] *Ibid.*, pp. 60-62

[23] Jerome J. Aliotta, *The Puerto Ricans*, New York, Chelsea House, 1991, pp. 13-14.

people of Puerto Rican origin or descent were living in the United States, the second largest6 group of Hispanic Americans.

As citizens possessing the right of legal entry and re-entry, the Puerto Rican population on the mainland has ebbed and flowed in response to economic conditions. In the seventies, as industries in New York declined and the national economy suffered from stagnation and recession, migration was minimal. At the same time, Puerto Ricans began to move to other parts of the Northeast and Middle Atlantic States.[24]

Mexicans

Mexican immigration across the border into the United States represents one of the largest population movements in this country's history. Drawn by the growing need for labor, from the cotton fields of Texas, to the farms, orchards, vineyards, and factories of California, Mexicans began entering the States in small but growing numbers after the turn of the century.[25]

Often they were subjected to systematic discrimination, as well as deportations. Chicano workers were actively sought by Anglo farmers, ranchers, and businessmen when labor was in short supply, but were often forcibly repatriated to Mexico when the economy slowed or fell into depression or recession. Notwithstanding these drawbacks, the Mexican-American population continues to increase, through a high rate of natural growth and immigration – both official and undocumented.[26] While less geographically concentrated than the Cubans or Puerto Ricans, over 13,000,000 people of Mexican origin or descent currently live in the United States. They remain a major presence throughout the Southwest.

Dominicans

Although Dominicans have migrated to the United States since the turn of the century, they have not done so in significant numbers until recently. Today, about one million Dominicans reside in this country, of which 85 percent are estimated to be immigrants. In 1961, the assassination of Generalissimo Rafael Trujillo, along with the resulting political and economic turmoil in the Dominican Republic, initiated increased immigration of Dominicans, primarily to New York City. Dominicans emigrate largely to escape their country's economic problems – an average annual inflation rate of 60 percent, an unemployment rate of 25 percent, and a four billion collar foreign debt in 1990. Dominican immigrants from all educational and economic levels have entered the United States by legal and illegal means.[27]

The estimated Dominican population in New York in 1990 was 800,000 out of a total Hispanic population of 2 million – a number that rivals that of the two traditionally largest Latino groups there – Puerto Ricans and Cubans. Yet, a sizeable number of New York residents is unaware of their presence because they are often mistaken for Puerto Ricans and

---

[24] *Ibid.*, pp. 40-41, 45-48, 62-65.

[25] Catalano, *Mexican Americans*, pp. 45-47; Mayberry, *Mexicans*, pp. 21-24; Thernstrom, *Harvard Encyclopedia of American Ethnic Groups*, pp. 702-704.

[26] *Ibid.*, pp. 48-55.

[27] Christopher Dwyer, *The Dominican Americans*, New York, Chelsea House, 1991, pp. 13-18.

section of Queens, neighborhoods rarely visited by many other New Yorkers.[28] Perhaps as many as half of New York's Dominicans are undocumented workers. Most are employed in the service and manufacturing sectors of the economy. Dominicans who were professionals and managers in their country are usually unsuccessful in acquiring similar employment status in the United States; frequently they have to accept jobs for which they are overqualified. But they still tend to enjoy a higher standard of living in the United States than they did in the Dominican Republic.[29]

To aid in their adjustment to the United States, Dominicans have established about 120 mutual benefit organizations in New York City alone. These associations, which provide recreational, cultural, civic and social services, tend to attract members based on regional ties, class interests, and family loyalties. Some groups such as the Council of Dominican Organizations, formed in 1972, fight for the rights of undocumented Dominicans; others offer free day care for children, family counseling, and English classes.[30]

Other Hispanic Americans

About five million Hispanic Americans living in the United States are classified by the Census Bureau as people of "other Hispanic origin." They have come in varying numbers over the years from places as diverse as Spain, and South and Central America. Central Americans comprise one of the most visible and fastest growing groups in this category. Driven from their homes by war, political oppression and poverty, they are arriving in even greater numbers, many as undocumented immigrants.

While these official figures reflect the continuing growth in the United States' Hispanic population, many observers maintain that they underestimate the actual number of Hispanics.

Table 2. Hispanics in the U.S. by Origin

Country of Origin	Population	Percent
Mexico	13,495,938	5.4
Puerto Rico	2,727,754	1.1
Cuba	1,043,932	.4
Other	5,086,435	2.0

Source: U.S. Department of Commerce. Bureau of the Census. *1990 Census of Population, General Population Characteristics. United States*. Washington, D.C., Government Printing Office, 1992.

---

[28] *Ibid.*, p. 16.

[29] Dwyer, *Dominican Americans*, p. 58.

[30] *Ibid.*, p. 66-68.

Ethnic Revitalization

The Hispanic peoples of the United States continue to grow in numbers, achievements, and ethnic awareness. In the decade of the 1960s, Hispanics of every origin began to realize and appreciate anew the diverse vitality of their shared cultural heritage, and their increasing potential for political and economic empowerment. Inspired, in part, by the struggles of black Americans to share equally and fully in the promises and opportunities of American life, Hispanic awareness was expressed in an increased pride and activism. The term Chicago, once considered demeaning by Mexican Americans, became an expression of pride as Hispanics grew more aware of their unique identity and contributions to America. The use of degrading stereotypes of Hispanics often found in films, television, and advertising was protested successfully.[31]

New organizations were founded to protect and extend the rights of Hispanic Americans. The long-established League of United Latin American Citizens was joined by the American G.I. Forum, the Mexican American Legal Defense and Education Fund the Puerto Rican Legal Defense and Education Fund, the National Association of Latino Elected and Appointed Officials, La Raza Unida, the Cuban American Foundation, and others. Hispanic Members of Congress established the Congressional Hispanic Caucus in 1976 to promote the interests of Hispanic Americans in the legislative arena.

Provisions of the Voting Rights Act were extended to areas in which Hispanics had historically been discouraged from voting by discriminatory practices. Bilingual education and election materials brought greater opportunity for Hispanic participation in the political process. The past 30 years have seen increases in the number of Hispanics holding public office, elective and appointive, throughout the United States.[32]

Total membership of the Congressional Hispanic Caucus during the 106th Congress is 17. Members of the Caucus are Lucille Roybal-Allard, Chair (CA), Xavier Becerra, (CA), Charles A. Gonzalez (TX), Luis V. Gutiérrez (IL), Rubén Hinojosa (TX), Matthew Martinez (CA), Robert Menendez (NJ), Grace Napolitano (CA), Solomon P. Ortiz (TX), Ed Pastor (AZ), Silvestre Reyes (TX), Ciro D. Rodriguez (TX), Carlos Romero-Barceló (PR), Loretta Sanchez (CA), José E. Serrano (NY), Robert Underwood (Guam), and Nydia Velázquez (NY).

In 1998, the National Association of Latino Elected and Appointed Officials identified 4,851 Hispanics holding public office at all levels of government in eight states with large Hispanic populations (Arizona, California, Colorado, Florida, Illinois, New Mexico, New York, and Texas). Texas, with 1,749, led the nation in the highest number of elected Hispanic officials in 1998, followed by Illinois and California with 1,114 and 789, respectively.[33]

A Hispanic American, William Richardson, has been appointed Secretary of Energy by President Clinton.

---

[31] Catalano, *Mexican Americans*, pp. 61-65.

[32] CRS Report by Garrine P. Laney, *The Voting Rights Act of 1965, As Amended: Its History and Current Issues* (Washington, 1995, pp. 17-20).

[33] Naleo Educational Fund, *The 1998 National Director of Latino Elected Officials*. Washington, National Association of Latino Elected and Appointed Officials, 1998, pp. 2, 16, 48, 56, 62, 108, 132, 138.

The scope of public service extends to many professions: education, the law, labor, and others. In each of these fields, there is a growing record of Hispanic achievement. Communications has been a natural field for expansion for a Hispanic population in which many speak exclusively Spanish or use Spanish in the homes. There are numerous Spanish-language radio stations in the United States. The Spanish International Network – SIN Television Network – began with a single station in San Antonio. Today its programming is broadcast in major metropolitan areas throughout the country.

Spanish-language newspapers have long been an important means of communication in the Hispanic community. New York's *El Diario-La Prensa*, Los Angeles' *La Opinion*, Miami's *Diario las Americas, El Manana* in Chicago, and *El Sol Texas* of Dallas are only the best known examples of a thriving industry.

The need for financial services in the barrio, such as check cashing, gave rise to a new type of Hispanic business, where commercial banks closed branches and restricted services in America's inner cities. For years, bodegas and other community oriented businesses have met these needs. Now they are being joined by more sophisticated operations, which not only cash checks, but also handle utility payments, mailbox rentals, and lottery ticket sales. Traditional banking services have been offered for many years at New York's Banco de Ponce and Banco Popular de Puerto Rico. In Miami, Republic National Bank, serving the Cuban American community, has grown to be among the largest financial institutions in populous Dada County.

Continued growth of America's Hispanic population has led to a parallel increase in efforts by producers and advertisers to appeal to this vital part of the national market. Hispanics spend more in the marketplace than the gross national product of many nations. Advertising firms such as Sosa and Associates of San Antonio are directing many of their sales campaigns to Hispanic patronage. The Hispanic-American market and business community are an essential resource for economic growth and show every indication of continuing to stimulate the economy in future decades.

ASPIRATIONS

Hispanic Heritage Month, commemorated between September 15 and October 15, of each year, seeks to increase the national awareness and understanding of, and respect for all Americans of Hispanic origin. Hispanic Americans are a diverse group. They came to America from different places, at different times, and for different reasons. Yet they share in a fundamental cultural identify, and a mutual aspiration to earn and enjoy the promise and benefits that America, at its best, extends to all. In this aspiration, they are united with all those who have come to the United States seeking freedom, security, and the chance to make better lives for themselves and their families.

BIOGRAPHICAL SKETCHES

Hispanic tradition has given birth to Hispanic achievement. Following are a few of the many Hispanics who have contributed to life in the United States in the areas of politics, education, science, sports, music, theater, dance, and film:

Linda Alvarado – (June 15, 1951-) Alvarado was born in Albuquerque, New Mexico. She attended Pomona College in California. In 1976, she founded Alvarado Construction, Inc., a commercial general contracting firm based in Denver, Colorado. It became one of the fastest growing Hispanic and woman-owned businesses in the country. She has assumed leadership roles in various civic and business affairs and has been the focus of articles in newspapers and magazines, including *Hispanic Business Magazine, Rocky Mountain Women at Work*, and *Latino Magazine*. An activist for Hispanics and women's business issues, she has given keynote presentations at Stanford University and other institutions of higher education and many national conferences. Alvarado is a founding member of the Committee of 200, a group of high-ranking women entrepreneurs that is comparable to the Business Round Table. The U.S. Hispanic Chamber of Commerce named her National Businesswomen of the Year in 1983. That same year *Hispanic Business Magazine* named her one of the 100 most influential Hispanics in America.[34]

Herman Badillo – (Aug. 21, 1929-) Badillo came to New York in 1940 at the age of eleven. He supported himself as an elevator operator and dishwasher. After graduating magna cum laude from the City College of New York with a degree in business administration, he attended Brooklyn Law School at night. Badillo graduated magna cum laude from law school in 1954. An advocate of social justice for the Puerto Rican community, he was elected president of the Bronx borough and used his position to bring sizable amounts of construction funds there. In 1970, Badillo became the first Puerto Rican elected to the House of Representatives of the U.S. Congress. He served in Congress for four terms, and resigned to become deputy mayor for operations of New York City during Mayor Edward Koch's administration. Having served in a number of capacities at the municipal level, Badillo is recognized for his extensive knowledge of the complex inner workings of the city of New York. Presently, Badillo is Chairman of City University of New York.[35]

Joan Baez – (Jan. 9, 1941-) Baez was born in Staten Island, New York of Mexican American descent. She has been popular as a singer and political activist since the 1960s. Baez learned to play the guitar at age twelve and began her professional career singing in coffee houses wile a student a Boston University. Her first public appearance was in 1959 at the Newport Folk Festival. Her beautiful soprano voice soon made her a popular performer. She has eight gold albums and many best-selling single recordings. Some of her popular hits were "Joe Hill," "Carry It On," "All My Trails," "Thank God," Greyhouse You're Gone," and "Raze the Prison to the Ground."

Among political causes she supported were Martin Luther King in his civil rights efforts and Cesar Chavez's movement to provide unions for agricultural workers. Baez was among

---

[34] *Hispanics, A Part of America's Excellence*, Washington, 1984, p. 3.

[35] Aliotta, *Puerto Rico*, p. 83; Duran de Chacon and Maria Isabel, *Hispanic Notables in the United States*, Albuquerque, Saguaro Publications, 1988, pp. 24-25.

the earliest protesters against the Vietnam War. She helped establish the Institute for the Study of Nonviolence. Today she remains concerned about the underprivileged.[36]

Fernando Bujones – (Mar. 9, 1955-) Bujones was born in Miami, Florida, but spent most of the first ten years of his life in Cuba. There he learned the basics of ballet. When his family returned to Miami, he received classical dance lessons from Jacques d'Amboise, a soloist in the New York City Ballet. Bujones underwent rigorous training at the School of American Ballet in New York City. Upon graduation he accepted an ensemble position with the American Ballet Theater in their corps de ballet. Six months later he graduated to principal roles. His talents attracted the attention of Antony Tudor, a British choreographer who has made major contributions to 20th-century dance. Bujones credits Tudor with teaching him to appreciate both the technical and artistic sides of dance. At the age of 19, Fernando Bujones became the first American to win a gold medal at the International Ballet Competition (the Olympics of the ballet world) in Varna, Bulgaria. For his execution of dances from *La Fille Mal Gardee, La Sylphide* and *Fancy Free* he was awarded not only fir first place prize, but received a special citation for technical mastery. Bujones received the New York Times' Artistic Award in 1985. He performs for the Boston Ballet and the American Ballet Theatre.[37]

Cesar Chavez – (Mar 31, 1927-April 22, 1993) A native of Arizona, Chavez worked as a migrant farm laborer in Arizona and California, after his father lost the family farm during the depression. Chavez's experiences and observations as a child prepared him for the role he was to play as a labor leader. He attended over 30 elementary schools and became a drop-out in the 7th grade to work full time as a grape packer. He suffered the discriminations common to Chicano farm workers; he recalled being removed from the "Anglo" section of movie theaters by the police, and his family being cheated out of their wages by employers.

As an adult, Chavez did volunteer work with the Community Service Organization (CSO) in San Jose. Later, he became a paid staffer, leading a successful voter registration drive in San Jose, addressing immigration problems of Chicanos, and organizing local chapters of the CSO in the San Joaquin Valley. In 19858, Chavez was promoted to general director of the CSO. In 1962, Chavez left the CSO, moved to Delano, California, and with $1,200 in savings started the National Farm Workers Association (NFWA). In three years, nearly 2,000 workers joined the Association. Filipino grape packers of the Agricultural Workers Organizing Committee (AWOC) went on strike in 1965. The NFWA and the AWOC merged to become the United Farm Workers Organizing Committee, affiliated with the AFL-CIO, in 1966.

The strike against grape growers lasted five years. Throughout the strike Chavez refused to abandon his non-violent strategy of using church meetings, sing-ins, and a personal fast to convince eleven major wine grape growers to sign contracts with the UFWOC. But table grape growers refused to contract with the UFWOC, so he employed other tactics to convince them to do so. A nation-wide boycott of all California grapes was begin in 1968, as labor leaders campaigned throughout the United States and Canada to convince people not to buy grapes. In 1970 the table grape growers signed contracts with the UFWOC. But Chavez

---

[36] Mayberry, *Mexicans*, p. 55; Catalano, *Mexican Americans*, p. 82; Duran de Chacon, *Hispanic Notables in the United States*, pp. 26-27.

[37] Gernand, *Cuban Americans*, pp. 97-99; Amy Unterburger, *Who's Who Among Hispanic Americans, 1992-1993*, Detroit, Gale Research, Inc., 1992, p. 85.

continued his efforts to improve working conditions for farm laborers until his death in 1993.[38]

Dennis Chavez – (April 8, 1888-Nov. 17, 1962) A native New Mexican, Chavez dropped out of school at 13 to work driving a delivery wagon. At 17, he was fired from his job because he refused to deliver food to strikebreakers. He studied at night to become a surveyor and later accepted a position as assistant engineer for the city of Albuquerque. In 1916, he was offered a clerkship in the office of U.S. Senator A. A. Jones. He entered Georgetown Law School, obtained his degree in 1920, and established a law practice. As a member of the State legislature Chavez introduced the first bill to provide free textbooks for public schools in New Mexico. In 1930 he was elected to the U.S. House of Representatives and re-elected two years later. His attempt to unseat U.S. Senator Bronson Cutting in 1934 failed, but when the Senator died, he was appointed to the vacancy. In 1936, Chavez won election on his own and was re-elected to the Senate for four more terms. Senator Chavez worked hard for his Mexican American constituents; he introduced legislation to provide for Equal Employment Opportunity in 1953. Chavez rose to become Chairman of the powerful Defense Appropriations Subcommittee. He supported enlarging the Army and Marine Corps, minimum strengths for the Reserves, quick development of the nuclear carrier, Polaris, and more conventional airpower. Senator Chavez died of a heart attack while campaigning for his party's ticket in New Mexico.[39]

Linda Chavez – (June 17, 1947-) A native New Mexican, Chavez moved with her family to Colorado at age ten. She earned her BA degree in English literature from the University of Colorado. Her graduate degrees were from the University of California and the University of Maryland. She is an educator and has held high positions in the Federal government. Chavez worked for the National Education Association and the American Federation of Teachers in Washington, D.C. in the 1970s. In 1977, President Jimmy Carter appointed her Special Assistant to the Deputy Assistant Secretary for Legislation in the U.S. Department of Health, Education, and Welfare. Chavez served as the first Hispanic woman on the U.S. Civil Rights Commission in 1983. She also was the director of President Reagan's White House Office of Public Liaison in 1985. In 1986, she ran for the U.S. Senate in Maryland. She serves on the board of directors for several corporations and for non-profit organizations. Currently, Chavez is president of the Center for Equal Opportunity.[40]

Roberto Walker Clemente – (Aug. 18, 1934-Dec. 21, 1972) Born in Puerto Rico, Clemente became a great baseball player with the Pittsburgh Pirates. He was an excellent hitter, batting a lifetime average of .317 and winning four National League batting championships. He had over 3,000 hits in his career. Clemente possessed a powerful throwing arm as well and in five seasons led the National League for throwing out batters. In 1966 he was named the league's Most Valuable Player. Clemente was a leader in an effort to aid victims of the 1972 earthquake in Nicaragua. The cargo plane, destined for Nicaragua, in which he was a passenger crashed at take off an San Juan International Airport. Puerto Rico

---

[38] Mayberry, *Mexicans*, p. 44; Catalano, *Mexican Americans*, p. 61; Duran de Chacon, *Hispanic Notables in the United States*, pp. 49-50; Roger W. Axford, *Spanish-Speaking Heroes*, Midland, Michigan, Pendall Publishing Company, 1973, pp. 5-8.

[39] Duran de Chacon, *Hispanic Notables in the United States*, pp. 52-54.

[40] Catalano, *Mexican Americans*, pp. 63-64; Mayberry, *Mexicans*, p. 53; Unterburger, *Who's Who Among Hispanic Americans*, p. 134.

observed three days of mourning in his honor. Roberto Clemente was elected to the Baseball Hall of Fame in 1973.[41]

Justino Diaz – (1940-) A native Puerto Rican, Diaz studied music at the University of Puerto Rico and the New England Conservatory. Since making his debut on October 23, 1963 with the New York Metropolitan Opera, Diaz has become one of their leading basses. He has appeared at world-renowned opera houses such as LaScala in Milan, the Hamburg State Opera, and the Vienna State Opera. Diaz has recorded performance of *Medea, La Wally*, and *Lucia di Lammermoor.*[42]

Jaime Escalante – (Dec. 31, 1930-) Escalante was born in La Paz, Bolivia. In 1954, he graduated from Normal Superior, a state teachers college, and married a fellow student, Fabiola Tapia. His wife's father and brothers were educated in California and she encouraged Escalante to emigrate. In 1963, he arrived in Los Angeles, Escalante worked as a cook during the day and in the evening pursued an AA degree in math and physics at Pasadena City College. When he applied for a job as a teacher, State authorities informed him that his Bolivian credentials were not acceptable and that he would have to repeat his entire college education plus an additional year in order to obtain a teaching certificate. Escalante obtained employment at an electronics plant. As he neared completion of a bachelors degree in mathematics at California State Los Angeles in 1973, he applied for and won a National Science Foundation scholarship for teachers. A year later, he was teaching mathematics at Garfield High, an inner city school in Los Angeles with a student population of over ninety-five percent Hispanic.

Using a combination of humor, nonchalance, and an appeal to team spirit, Escalante was able to overcome the deteriorating physical plant, and problems of poverty and ignorance to effectively teach his Hispanic students mathematics. Escalante added Advanced Placement (AP) calculus to his class load, because he though his students needed a goal and because the AP examination imposed a valid outside measure of how *he* was doing. The motto of his calculus class is, "Calculus need not be made easy; it is easy already." In 1982, his students took and passed the rigorous three-hour AP calculus test for college-bound students taken by less than four percent of seniors nationally. The Educational Testing Service, which administers the test, however, challenged the validity of the examinations taken by 14 of 18 Garfield students. They were retested and all passed the examinations, some with perfect scores. In 1987, 129 of Escalante's students took the AP calculus examination, and two-thirds of them passed. According to Garfield High principal Maria Elena Tostado, the achievements of Jaime Escalante's students destroyed an entrenched belief that students at the school could not understand such advanced concepts and that attempts to teach them would end in failure. Seniors at Garfield have gone on to attend such prestigious universities as Harvard, Stanford, and Yale, and have realized distinguished careers with such agencies as the Jet Propulsion Laboratories. Their success attracted the attention of journalists and other well-wishers. A movie, "Stand and Deliver," was based on the experiences of Jaime Escalante and his students at Garfield High.[43]

---

[41] *Hispanics, A Part of America's Excellence*, p. 11; Aliotta, *Puerto Ricans*, pp. 87-88.

[42] Aliotta, *Puerto Ricans*, p. 93.

[43] *Christian Science Monitor*, March 24, 1988, pp. 1, 28; *Los Angeles Times Magazine*, November 27, 1988, pp. 24-26, 30-31, 40-42; Unterburger, *Who's Who Among Hispanic Americans*, p. 200.

Gloria Estefan – (1958-) Born in Havana, Cuba, Estefan is a popular singer and songwriter. She received a BA degree in psychology from the University of Miami in 1978. She has also been accorded a wide range of honors and awards: Best New Pop Artist by Billboard Magazine in 1986, the American Music Award in 1989, and Lo Nuestro Latin Music Awards and Crossover Artist of the Year in 1990. Some of her hit albums are *Eyes of Innocence, Primitive Love, Let It Loose*, and *Cuts Both Ways*.[44]

Jose Feliciano – (Jan. 29, 1956-) A native Puerto Rican, Jose Feliciano was born blind, a victim of glaucoma. At five years of age he and his family moved to New York City. Feliciano has mastered many musical instruments, including the 6- and 12-string guitars, the bass, banjo, mandolin, organ, bongo drums, piano, harpsichord, harmonica, and trumpet. He began his career performing in coffeehouses in Greenwich Village. In 1968, he achieved stardom with his Latin-soul version of "Light My Fire." Some of his albums are *The Voice and Guitar of Jose Feliciano, A Bag Full of Soul*, and *Feliciano!* His unorthodox blues-rock rendition of "The Star-Spangled Banner" before the 1968 World Series game in Detroit broadened his popularity beyond the Hispanic community.[45]

Ernesto Galarza – (1904-1984) A scholar and activist, Galarza was born in Mexico. His family immigrated to California, where he attended public schools in Sacramento. He worked his way through Occidental College by tutoring pupils in languages and history and serving as a research assistant for the Foreign Policy Association. Galarza went on to get his M.A. from Stanford and his Ph.D. in sociology from Columbia University. Dr. Galarza wrote an account of managed migration of Mexican farm workers to California from 1942 to 1960, *Merchants of Labor*. Prior to obtaining a formal education and becoming a teacher, writer and social critic, Galarza had worked for years as a migrant farm worker, a cannery hand, and a court interpreter. He was involved in labor strikes against some of the most powerful organized groups in California, such as the Associated Farmers of California, banks, and insurance companies. After retiring from San Jose State College, Dr. Galarza continued his efforts to improve the lot of Mexican Americans.[46]

Fabian Garcia – (Jan. 20, 1871-Aug. 6, 1948) Garcia was born in Mexico but came to the Territory of New Mexico to live with his grandmother as a young child following the death of his parents. He graduated from New Mexico College of Agriculture and Mechanic Arts in 1890. While at college he became interested in the habits of the codling moth and the wooly aphid because they were bothersome fruit pests in orchards in New Mexico. In 1895 he was appointed meteorologist and assistant in horticulture for the Agricultural Extension Station. He devoted his life to improving the agriculture of New Mexico. His first publication, in 1902, was *Spraying Orchards for Codling Moth*. Dr. Garcia initiated a life history study of the codling moth whereby it could be controlled more effectively.

For years he summarized and translated into Spanish short bulletins on insects for distribution to Spanish speaking farmers. He used the opportunity afforded by the Farmer's Institute and the Extension Service to visit nearly every agricultural community in New Mexico and to discuss in both English and Spanish any agricultural problems of farmers. Dr. Garcia's major contribution to horticulture are the yellow and white Grano varieties of onions

---

[44] Unterburger, *Who's Who Among Hispanic Americans*, p. 207.

[45] Aliotta, *Puerto Ricans*, pp. 97-98.

[46] Duran de Chacon, *Hispanic Notables in the United States*, pp. 73-84; Catalano, *Mexican Americans*, p. 76.

and the *No. 9 Chile Pepper* bulletin. On his retirement the Experiment Station gave him the title "Director Emeritus of the Experiment Station and Professor Emeritus of Horticulture." Upon his death he bequeathed $85,300 to his Alma Mater to build a dormitory for poor Spanish-surnamed youths.[47]

Gus Garcia – (1916-June 3, 1964) Born in Laredo, Texas, Garcia was valedictorian of his graduation class at Jefferson High School. He won a scholarship to the University of Texas, receiving both his BA and LLB degrees from there. He worked as assistant district attorney for Bexar County and the city of San Antonio. Gus Garcia was the chief counsel in *Hernandez v. Texas*. He argued the case before the U.S. Supreme Court and in the words of the Texas Bar Journal, "awed the U.S. Supreme Court with his arguments" in the case. In 1954, fourteen days before the landmark *Brown* case, the Supreme Court unanimously found that the exclusion of Mexican Americans from petit juries, grand juries, or Jury Commissions was unconstitutional and illegal. For the rest of his life he fought to defend Mexican Americans, but he was largely unappreciated by the Mexican-American community. Ahead of his time in his efforts to draw attention to the plight of his people, Garcia died a victim of alcoholism and loneliness. Today, Mexican-American activists are giving Gus Garcia the recognition that he deserves.[48]

Hector P. Garcia – (Jan. 17, 1914-1996) The Garcia family moved from Mexico to Mercedes, Texas when Hector P. Garcia was four years old. Garcia attended local schools and graduated with BA and MD degrees from the University of Texas in 1936 and 1940, respectively. As a volunteer in the U.S. Army infantry, he earned a Bronze Star with six battle stars. He was transferred to the Corps of Engineers and finished the war in the Medical Corps. After establishing his medical practice, Dr. Garcia became increasingly convinced that no matter how valiantly Mexican-Americans defended the flag during wars, they would still be treated as second class citizens. To correct this injustice he founded the American G.I. Forum, a veteran's family organization committed to freedom and education.

Sometimes compared to the Urban League for African-Americans, the American G.I. Forum offered assistance whenever injustice occurred against Mexican-Americans. Several cases handled by the Forum have become bench marks in Mexican-Americans' efforts to achieve justice – the Hernandez case, the Perez case and the Judge Chargin case are a few. While practicing his profession, two Presidents, John F. Kennedy and Lyndon B. Johnson, called upon Dr. Garcia to serve in a number of capacities, including alternate delegate to the United Nations with the rank of Ambassador and Member of the U.S. Commission on Civil Rights. Dr. Garcia's life has been dedicated to improving the quality of life for people. The Texas Council on Negro Organizations awarded him the Bronze Plaque in 1955, just one of many honors that he has received for his civic efforts.[49]

Roberto Goizueta – (Dec. 8, 1954-1997) At the age of 18, Goizueta came to the United States, enrolled in a prep school (the Cheshire Academy) and graduated as class valedictorian. In 1976 he obtained a BS degree in chemical engineering from Yale University. Following graduation from college, a Coca Cola plant in Havana hired him as a quality-control chemist. For 26 years he worked for the Coca Cola corporation, assuming increasingly responsible positions as head of the company's Caribbean operations, as second in commend of the Latin

[47] Duran de Chacon, *Hispanic Notables in the United States*, pp. 75-76.

[48] Duran de Chacon, *Hispanic Notables in the United States*, pp. 79-80.

[49] Duran de Chacon, *Hispanic Notables in the United States*, pp. 82-83.

American division, and finally, in 1981, as its chairman and chief executive. Although his Cuban heritage caused some dissension among members of the board of directors, his bilingualism and Latin background gave him a professional advantage in a company that received two-thirds of its earnings from outside the United States. Since becoming chairman and chief executive officer, Goizueta has diversified Coca-Cola's holdings and helped boost the company's stock by nearly 60 percent.[50]

Horacio Gutierrez – (1948-) In 1959, two years before his family immigrated from Cuba, Gutierrez made his piano debut with the Havana Symphony Orchestra at the age of eleven. He studied with Sergei Tarnowsky, the former teacher of the virtuoso Vladimir Horowitz, with whom Gutierrez has been compared favorably. In 1970, Gutierrez played in and won a silver medal at the prestigious Tchaikovsky Competition in Moscow. With this accomplishment his professional career was launched. On returning home Gutierrez began world tours, performing about 70 concerts a year. Gutierrez has played with the world's most reputed orchestras. He won the Avery Fisher Prize, awarded to young artists of achievement.[51]

Mari-Luci Jamarillo – (Jan. 19, 1928-) A native of Las Vegas, New Mexico, Jamarillo worked her way through college at New Mexico Highlands University, graduating in 1955 with a BA degree and in 1959 with a MA degree. She received a Ph.D. in education from the University of California of California in 1964. From 1965 to 1977 she was a professor of education at the University of New Mexico. Dr. Jamarillo has also served as an administrator in Latin American education programs at her alma mater. During this period, the U.S. Agency for International Development called on her expertise as a consultant in education, sending her to represent the United States in 21 nations around the world. In 1977, she was appointed by President Jimmy Carter, and confirmed by the Senate, as Ambassador to Honduras, the first woman ambassador of Hispanic descent.[52]

Juan Marichal – (Oct. 20, 1938-) Marichal was born in Laguna Verde, the Dominican Republic. After his father's death, he was reared by his mother and older brother. He did not complete high school, opting instead to play baseball, first as an amateur for several teams and then professionally for the Escogido Leones. In 1960 he joined the San Francisco Giants of the National League. His size (six feet, 180 pounds), varied delivery, and high-kicking windup consistently kept batters off balanced. From 1963-1969, Marichal won more games than any other pitcher in baseball. During his sixteen-year pro career he won 243 games and was named to the All-Star Game eight times. In 1983, Juan Marichal was the first Latin American admitted to the Baseball Hall of Fame by the normal selection process. (Roberto Clemente was admitted by special vote in 1972 after his accidental death.) Marichal is said to have set the pitching standards to which other Dominican players aspire.[53]

Luis Munoz Marin – (Feb. 18, 1898-April 30, 1980) Munoz Marin was born in Puerto Rico the year the United States assumed sovereignty over the island. He was reared in both Puerto Rico and the United States, arriving in the states for the first time at the age of three. In 1931, Munoz Marin, now married, returned to Puerto Rico. He used the newspaper founded

---

[50] Gernand. *Cuban Americans* pp. 100-101; Unterburger, *Who's Who Among Hispanic Americans*, p. 277.

[51] Gernand, *Cuban Americans*, pp. 96-97.

[52] Duran de Chacon, *Hispanic Notables in the United States*, pp. 98-99.

[53] Dwyer, *Dominican Americans*, pp. 87-88.

by his father, *La Democracia*, as a vehicle to explain his political ideas. Munoz Marin also used his personal charisma to attract a devoted group of followers. He joined the Liberal Party in 1932 and was elected to a four-year term as senator-at-large. In 1938, he formed his own party, the Popular Democratic Party. Munoz Marin made a concerted effort to raise the level of political awareness and democratic understanding among the masses or Puerto Ricans. In 1948, he became the first elected Governor of Puerto Rico and served in that capacity until his retirement in 1964.

Believing that the economic relationship between Puerto Rico and the United States was highly desirable but that the political one was not, Munoz Marin endorsed an alternative status – the Associated People of Puerto Rico, which would be irrevocable unless changed by mutual consent. He supported changing the Organic Act and passage of Public Law 600 by Congress in 1950. P.L. 600 gave Puerto Ricans an opportunity to draft their own constitution and gave the Governor a chance to construct a new type of relationship with the United States, commonwealth status, which he believed gave Puerto Rico full political dignity and juridical equality.[54]

Vilma S. Martinez – (Oct. 17, 1943-) Born in San Antonio, Texas, Martinez was the eldest of five children. She was the first in her family to attend college, graduating from the University of Texas in 1964. In 1967, she received her law degree from Columbia Law School. From 1967 to 1970 she handled general civil rights litigation for the NAACP Legal Defense and Education Fund. Her career also included stints at the New York State Division of Human Rights and a law firm. For nearly ten years (1973-1982) she served as President and General Counsel for the Mexican-American Legal Defense and Education Fund (MALDEF). During her tenure as president, MALDEF became a national organization, with six offices and a budget in the millions of dollars. On leaving MALDEF, Martinez joined the prestigious law firm of Munger, Tolles and Rickershauser in Los Angeles. She has served on the board of directors of major corporations and is involved in education and voter registration efforts.[55]

Gloria Molina – (May 31, 1948-) Born in Montebello, California, Molina was the eldest of ten children. On graduating from high school, she attended East Los Angeles College, but dropped out to help provide for her family after her father had an accident. Later, she became active in politics, serving as an administrative assistant for Assemblyman Art Torres of the 56th Assembly District. She served as the California Deputy Director for the Carter/Mondale Election Committee in 1976, before moving to Washington, D.C., in 1977 to assume positions in the Carter administration, first as Deputy Director of Presidential Personnel and then as Director of Intergovernmental and Congressional Affairs for the U.S. Department of Health and Human Services. Molina returned to California to work as Chief Deputy in the Los Angeles office of the California Speaker of the House, Willie Brown. In 1982, Molina became California's first Hispanic woman legislator. Nearly ten years later, in 1991, she became the first woman and Hispanic-American to be elected to the Los Angeles County Board of Supervisors.[56]

Joseph Monserrat – (Sept. 17, 1921-) Known as the first Hispanic to head the Board of Education for New York City, Monserrat was born in Puerto Rico. He came to New York

---

[54] Aliotta, *Puerto Ricans*, pp. 31-35, 82-83.

[55] *Hispanics, A Part of America's Excellence*, p. 22.

[56] *Hispanics, A Part of America's Excellence*, p. 23.

when he was three years old. He lived in a foster home for seven years until his father remarried and claimed custody of him. After attending public schools he joined the United States Air Force. Monserrat pursued studies in social work at Columbia University and the New School for Social Research. He obtained work in the settlement houses and as a member of the New York City Youth Board was one of the early social workers to work with gangs.

For many years he headed the Migration Division, Department of Labor, of the Commonwealth of Puerto Rico and helped thousands of persons come to the mainland. During his tenure strong contracts were signed with growers to insure that migrant laborers would not be exploited. Each group of workers was required to have an English teacher accompany the pickers, enabling migrants to learn to read, write, and do arithmetic.[57]

Rita Moreno – (Dec. 11, 1931-) Known for her acting and singing talents, Moreno is the only performer in the history of American show business to win the most prestigious awards in the motion picture, television, theater, and record industries – the Oscar, Emmy, Tony, and Grammy, respectively. She won the Oscar in 1962, for Best Supporting Actress in the film "West Side Story." In 1972, the Grammy was awarded her for her singing on *The Electric Company* album. Three years later, she received a Tony for her role as Goggie Gomez in the Broadway stage show "The Ritz." And, in 1977 and 1978 she received an Emmy for a variety appearance on "The Muppet Show" and a dramatic role in "The Rockford Files."[58]

Antonia Novello – (Aug. 23, 1944-) A native of Puerto Rico, Novello attended the University of Puerto Rico in Rio Piedras, majoring in biology. Her medical degree was obtained at the University of Puerto Rico at San Juan, graduating in 1970. She did her internship at the University of Michigan. While at Michigan she was named the Intern of the Year, the first woman to receive such an award. After two years she left private practice to work for the U.S. Public Health Service where the emphasis on teaching people how to stay healthy appealed to her. While there she presented a government report showing that AIDS was the number nine cause of death among children under four years of age, and warned that the number of teenagers infected with AIDS was probably higher than people realized.

In 1989 President George Bush nominated her for the post of Surgeon General of the United States. The Surgeon General is primarily responsible for helping to shape this country's policies on health-related issues such as alcohol, nutrition, AIDS, and smoking. In 1990, the Senate confirmed Dr. Novello's appointment and she became the first woman and first Hispanic Surgeon General. Her favorite good health motto was "good science and good sense." "Good science" meant learning as much as possible about disease; "good sense" required people to think about their actions and to be careful.[59]

Tito Puente – (April 20, 1923-) Born in New York City, Puente is of Puerto Rican descent. He displayed his musical talent at an early age and began receiving piano lessons at age seven. By his early teens Puente was playing regularly with a combo called the Happy Boys. While serving in the Navy during World War II, he taught himself to play the saxophone. After the War he attended the Juilliard School of Music and worked as a sideman and arranger for a number of musicians. In 1956, RCA Victor released his very popular album, *Puente Goes Jazz*. Puente's perennial bestseller, "Dance Mania" was released in 1958.

[57] Axford, *Spanish-Speaking Heroes*, pp. 19-21.

[58] Aliotta, *Puerto Ricans*, pp. 90-92; *Hispanics, A Part of America's Excellence*, p. 24.

[59] Joan C. Hawxhurst and Antonia Novello, *U.S. Surgeon General*, Brookfield, Connecticut, Millbrook Press, 1993, pp. 11-15, 19, 21.

Tito Puente has received numerous honors, including awards from *Metronome, DownBeat*, and *Playboy* magazines and three Grammys. He plays in clubs in the New York City area almost daily.[60]

Cruz Reynoso – (May 2, 1931-) A native California, Reynoso is nationally known as a champion of Hispanic rights. His college education was obtained at Fullerton Junior College and Pomona College where he graduated with honors. He pursued graduate studies in economics and United States history at George Washington University before attending law school at Boalt Hall in Berkeley, California. He obtained his law degree in 1958 and studied constitutional law for a year at the National University of Mexico on a Ford Foundation Fellowship. Reynoso served as associated general counsel of the Equal Employment Opportunity Commission and staff secretary to California Governor Edmund G. Brown, Jr. For four years he served with the California Rural Legal Assistance Program, first as deputy director in 1968 and then as director. He received the Loren Miller Legal Services Award from the State Bar of California.

Besides working on the boards of many civic organizations, Reynoso was a member of a Select Congressional Committee on Immigration and Refugee Policy from 1979-91. In 1980, he was a U.S. delegate to the United Nations Commission on Human Rights in Geneva, Switzerland. He has served as associate justice on the Court of Appeals of California, Third Appellate District as well as professor of law at the University of New Mexico. In 1982, Cruz Reynoso became the first Mexican-American appointed to the California Supreme Court. Formerly a board member of the Mexican American Legal Defense and Educational Fund, Reynoso currently serves on the board of Children NOW and the Latino Issues Forum. A professor of law at the University of California at Los Angeles School of Law, he was appointed to a six-year term on the U.S. Commission on Civil Rights in 1993.[61]

Ruben Salazar – (1928-Aug. 29, 1970) Born in Mexico, Salazar became a U.S. citizen at the age of 21. He received the BA degree in Journalism from the University of Texas at El Paso. After graduating from college, he worked for newspapers in California. For ten years he was a reporter at the *Los Angeles Times* with assignments in Viet Nam, Panama, and Mexico, before returning to the States to cover the Mexican-American community, particularly in East Los Angeles. Salazar also served as the News Director on KMEX-TV, a Spanish language television station. As he became more involved in the concerns of the Chicano movement, he became more militant. Salazar reported on police abuses and supposedly was prepared to expose an alleged pattern of suicides of Chicanos in police custody when he was killed during a Mexican-American anti-war parade and rally. He was hit in the head by a tear gas projectile fired by a deputy sheriff. Some Mexican-Americans never accepted Police Chief Edward M. Davis' finding that the death was accidental. The publisher of the *Los Angeles Times*, Otis Chandler, complimented Salazar on his contribution to the newspaper, noting his honesty and grasp of the problems of Mexican-Americans and his success in using the media to make the larger community aware of the injustices.[62]

Arthur A. Schomburg – (1874-1938) A book collector and scholar, Schomburg was born in San Juan, Puerto Rico. Schomburg graduated from the Institute of Instruction in San

---

[60] Aliotta, *Puerto Ricans*, pp. 95-97; *Hispanics, A Part of America's Excellence*, p. 29.

[61] *Hispanics, A Part of America's Excellence*, p. 31; Unterburger, *Who's Who Among Hispanic Americans*, p. 56.

[62] Duran de Chacon, *Hispanic Notables in the United States of North America*, pp. 155-56.

Juan, then attended St. Thomas College in the Virgin Islands. In 1891 he emigrated to New York and became involved in many activities affecting Puerto Ricans in the early 20th century. He cofounded the Negro Society for Historical Research in 1911, and headed the American Negro Academy in 1922. His famous collection on African culture, housed in the Schomburg Center for Research in Black Culture of the New York Public Library, contains books, pamphlets, manuscripts, photographs, art objects and recordings on virtually every aspect of black life from ancient Africa to the present.[63]

Piri Thomas – (Sept. 30, 1928-) Thomas is a Puerto Rican writer who grew up in East Harlem. At the age of 22 he was imprisoned for armed robbery. While in prison Thomas began to write, but the product of his labor of four years was accidentally destroyed after his release from prison. In 1967, he completed *Down These Mean Streets*, a critically acclaimed autobiography about life as a Puerto Rican in Spanish Harlem. Thomas' two-act play, *The Golden Streets* premiered in 1970 at the Puerto Rican Traveling Theatre in New York City. A former drug addict himself, Thomas has contributed to drug rehabilitation programs in Harlem and Puerto Rico. Since 1967 he has been staff associate with the Center for Urban Education in New York City. Thomas also is vice president of Third World Cinema Productions.[64]

Lee Trevino – (Dec. 1, 1939-) A native Texan, Trevino is popularly known as "Supermex." He was a U.S. Marine and worked at odd jobs and as an assistant professional at golf courses in Texas before jointing the Professional Golfers' Association of America Tour in 1967. He was soon recognized as one of the finest players in the world. In 1970 he led all golfers in prize earnings. The following year he became the first to win the U.S., British, and Canadian Opens in the same year. Trevino twice won both the prestigious U.S. Open (1968 and 1971) and the British Open (1971 and 1972). In 1981, Trevino was inducted into the World of Golf Hall of Fame. He won the U.S. Senior Open in 1990, becoming the first Senior PGA Tour player to exceed the money-winning total of the leader on the regular tour.[65]

SOURCES

Adams, James Truslow. *Dictionary of American History*. New York, Charles Scribner's Sons, 1951.

Aliotta, Jerome J. *The Puerto Ricans*. New York, Chelsea House Publishers, 1991.

Axford, Roger W. *Spanish-speaking Heroes*. Midland, Michigan, Pendell Publishing Company, 1973.

Bowers, Jean, *Hispanic Heritage: Bibliography-in-Brief*. Washington, Congressional Research Service, Library of Congress, Washington, 1993. 4 p.

---

[63] Low, W. Augustus, *Encyclopedia of Black America*. New York, McGraw-Hill Book Company, 1981, pp. 742-43; Harry A. Ploski, *The Negro Almanac, A Reference Work on the African American*, Detroit, Gale Research, Inc., pp. 742-43.

[64] Aliotta, *Puerto Ricans*, p. 84; Harry A. Ploski, *The Negro Almanac, A Reference Work on the African American*, Detroit, Gale Research, Inc., 1989, pp. 220, 1030, 1366; W. Augustus Low, *Encyclopedia of Black America*, New York, McGraw-Hill Book Company, 1981, pp. 742-43.

[65] Catalano, *Mexican Americans*, p. 81; *Hispanics, A Part of America's Excellence*, p. 34.

Camarillo, Albert. *Chicanos in a Changing Society*. Cambridge, Massachusetts, Harvard University Press, 1979.

Catalano, Julie. *The Mexican Americans*. New York, Chelsea House Publishers, 1988.

Christian Science Monitor, March 24, 1988. p. 1, 28.

Duran de Chacon, Maria Isabel, ed. *Hispanic Notables in the United States of North America*. Albuquerque, Saguaro Publications, vol. 3, 1978. 1999.

Dwyer, Christopher. *The Dominican Americans*. New York, Chelsea House Publishers, 1991.

Encyclopedia of Americana, International Edition. Danbury, Connecticut, Grolier, Inc., vol. 27, 1987.

Federal Writers Project of the Works Projects Administration for the State of California. *California, A Guide to the Golden State*. New York, Hastings House, 1968. (American Guide Series)

Federal Writers Project of the Works Projects Administration for the State of Florida. *Florida, A Guide to the Southernmost State*. New York, Oxford University Press, 1949. (American Guide Series)

Federal Writers Project of the Works Projects Administration for the State of Texas. *Texas, A Guide to the Lone Star State*. New York, Hastings House, 1949. (American Guide Series)

Fulton, Maurice G. and Paul Horgan. *New Mexico's Own Chronicle, Three Races in the Writings of Four Hundred Years*. Dallas, Banks Upshaw and Company, 1937.

Gernand, Renee. *The Cuban Americans*. New York, Chelsea House Publishers, 1988.

Hawxhurst, Joan C. *Antonia Novello, U.S. Surgeon General*. Brookfield, Connecticut, The Millbrook Press, 1993.

Hispanics – A Part of America's Excellence. Washington, D.C., 1984.

Johnson, Roberta Ann. *Puerto Rico, Commonwealth or Colony?* New York, Praeger Publishers, 1980.

Los Angeles Times Magazine. November 17, 1988. p. 24-42.

Low, W. Augustus, ed. *Encyclopedia of Black America*. New York, Charles Scribner's Sons, Vol. 19, 1936.

Mayberry, Jodine. *Mexicans*. New York, Franklin Watts, Inc., 1990.

Moore, Joan and Harry Pachon. *Hispanics in the United States*. Englewood Cliffs, New Jersey, Prentice-Hall, Inc., 1985.

Naleo Educational Fund. *The 1997 National Roster of Hispanic Elected Officials*. Washington, D.C., National Association of Latino Elected and Appointed Officials, 1997.

Ploski, Harry A. and James Williams. *The Negro Almanac, A Reference Work on the African American*. Detroit, Gale Research Inc., 1989.

Salaz, Ruben Dario. *Cosmic: The La Raza Sketch Book*. Santa Fe, New Mexico, Blue Feather Press, 1975.

Shorris, Earl. *Latinos, A Biography of the People*. New York, W. W. Norton and Company, 1992.

Thernstrom, Stephan, ed. *Harvard Encyclopedia of American Ethnic Groups*. Cambridge, Massachusetts, Harvard University Press, 1980.

Unterburger, Amy L., ed. *Who's Who Among Hispanic Americans, 1992-93*. Detroit, Gale Research Inc., 1992.

Weber, David J. *The Spanish Frontier in North America*. New Haven, Yale University Press, 1992.

Zavala, Lorenzo de. *Journey to the United States of America*. Austin, Texas, Shoal Creek Publishers, Inc., 1980.

Chapter 4

LATINO POLITICAL PARTICIPATION AND REPRESENTATION IN ELECTIVE OFFICE

Kevin Coleman

SUMMARY

America's Latino population is on the verge of becoming the largest minority group in the country, a phenomenon that is significant with respect to the representational responsibilities of Members of Congress. After several decades of rapid population growth, Latinos will surpass African Americans as the largest minority group early in the next century, according to the Census Bureau projections. By 2010, Latinos are projected to be 13.8% of the national population (African Americans are projected to be 13.5%), and 16.3% of the population a decade later. And although Latino voting participation had remained static for decades, despite the intervening increase in population, results from the 1996 and 1998 elections suggest that an increase in political participation may have begun. In Presidential elections, Latino turnout increased from 28.9% to 44.3% between 1992 and 1996. As a percentage of those who voted in recent elections, Latinos were 3% of the electorate in 1994 and about 5% in 1998, according to exit polls. The number of Latinos in Congress remained unchanged after the 1998 election, although several new members were elected to replace retiring officeholders. In states with large Latino populations, California and Texas for example, Latino voters cast 14% and 16% of the vote, respectively, in the 1998 elections. These factors may point to a groundswell in Latino participation, but to fully translate the rapid increase in population into political power will require even higher rates of Latino voter participation than in the past. This report will be updated to reflect the results of the 2000 general election.

By the time England established a permanent new world settlement at Jamestown in 1607, Spain's colonial empire spanned both American continents, from Cape Horn to what is now Canada. Shortly after Columbus's expeditions for Spain, explorers and missionaries founded colonies at Hispaniola (the Dominican Republic) in 1496, Puerto Rico in 1508, and Cuba in 1511. Within a century, Spanish missions extended across southwestern North

America from St. Augustine (Florida, 1565) to Santa Fe (1609): "There has been no other conquest like this in the annals of the human race. In one generation, the Spaniards acquired more new territory than Rome conquered in five centuries."[1]

By the beginning of the 17th century, as French and English colonization of North America gained momentum, Spain's power had begun to ebb. England had repelled Spain's attempt to invade the British Isles in 1588 and destroyed the Spanish fleet. Spain's effort to maintain its far-flung empire further burdened the nation and, over the next two centuries, its empire receded as the result of competition from other European colonizers and armed conflict.

Although Spain had claimed much of the North American interior, Spain's presence was found primarily in missions scattered along the Gulf coast and across the southwest to California. A series of agreements transferred the Louisiana territory, once claimed by Spain, back and forth between Spain and France until France sold the area to the United States in 1803. The U.S. nearly doubled its size by acquiring Louisiana, a vast region that extended from the Mississippi River to the Rocky Mountains. Shortly thereafter, Spain accepted the transfer of east and west Florida to the U.S., under the Transcontinental Treaty of 1819. Mexico declared independence from Spain in 1823, and Texas subsequently declared independence from Mexico in 1836. The U.S. annexed Texas in 1845. Following the Mexican-American War, the U.S. acquired lands north of the Rio Grande river under the Treaty of Guadalupe Hidalgo (1848) and the Gadsden Purchase (1853). Under the terms of the Treaty of Paris (1898) that ended the Spanish-American War, Spain lost its remaining possessions in Cuba, Puerto Rico, and the Philippines.

Spain's cultural influence on the territory that became the United States remained long after the Spanish Empire collapsed. Explorers, missionaries, and conquistadors had pushed the boundaries of European settlement in the Americas and created a distinct people and culture, with the Spanish language as the common element. When the United States expanded to the Pacific, the Spanish-speaking people of the west and southwest, and the settlements they established at San Francisco, Santa Fe, and San Diego, became part of the new nation.

Until immigration laws were revised in 1965, most Latinos in the U.S. were of Mexican descent. Cuban communities in Florida, New Orleans, and New York can be traced to the 19th century, and a Puerto Rican community emerged in New York in the 1930s, but most of the Latino population in the 1950s was found in the Southwest, including the descendants of the Spanish who originally settled the territory when it was called New Spain. The Immigration and Nationality Act of 1965 (79 Stat. 911) eased previous restrictions on immigration and established a 120,000 a year limit on immigration from countries in the Western Hemisphere. Latino immigration to the U.S. has increased sharply since then, reinforced by migration from South and Central American countries because of political and social unrest. From 1950 to 1990, the Latino population of the U.S. grew by an estimated 265%, whereas the total population grew by approximately 50% during these four decades.[2] Latinos will be the largest minority group in the country within a decade, according to the Census Bureau, a

---

[1] Samuel E. Morison, Henry Steele Commager, and William E. Leuchtenburg. *The Growth of the American Republic.* (New York: Oxford University Press, 1980), vol. 1, P. 29.

[2] Edna Acosta-Belén and Barbara R. Sjostrom. *The Hispanic Experience in the United States: Contemporary Issue and Perspectives.* (New York: Praeger, 1988), P. 10.

phenomenon which has focused greater attention on Latino voters and their impact on electoral politics.

VOTING PATTERNS IN NATIONAL ELECTIONS

Latino voters display a strong tendency to support Democratic candidates for federal office, particularly in U.S. House elections. Since 1980, Latino voters cast between 61% and 76% of their voters for Democratic House candidates, according to exit polls. In Presidential elections since 1976, Latino voters cast between 59% and 76% of their ballots for the Democratic nominee. Among major racial and ethnic groups, Latino voter loyalty to Democratic candidates is surpassed only by black support for Democrats.

Table 1. Voting Patterns by Race and Hispanic
Origin in Presidential Elections, 1980-1996

		National vote	Hispanic	Black	White	Asian
1980	Reagan (R)	51%	33%	11%	56%	na
	Carter (D)	41%	59%	85%	36%	na
	Anderson (I)	7%	6%	3%	7%	na
1984	Reagan (R)	59%	37%	9%	64%	na
	Mondale (D)	40%	62%	90%	35%	na
1988	Bush (R)	53%	30%	12%	59%	na
	Dukakis (D)	45%	69%	86%	40%	na
1992	Clinton (D)	43%	62%	82%	39%	29%
	Bush (R)	38%	25%	11%	41%	55%
	Perot (I)	19%	14%	7%	20%	16%
1996	Clinton (D)	49%	72%	84%	43%	42%
	Dole (R)	41%	21%	12%	46%	48%
	Perot (I)	8%	6%	4%	9%	8%

Source: Marjorie Connelly, Portrait of the Electorate, *The New York Times*, Nov. 10, 1996, p. 28.

Despite an overall tendency to support Democrats, Latinos are not a monolithic voting bloc, and occasionally provide strong support for Republican candidates. For example, 61% of Latinos voted for Republican Jeb Bush in the 1998 Florida governor's race, while 65% voted for Democrat Bob Graham in the U.S. Senate race.[3] In Texas, George W. Bush won 49% of the Latino vote in the 1998 governor's race.[4]

---

[3] CNN Allpolitics Election Night 1998. [http://cnn.com/ELECTIONS/1998/stated/FL/exit.poll.html], visited Apr. 21, 1999.

[4] The Associated Press, *Election Results for Hispanics*, [http://www.infobeat.com/stories/cgi/story.cig?id+2560106407-ae2], visited June 29, 1999.

VOTING PARTICIPATION

In several large states, Latino voters were a significant percentage of the electorate in 1998: 16% in Texas, 14% in California, 70% in Florida, and, 6% in New York. Because Latinos are a growing proportion of the electorate in certain places, they have the potential to affect the outcome of some elections, especially in close races.

Table 2. Latino Voting Participation in Presidential Elections, 1976-1996

	1976	1980	1984	1988	1992	1996
Latino	31.8%	29.9%	32.6%	28.8%	28.9%	44.3%
White	60.9%	60.9%	61.4%	59.1%	63.3%	60.7%
Black	48.7%	50.5%	55.8%	51.5%	54.0%	53.0%
Asia	na	na	na	na	27.3%	45.0%

Source: U.S. Bureau of the Census, "Voting and Registration in the Election of November 1996," [http://www.census.gov/population/www/socdemo/voting.html], visited Mar. 3, 1998.

Latino voter turnout in Presidential elections increased sharply from 28.9% in 1992 to 44.3% in 1996, exceeding 30% for the first time since 1984. Latinos still lag behind all other groups in turnout, but in 1996, Asian American and Latinos voted at much higher rates than in 1992, while turnout for whites and Blacks declined between 1992 and 1996.

REPRESENTATION AMONG ELECTED OFFICIALS

The 106th Congress includes 21 Latinos and several new Members were elected to replace retiring Latino officeholders: Charlie Gonzalez replaced Henry B. Gonzalez in Texas's 20th district and Grace Napolitano replaced Estaban Torres in California's 34th district. Joe Baca was elected to California's 42nd district in a special election on November 16, 1999. All current Latino Members serve in the House of Representatives.

At the State level, Latinos were elected to statewide office in California (lieutenant governor), Texas (railroad commissioner), Colorado (Attorney General), and New Mexico (Attorney General, State Auditor, Secretary of State, and State Treasurer) in 1998. In California, Lieutenant Governor Cruz Bustamante became the first Latino elected to statewide office since 1871, when Romualdo Pacheco was elected lieutenant governor.[5] The number of Latino state legislators nationwide increased from 169 to 186 (51 state senators and 135 representatives), including the election of Latinos to the Michigan and Wisconsin legislatures for the first time.[6]

---

[5] Pacheco was seated on October 17, 1877, but the House Committee on Elections subsequently voted to seat his opponent. He was, however, reelected to the House in 1878 and served two full terms. Hispanic Americans in Congress, the Library of Congress, [http://www.loc.gov/rr/Hispanic/congress/Pacheco.html], visited Sept. 9, 1999.

[6] National Association of Latino Elected Officials.

Table 3. Latino Members in the 106th Congress

Name	State or Territory and Congressional District	Years of Service
Joe Baca, D	California, 42	1999-present
Xavier Becerra, D	California, 30	1992-present
Henry Bonilla, R	Texas, 23	1992-present
Lincoln Diaz-Balart, R	Florida, 21	1992-present
Charlie Gonzalez, D	Texas, 20	1998-present
Luis V. Gutierrez, D	Illinois, 4	1992-present
Rubén Hinojosa, D	Texas, 15	1996-present
Matthew G. Martinez, D	California, 31	1982-present
Robert Menéndez, D	New Jersey, 13	1992-present
Grace F. Napolitano, D	California, 34	1998-present
Solomon P. Ortiz, D	Texas, 27	1982-present
Ed Pastor, D	Arizona, 2	1991-present
Silvestre Reyes, D	Texas, 16	1996-present
Ciro Rodriquez, D	Texas, 28	1997-present
Carlos Romero-Barceló, D	Puerto Rico	1992-present
Ileana Ros-Lehtinen, R	Florida, 18	1989-present
Lucille Roybal-Allard, D	California, 33	1992-present
Loretta Sanchez, D	California, 46	1996-present
José E. Serrano, D	New York, 16	1990-present
Robert A. Underwood, D	Guam	1992-present
Nydia Velázquez, D	New York, 12	1992-present

Source: Charles Pope, "New Congress is Older, More Politically Seasoned," *Congressional Quarterly Weekly Report*, Jan. 9, 1999, p. 62.

The first Latino Member of Congress, Delegate Joseph Marion Hernandez of the Territory of Florida, took office in 1822. The first Latino Member elected from a state was Romualdo Pacheco of California, who won by a margin of one vote in the 1876 election. Since then, 38 Latino Members have been elected to Congress from the states.[7] Thirty-five of the 38 Latino Members elected from the states have served in the U.S. House of Representative; three served in the U.S. Senate. The first Latino Member of the Senate was Dennis Chavez of New Mexico, who was elected in 1936. The most recent Latino Member of the Senate was Joseph M. Montoya of New Mexico who was defeated in his re-election bid in 1976, having first been elected in 1964. The 103rd Congress included 21 Latino members, the highest number ever elected to Congress to date.

In addition to the Latino Members elected from the states, others have served in Congress as resident commissioners from Puerto Rico, as non-voting delegates from Guam and the Virgin Islands, and as territorial delegates prior to their state's admission to the Union. Latino Members who have served in Congress in these positions include 10 territorial delegates, 16

---

[7] This figure excludes territorial delegates, resident commissioners of Puerto Rico, and delegates from Guam and the Virgin Islands.

resident commissioners of Puerto Rico, and two non-voting delegates from Guam and one from the Virgin Islands.

Although Latinos have served in the Congress since the 1820s, some political milestones have been reached only recently. Ileana Ros-Lehtinen's election to Congress in 1988 was a first for Latinas and Cuban-Americans; in 1992, Nydia Velázquez was the first Puerto Rican woman, and Lucille Roybal-Allard the first Mexican American woman, elected to Congress.

Between 1984 and 1998, the number of Latinos in Congress has more than doubled (from nine to 20), and the number of state legislators increased from 105 to 186. There were five Latino statewide elected officials in 1984 and nine following the 1998 election.

Latino Federal and State Elected Officials, 1984-1998

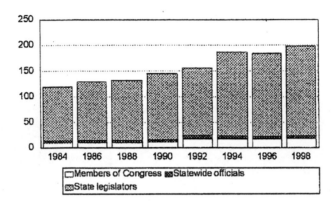

Source: National Association of Latino Elected Officials.

BIBLIOGRAPHY

1990 census counts of detailed race and
Hispanic origin data for Twin Cities
metropolitan area communities.
Published/Created: St. Paul, MN:
Metropolitan Council, 1991.
Related Authors: Metropolitan Council
of the Twin Cities Area. United States.
Bureau of the Census.
Related Titles: Census counts of detailed
race and Hispanic origin data for Twin
Cities metropolitan area communities.
Description: iii, 77 p.; 28 cm.
Notes: "August 1991." "The data in this
report have been prepared by the United
States Census Bureau ..."--P. ii.
Subjects: Minorities--Minnesota--
Minneapolis Metropolitan Area
Statistics. Minorities--Minnesota--Saint
Paul Metropolitan Area Statistics.
Demographic surveys--Minnesota--Saint
Paul Metropolitan Area. Demographic
surveys--Minnesota--Minneapolis
Metropolitan Area. Hispanic Americans-
-Minnesota--Saint Paul Metropolitan
Area--Statistics. Hispanic Americans--
Minnesota--Minneapolis Metropolitan
Area--Statistics. Saint Paul Metropolitan
Area (Minn.)--Census, 1990.
Minneapolis Metropolitan Area (Minn.)-
-Census, 1990. Saint Paul Metropolitan
Area (Minn.)--Population. Minneapolis
Metropolitan Area (Minn.)--Population.
Series: Publication (Metropolitan
Council of the Twins Cities Area); no.
320-91-055.
LC Classification: HA730.M6 A14 1991
Dewey Class No.:
305.8/009776/57909049 20

1990 census of population. Persons of
Hispanic origin in the United States.
Published/Created: Washington, DC:
U.S. Dept. of the Commerce, Economics
and Statistics Administration, Bureau of
the Census: For sale by the Supt. of
Docs., U.S. G.P.O., [1993]
Related Titles: Persons of Hispanic
origin in the United States.
Description: 1 v. (various pagings): ill.;
28 cm.
Notes: At head of 1990 CP-3-3. "Issued
August 1993." Chiefly tables. Shipping
list no.: 93-0546-P. 003-024-08705-7
(GPO) Includes bibliographical
references.
Subjects: Hispanic Americans--Census,
1990. United States--Census, 21st, 1990.
LC Classification: E184.S75 C46 1993
Govt. Doc. No.: C 3.223/10:1990 CP-3-3

1990 Hispanic census counts, metro and
greater Minnesota: reference charts and
maps.
Published/Created: St. Paul, Minn.:
Spanish Speaking Affairs Council,
[1991]

Related Authors: Minnesota. Spanish Speaking Affairs Council.
Description: iii, 29 p.: ill, maps; 28 cm.
Notes: "April 1, 1991."
Subjects: Hispanic Americans--Minnesota--Census. Minnesota--Census, 1990. United States--Census, 21st, 1990.
LC Classification: F615.S75 A15 1991

1990 population by race and Hispanic origin for Wisconsin counties and municipalities.
Published/Created: Madison, Wis. (101 S. Webster St., 6th Flr., P.O. Box 7868, Madison, 53707-7868): Demographic Services, Wisconsin Dept. of Administration, [1991]
Related Authors: Wisconsin. Demographic Services Center.
Description: 1 v. (unpaged); 28 cm.
Notes: Cover title. "March 5, 1991." Includes errata sheet. "26-0391."
Subjects: Minorities--Wisconsin--Statistics. Hispanic Americans--Statistics. Wisconsin--Population--Statistics. United States--Census, 21st, 1990.
LC Classification: HA711.5 1990a
Dewey Class No.: 305.8/009775021 20

A coordinated approach to raising the socio-economic status of Latinos in California / editors: Elias Lopez, Ginny Puddefoot, Patricia Gándara.
Published/Created: Sacramento, CA (900 N Street, Suite 300, Sacramento, 94237-0001): California Research Bureau, California State Library, [2000].
Related Authors: Lopez, Elias. Puddefoot, Ginny. Gandara, Patricia C. California State Library. California Research Bureau.
Description: 63 leaves: ill.; 28 cm.
Notes: "March 2000." "Prepared at the request of the Latino Legislative Caucus, the Hispanic Republican Caucus, and the

Assembly Committee on Education." "CRB-00-003." Includes bibliographical references.
Subjects: Hispanic Americans--Government policy--California. Hispanic Americans--California--Economic Conditions. Hispanic Americans--Education--California. Hispanic Americans students--California.
LC Classification: F870.S75 C66 2000

A guide to hispanic Texas / edited by Helen Simons and Cathryn A. Hoyt; compiled with the assistance of Ann Perry and Deborah Smith.
Edition Information: 1st abridged ed.
Published/Created: Austin: University of Texas Press, 1996.
Related Authors: Simons, Helen, 1939- Hoyt, Catherine A.
Related Titles: Hispanic Texas.
Description: xv, 347 p.: ill., maps; 28 cm.
ISBN: 0292777094 (pbk.: alk. paper)
Notes: Abridged ed. of: Hispanic Texas. Includes bibliographical references (p. [325]-335) and index.
Subjects: Historic sites--Texas--Guidebooks. Hispanic Americans--Texas--History. Texas--Guidebooks.
LC Classification: F387 .G88 1996
Dewey Class No.: 917.6404/63 20

A Hispanic look at the Bicentennial / David Cardus, editor.
Published/Created: Houston, Tex.: Institute of Hispanic Culture of Houston, c1978.
Related Authors: Cardus, D., 1922- Institute of Hispanic Culture of Houston (Tex.)
Description: viii, 207 p.: ill.; 24 cm.
Notes: Papers presented at a symposium held in Houston, Tex., Oct. 8-9, 1976 and organized by the Institute of Hispanic Culture of Houston. English

and Spanish. Includes bibliographical references.
Subjects: Hispanic Americans--History--Congresses. American Revolution Bicentennial, 1776-1976--Congresses. United States--Civilization--Spanish influences Congresses.
LC Classification: E169.1 .H62
Dewey Class No.: 973/.04/68

Abalos, David T.
La Comunidad Latina in the United States: personal and political strategies for transforming culture / David T. Abalos.
Published/Created: Westport, CT: Praeger, 1998.
Description: x, 201 p.; 24 cm.
ISBN: 0275958922 (alk. paper) 0275958930 (pbk.: alk. paper)
Notes: Includes bibliographical references (p. [185]-191) and index.
Subjects: Hispanic Americans--Cultural assimilation. Hispanic Americans--Ethnic identity. Hispanic Americans--Conduct of life.
LC Classification: E184.S75 A618 1998
Dewey Class No.: 305.868073 21

Abalos, David T.
Latinos in the United States: the sacred and the political / David T. Abalos.
Published/Created: Notre Dame, Ind.: University of Notre Dame Press, c1986.
Description: xviii, 204 p.: 1 ill.; 24 cm.
ISBN: 0268012776 :
Notes: Includes index. Bibliography: p. 185-196.
Subjects: Hispanic Americans--Ethnic identity. Hispanic Americans--Cultural assimilation.
LC Classification: E184.S75 A63 1986
Dewey Class No.: 305.8/68073 19

Achieving a representative federal workforce: addressing the barriers to Hispanic participation: a report to the President and the Congress of the United States / by the U.S. Merit Systems Protection Board.
Published/Created: Washington, DC: The Board: [For sale by the U.S. G.P.O., Supt. of Docs., 1997]
Description: vi, 21 p.; 28 cm.
ISBN: 0160491908 :
Notes: Cover title. Shipping list no.: 97-0364-P. "September 1997"--1st prelim. leaf. Includes bibliographical references.
Additional Form Avail.: Also available via Internet from the Merit Systems Protection Board web site (PDF file only).
Subjects: Hispanic Americans in the civil service.
LC Classification: JK723.H55 U55 1997
Govt. Doc. No.: MS 1.2:H 62

Achieving equitable access: studies of health care issuesaffecting Hispancs and African Americans / Marsha D. Lillie-Blanton, Wihelmina A. Leigh, and Ana I. Alfaro-Correa, editors.
Published/Created: Washington, D.C.: Joint Center for Political and Economic Studies Press; Lanham, MD; Distributed by arrangement with University Press of America, c1996.
Related Authors: Lillie-Blanton, Marsha D. Leigh, Wilhelmina. Alfaro-Correa, Ana I. Joint Center for Political and Economic Studies (U.S.)
Description: ix, 212 p.: ill.; 24 cm.
ISBN: 0761803777 (cloth: alk. paper) 0761803785 (pbk.: alk. paper) 0761803785 (pbk.: alk. paper)
Notes: Includes bibliographical references.
Subjects: Afro-Americans--Medical care. Hispanic Americans--Medical care. Health services accessibility--United States. Medical care--Utilization--United States.

LC Classification: RA448.4 .A34 1996
Dewey Class No.: 362.1/089/68073 20

Advances in bilingual education research /
Eugene E. García, Raymond V. Padilla,
editors.
Published/Created: Tucson: University
of Arizona Press, c1985.
Related Authors: García, Eugene E.,
1946- Padilla, Raymond V.
Description: xi, 328 p.: ill.; 24 cm.
ISBN: 0816509220 (alk. paper)
Notes: Includes bibliographies and
index.
Subjects: Education, Bilingual--United
States. Hispanic Americans--Education.
Code switching (Linguistics)--United
States. Bilingualism in children--United
States.
LC Classification: LC3731 .A58 1985
Dewey Class No.: 371.97/00973 19

Aros, Andrew A., 1944-
The latin music handbook / Andrew A.
Aros.
Published/Created: Diamond Bar, Calif.:
Applause Publications, c1978.
Description: 103 p.; 22 cm.
Notes: Discography: p. [15]-60.
Subjects: Latin Americans--Music--
Directories. Hispanic Americans--Music-
-Directories. Popular music--Latin
America--Directories. Popular music--
United States--Directories. Popular
music--Latin America--Discography.
Popular music--United States--
Discography.
LC Classification: ML19 .A76
Dewey Class No.: 789.9/13617268/0973

Assessment and access: Hispanics in higher
education / edited by Gary D. Keller,
James R. Deneen, and Rafael J.
Magallán.
Published/Created: Albany, N.Y.: State
University of New York Press, c1991.

Related Authors: Keller, Gary D.
Deneen, James R. Magallán, Rafael J.,
1945-
Description: viii, 333 p.: ill.; 24 cm.
ISBN: 0791407799 (alk. paper)
0791407802 (pbk.: alk. paper)
Notes: Includes bibliographical
references (p. 275-312) and index.
Subjects: Hispanic Americans--
Education (Higher) College entrance
achievement tests--United States.
Series: SUNY series, United States
Hispanic studies
LC Classification: LC2670.6 .A87 1991
Dewey Class No.: 378.1/98/298073 20

Assimilation and socioeconomic
advancement of Hispanics in the U.S. /
by the Population Reference Bureau, Inc.
Published/Created: Washington, DC:
The Bureau, 1989.
Related Authors: O'Hare, William P.
Population Research Bureau.
Description: 72 p.; 28 cm.
Notes: On cover: "By Dr. William P.
O'Hare." "While the primary author ... is
William O'Hare ... numerous other
current and former Population Reference
Bureau staff members contributed to the
study"--Verso of t.p. Includes
bibliographical references.
Subjects: Hispanic Americans--Statistics.
Hispanic Americans--Economic
conditions--Statistics. Hispanic
Americans--Social conditions--Statistics.
Series: Staff working papers (Population
Research Bureau)
LC Classification: E184.S75 A87 1989

Augenbraum, Harold.
Latinos in English: a selected
bibliography of Latino fiction writers of
the United States / edited by Harold
Augenbraum; research compiled by
Hilda Mundo-Lopez and Harold
Augenbraum; introduction by Ilan

Stavans; text edited by Terry Quinn.
Published/Created: New York, NY:
Mercantile Library of New York, 1992.
Related Authors: Mundo-Lopez, Hilda.
Quinn, Terry, 1945-
Description: 121 p.; 22 cm.
Notes: Includes indexes.
Subjects: American fiction--Hispanic
American authors--Bibliography.
Hispanic Americans in literature--
Bibliography.
LC Classification: Z1229.H57 A94 1992
PS153.H56
Dewey Class No.: 016.813008/0868 20

Awash in the mainstream: Latino politics in
the 1996 elections / edited by Rodolfo O.
de la Garza, Louis DeSipio.
Published/Created: Boulder, Colo.:
Westview Press, 1999.
Related Authors: De la Garza, Rodolfo
O. DeSipio, Louis.
Description: xiii, 283 p.; 24 cm.
ISBN: 0813366860 (hc.: acid-free paper)
Notes: Includes bibliographical
references and index.
Subjects: Hispanic Americans--Politics
and government. Elections--United
States--History--20th century. United
States--Politics and government--1993-
2001.
LC Classification: E184.S75 A93 1999
Dewey Class No.: 323.1/168073 21

Axford, Roger W.
Spanish-speaking heroes [by] Roger W.
Axford.
Published/Created: [Midland, Mich.]
Pendell Pub. Co. [1973]
Description: xii, 85 p. illus. 24 cm.
ISBN: 0878120416
Summary: Brief biographies of twenty-
three Spanish-speaking men and women
who have achieved prominence in a
variety of fields.
Subjects: Hispanic Americans--

Biography--Juvenile literature. Hispanic
Americans.
LC Classification: E184.S75 A95
Dewey Class No.: 301.45/16/872073 920
B

Baker, Nancy R.
Hispanics in Ohio: general social and
economic characteristics / Nancy R.
Baker.
Published/Created: Columbus, Ohio:
Commission on Spanish Speaking
Affairs, [1985]
Related Authors: Ohio. Commission on
Spanish Speaking Affairs.
Description: iii, 72 p.; 28 cm.
Notes: "April 1985." "CP13."
Subjects: Hispanic Americans--Ohio--
Census, 1980. Ohio--Census, 1980.
United States--Census, 20th, 1980.
LC Classification: F500.S75 B34 1985
Dewey Class No.: 305.8/680771/021 20

Baker, Nancy R.
Ohio Hispanics by national origin:
general social and economic
characteristics / Nancy R. Baker.
Published/Created: Columbus, Ohio:
Commission on Spanish Speaking
Affairs, [1985]
Related Authors: Ohio. Commission on
Spanish Speaking Affairs.
Description: iii, 58 p.; 28 cm.
Notes: "May, 1985." "CP14."
Bibliography: p. 58.
Subjects: Hispanic Americans--Ohio--
Statistics. Ohio--Population--Statistics.
LC Classification: F500.S75 B35 1985
Dewey Class No.: 304.6/089680771 19

Barrio ballots: Latino politics in the 1990
elections / edited by Rodolfo O. de la
Garza, Martha Menchaca, and Louis
DeSipio; with a foreword by Sidney
Verba.
Published/Created: Boulder, Colo.:

Westview Press, 1994.
Related Authors: De la Garza, Rodolfo
O. Menchaca, Martha. DeSipio, Louis.
Description: xiv, 205 p.; 23 cm.
ISBN: 0813385733 (soft: alk. paper)
Notes: Includes bibliographical
references (p. 194-196) and index.
Subjects: Hispanic Americans--Politics
and government. Elections--United
States--History--20th century. United
States--Politics and government--1989-
1993.
LC Classification: E184.S75 B37 1994
Dewey Class No.: 323.1/168 20

Barrio streets, carnival dreams: three
generations of Latino artistry / edited by
Lori Marie Carlson.
Edition Information: 1st ed.
Published/Created: New York: H. Holt,
c1996.
Related Authors: Carlson, Lori M.
Description: xvi, 127 p.: ill.; 22 cm.
ISBN: 0805041206
Summary: A collection of Latino
literature, poetry, artwork, and
commentary celebrating the
contributions of three generations of
twentieth century Americans of
Mexican, Caribbean, and South
American descent.
Notes: Includes index.
Subjects: Children's literature, American-
-Hispanic American authors. Hispanic
Americans--Literary collections.
Hispanic Americans--Juvenile literature.
Hispanic Americans in art. Hispanic
Americans--Literary collections.
American literature--Hispanic American
authors Collections. Hispanic Americans
in art.
Series: Edge books
LC Classification: PZ5 .B27 1996
Dewey Class No.: [Fic] 20

Barrios and borderlands: cultures of Latinos
and Latinas in the United States / [edited
by] Denis Lynn Daly Heyck.
Published/Created: New York:
Routledge, 1994.
Related Authors: Heyck, Denis Lynn
Daly.
Description: xviii, 485 p.: ill.; 26 cm.
ISBN: 0415903947: 0415903955 (pbk.) :
Notes: Includes bibliographical
references (p. 454-456) and index.
Subjects: American literature--Hispanic
American authors. Hispanic Americans--
Literary collections. Hispanic
Americans.
LC Classification: PS508.H57 B37 1994
Dewey Class No.: 810.8/0868 20

Basurto, Elia.
Hispanics in Wisconsin, 1980: a
chartbook: a demographic profile of the
Hispanic and total population in
Wisconsin / produced cooperatively by
Elia Basurto, Doris P. Slesinger, and
Eleanor Cautley.
Published/Created: Madison, Wis.:
Applied Population Laboratory,
University of Wisconsin-Madison,
[1985]
Related Authors: Slesinger, Doris
Peyser. Cautley, Eleanor.
Description: iv, 70 p.: ill.; 28 cm.
Notes: "December 1985."
Subjects: Hispanic Americans--
Wisconsin--Census, 1980. Wisconsin--
Census, 1980. United States--Census,
20th, 1980.
Series: Population series (Madison,
Wis.); no. 80-5.
LC Classification: F590.S75 B37 1985
Dewey Class No.: 304.6/089680775 19

Bean, Frank D.
The Hispanic population of the United
States / Frank D. Bean and Marta Tienda
for the National Committee for Research

on the 1980 Census.
Published/Created: New York: Russell
Sage Foundation, c1987.
Related Authors: Tienda, Marta.
National Committee for Research on the
1980 Census.
Description: xxiv, 456 p.: ill.; 25 cm.
ISBN: 0871541041 (alk. paper):
087154105X (pbk.: alk. paper) :
Notes: Includes indexes. Bibliography: p.
419-433.
Subjects: Hispanic Americans--Social
conditions. Hispanic Americans--
Economic conditions.
Series: The Population of the United
States in the 1980s
LC Classification: E184.S75 B4 1987
Dewey Class No.: 305.8/68073 19

Benavidez, Roy P.
Medal of honor: a Vietnam warrior's
story / Roy Benavidez with John R.
Craig; foreword by H. Ross Perot.
Published/Created: Washington, D.C.:
Brassey's, c1995.
Related Authors: Craig, John R.
Description: xvi, 211 p.: ill.; 25 cm.
ISBN: 0028810988
Notes: Includes index.
Subjects: Benavidez, Roy P. United
States. Army--Hispanic Americans.
Vietnamese Conflict, 1961-1975--
Veterans--United States Biography.
Medal of Honor--Biography.
LC Classification: U53.B39 A3 1995
Dewey Class No.: 956.704/33473/092 B
20

Bermúdez, Andrea B., 1941-
Doing our homework: how schools can
engage Hispanic communities / by
Andrea B. Bermúdez.
Published/Created: Charleston, WV:
ERIC Clearinghouse on Rural Education
and Small Schools, c1994.
Related Authors: ERIC Clearinghouse on

Rural Education and Small Schools.
Description: viii, 92 p.: ill.; 23 cm.
ISBN: 1880785110 :
Notes: Includes bibliographical
references (p. 81-91).
Subjects: Hispanic Americans--
Education. Education--Parent
participation--United States. Home and
school--United States.
LC Classification: LC2670 .B47 1994
Dewey Class No.: 371.97/68073 20

Berry-Cabán, Cristóbal S., 1953-
Hispanics in Wisconsin: a bibliography
of resource materials = Hispanos en
Wisconsin: una bibliografía de
materiales de recurso / compiled by
Cristóbal S. Berry-Cabán with the
assistance of Sarah H. Cooper, Donna J.
Sereda, DAle E. Treleven.
Published/Created: Madison: State
Historical Society of Wisconsin, 1981.
Related Titles: Hispanos en Wisconsin.
Description: 258 p.; 23 cm.
ISBN: 087020209X
Subjects: Hispanic Americans--
Wisconsin--Bibliography--Union lists.
Catalogs, Union--Wisconsin. Wisconsin-
-Ethnic relations--Bibliography--Union
lists.
LC Classification: Z1351 .B47 1981
F590.S75
Dewey Class No.: 016.9775/00468 19

Beyond Ellis Island: Hispanics--immigrants
and Americans.
Published/Created: Washington, D.C.
(20 F St., NW, 2nd fl., Washington
20001): National Council of La Raza,
Office of Research, Advocacy, and
Legislation, c1986.
Related Authors: National Council of La
Raza. Office of Research, Advocacy, and
Legislation.
Description: i, 42 p.; 28 cm.
Notes: "June 1986." Bibliography: p.

[41]-42.
Subjects: Latin Americans--Cultural
assimilation--United States. Hispanic
Americans--History. United States--
Emigration and immigration--
Government policy.
LC Classification: JV6795 1986
Dewey Class No.: 325.73 19

Bilingual education for Hispanic students in
   the United States / editors, Joshua A.
   Fishman, Gary D. Keller.
   Published/Created: New York: Teachers
   College Press, 1982.
   Related Authors: Fishman, Joshua A.
   Keller, Gary D.
   Description: 502 p.; 24 cm.
   ISBN: 0807726036 (pbk.) 0807726559
   Notes: Includes bibliographies and
   index.
   Subjects: Hispanic Americans--
   Education. Education, Bilingual--United
   States. Bilingualism--United States.
   Language acquisition--United States.
   Series: Bilingual education series
   LC Classification: LC2669 .B54
   Dewey Class No.: 371.97/68/073 19

Borderless borders: U.S. Latinos, Latin
   Americans, and the paradox of
   interdependence / edited by Frank
   Bonilla ... [et al.].
   Published/Created: Philadelphia: Temple
   University Press, 1998.
   Related Authors: Bonilla, Frank.
   Description: xiii, 290 p.: ill.; 24 cm.
   ISBN: 1566396190 (cloth: alk. paper)
   1566396204 (paper: alk. paper)
   Notes: Includes bibliographical
   references (p. 231-275) and index.
   Subjects: Hispanic Americans--Politics
   and government. Hispanic Americans--
   Social conditions. Hispanic Americans--
   Economic conditions. United States--
   Ethnic relations. United States--
   Relations--Latin America. Latin

America--Relations--United States.
LC Classification: E184.S75 B674 1998
Dewey Class No.: 305.868073 21

Boyd, E. (Elizabeth), 1903-1974.
   Popular arts of Spanish New Mexico
   [by] E. Boyd.
   Published/Created: Santa Fe, Museum of
   New Mexico Press, 1974.
   Description: viii, 518 p. illus. (part col.)
   29 cm.
   ISBN: 0890130647
   Notes: Bibliography: p. 484-500.
   Subjects: Folk art--New Mexico. Latin
   Americans--New Mexico--Social life
   and customs. Hispanic Americans--New
   Mexico--Social life and customs.
   LC Classification: NK835.N5 H32
   Dewey Class No.: 745/.09789

Bradby, Denise.
   Language characteristics and academic
   achievement: a look at Asian and
   Hispanic eighth graders in NELS:88 /
   Denise Bradby.
   Published/Created: Washington, D.C.:
   National Center for Education Statistics,
   U.S. Dept. of Education, Office of
   Educational Research and Improvement:
   For sale by U.S. G.P.O., Supt. of Docs.,
   [1992]
   Related Authors: National Center for
   Education Statistics.
   Description: xvi, 184 p.: ill.; 28 cm.
   ISBN: 016036115X :
   Notes: Item 461-D-5 Shipping list no.:
   92-162-P. "February 1992." "NCES 92-
   479." S/N 065-000-00483-6 (GPO)
   Includes bibliographical references.
   Subjects: Eighth grade (Education)--
   Statistics. Language and education--
   United States--Statistics. Linguistic
   minorities--Education (Secondary)--
   United States--Statistics. Asian
   Americans--Education (Secondary)--
   Statistics. Hispanic Americans--

Education (Secondary)--Statistics.
Education, Bilingual--United States--
Statistics. Academic achievement--
United States--Statistics.
Series: Statistical analysis report
(National Center for Education Statistics)
LC Classification: LC3726 .B73 1992
Dewey Class No.: 371.97 20
Govt. Doc. No.: ED 1.302:L 26

Bridging boundaries: the pastoral care of
U.S. Hispanics / edited by Kenneth G.
Davis and Yolanda Tarango.
Published/Created: Scranton: University
of Scranton Press; Tonawanda, NY:
University of Toronto Press [distributor],
c2000.
Related Authors: Davis, Kenneth G.,
1957- Tarango, Yolanda.
Description: xvi, 144 p.; 24 cm.
ISBN: 0940866811 (hardback)
094086682X
Notes: Includes bibliographical
references (p. 133-140) and index.
Subjects: Church work with Hispanic
Americans. Hispanic American
Catholics--Religious life.
LC Classification: BX1407.H55 B75
1999
Dewey Class No.: 282/.73/08968 21

Bridging cultures: an introduction to
Chicano/Latino studies / edited by Mario
T. García.
Published/Created: Dubuque, Iowa:
Kendall/Hunt Pub. Co., c2000.
Related Authors: García, Mario T.
Description: xv, 234 p.; 24 cm.
ISBN: 0787270776
Notes: Includes bibliographical
references.
Subjects: Mexican Americans. Hispanic
Americans.
LC Classification: E184.M5 B7 2000
Dewey Class No.: 973/.046872073 21

California Hispanic perspectives / [project
directors, Rodolfo O. de la Garza, Harry
Pachon].
Published/Created: Claremont, CA:
Tomás Rivera Center, 1996.
Related Authors: De la Garza, Rodolfo
O. Pachon, Harry. Tomás Rivera Center.
Description: 14 p.: ill.; 28 cm.
Notes: "A Tomás Rivera Center survey"-
-Cover.
Subjects: Hispanic Americans--
California--Attitudes. Public opinion--
California.
LC Classification: F870.S75 C35 1996
Dewey Class No.: 305.868/0794 21

Camarillo, Albert.
Chicanos in a changing society: from
Mexican pueblos to American barrios in
Santa Barbara and southern California,
1848-1930 / Albert Camarillo; [with a
new preface by the author].
Published/Created: Cambridge, Mass.:
Harvard University Press, c1996.
Description: xxii, 326 p.: ill.; 21 cm.
ISBN: 0674113969 (pbk.) 0674113977
(p. [4] of cover)
Notes: Original ed. published in 1979.
Includes bibliographical references (p.
[301]-316) and index.
Subjects: Mexican Americans--
California--Santa Barbara--History.
Mexican Americans--California,
Southern--History. Hispanic American
neighborhoods--California--Santa
Barbara. Hispanic American
neighborhoods--California, Southern.
Santa Barbara (Calif.)--History.
California, Southern--History.
LC Classification: F869.S45 C25 1996
Dewey Class No.: 979.4/9/0046872073
21

Carrillo, Louis.
Oscar de la Renta / by Louis Carrillo.
Published/Created: Austin, Tex.:

Raintree Steck-Vaughn, c1996.
Description: 48 p.: ill. (some col.); 25 cm.
ISBN: 0817239804 0811497879 (pbk.)
Summary: Narrates the story of the Dominican-American who had studied art in Spain but gave up painting in order to pursue a career as a fashion designer.
Notes: Includes bibliographical references (p. 47) and index.
Subjects: De la Renta, Oscar--Juvenile literature. De la Renta, Oscar. Fashion designers--United States--Biography--Juvenile literature. Costume design--United States--History--20th century Juvenile literature. Hispanic Americans--Biography--Juvenile literature. Fashion designers. Costume design. Hispanic Americans--Biography.
Series: Contemporary Hispanic Americans
LC Classification: TT505.D4 C37 1996
Dewey Class No.: 746.9/2/092 B 20

Chase, Richard A., Ph.D.
Minnesota Latino needs and resources assessment / by Richard A. Chase, Suzanne Zerger, Lisa Sass Zaragoza.
Published/Created: St. Paul, Minn.: Wilder Research Center, [1995]
Related Authors: Zerger, Suzanne. Zaragoza, Lisa Sass. Wilder Research Center. Minnesota. Spanish Speaking Affairs Council.
Description: vii, 191 p.; 28 cm.
Notes: "For Spanish Speaking Affairs Council, through a grant from the McKnight Foundation." "May, 1995."
Subjects: Hispanic Americans--Minnesota--Social conditions Statistics. Hispanic Americans--Minnesota--Economic conditions Statistics. Minnesota--Social conditions--Statistics. Minnesota--Economic conditions--Statistics.
LC Classification: F615.S75 C47 1995

Dewey Class No.: 305.868/0776 20

Chavez, Angelico, 1910-
Origins of New Mexico families: a genealogy of the Spanish colonial period / by Angélico Chávez; new foreword by Thomas E. Chávez.
Edition Information: Rev. ed.
Published/Created: Santa Fe: Museum of New Mexico Press, 1992.
Related Authors: Chavez, Angelico, 1910- Origins of New Mexico families in the Spanish colonial period.
Description: xxi, 441 p.; 28 cm.
ISBN: 0890132399
Notes: Rev. ed. of: Origins of New Mexico families in the Spanish colonial period. Includes bibliographical references (p. 439-441).
Subjects: Hispanic Americans--New Mexico--Genealogy. Spaniards--New Mexico--Genealogy. Mexican Americans--New Mexico--Genealogy. New Mexico--Genealogy.
LC Classification: F805.S75 C47 1992
Dewey Class No.: 929/.3789/08968 20

Chávez, Gene T.
La comunicación: curriculum unit / Gene T. Chávez.
Published/Created: Santa Cruz, CA: Network Publications, 1989.
Related Titles: Comunicación curriculum unit.
Description: 196 p.: ill.; 28 cm.
ISBN: 0941816796
Notes: English and Spanish Includes bibliographical references (p. 195-196).
Subjects: Interpersonal relations--Study and teaching (Elementary) United States. Interpersonal communication--Study and teaching (Elementary)--United States. Hispanic Americans--Ethnic identity.
Series: Latino family life education curriculum series
LC Classification: HM132 .C4235 1989

Dewey Class No.: 372.6/043 21

Chavez, Linda.
Out of the barrio: toward a new politics
of Hispanic assimilation / Linda Chavez.
Published/Created: [New York, N.Y.]:
BasicBooks, c1991.
Description: xii, 208 p.; 22 cm.
ISBN: 0465054307 :
Notes: Includes bibliographical
references (p. [173]-196) and index.
Subjects: Hispanic Americans--Cultural
assimilation. Hispanic Americans--
Politics and government.
LC Classification: E184.S75 C48 1991
Dewey Class No.: 305.868 20

Chavis, David M.
The state of Hispanics in Camden
County: Camden County Board of
Freeholders Hispanic Advisory
Commission / submitted by Center for
Community Education, School of Social
Work, Rutgers-the State University;
[written and prepared by: David Chavis,
Laurie Nsiah-Jefferson, Laura Miller].
Published/Created: New Brunswick,
N.J.: The Commission, c1992.
Related Authors: Nsiah-Jefferson,
Laurie. Miller, Laura. Camden County
(N.J.). Board of Freeholders. Hispanic
Advisory Commission. Rutgers
University. Center for Community
Education.
Description: 1 v. (various pagings): ill.;
28 cm.
Notes: Cover title. "February, 1992."
Includes bibliographical references.
Subjects: Hispanic Americans--New
Jersey--Camden County--Social
conditions. Camden County (N.J.)--
Social conditions.
LC Classification: F142.C16 C48 1992
Dewey Class No.: 974.9/8700468 20

Chicano psychology / edited by Joe L.
Martinez, Jr., and Richard H. Mendoza.
Edition Information: 2nd ed.
Published/Created: Orlando: Academic
Press, 1984.
Related Authors: Martinez, Joe L.
Mendoza, Richard H.
Description: xxii, 456 p.; 24 cm.
ISBN: 0124756603 (alk. paper)
Notes: Includes bibliographies and
index.
Subjects: Mexican Americans--
Psychology. Mexican Americans--
Mental health. Mexican Americans--
Education. Language arts. Bilingualism--
United States. Hispanic Americans--
Psychology.
LC Classification: E184.M5 C45 1984
Dewey Class No.: 305.8/6872/073 19

Cockcroft, James D.
Latinos in the making of the United
States / James D. Cockcroft.
Published/Created: New York: F. Watts,
c1995.
Description: 191 p.: ill.; 24 cm.
ISBN: 0531112098
Notes: Includes bibliographical
references (p. 183-186) and index.
Subjects: Hispanic Americans. Hispanic
Americans--History. Hispanic
Americans--History.
Series: The Hispanic experience in the
Americas
LC Classification: E184.S75 C64 1995
Dewey Class No.: 973/.0468 20

Cockcroft, James D.
Latinos in the struggle for equal
education / James D. Cockcroft.
Published/Created: New York: Franklin
Watts, c1995.
Description: 191 p.: ill.; 24 cm.
ISBN: 0531112268 (alk. paper)
Summary: Describes the struggle of
Hispanic Americans to get an equal

education, with an emphasis on New York City and the Southwest.
Notes: Includes bibliographical references (p. 185-186) and index.
Subjects: Hispanic American students--Education--Juvenile literature. Educational equalization--United States--Juvenile literature. Hispanic Americans--Education. Education, Bilingual.
Series: The Hispanic experience in the Americas
LC Classification: LC2669 .C63 1995
Dewey Class No.: 371.97/68/073 20

Cockcroft, James D.
The Hispanic struggle for social justice: the Hispanic experience in the Americas / James D. Cockcroft.
Published/Created: New York: F. Watts, c1994.
Description: 160 p., [16] p. of plates: ill.; 24 cm.
ISBN: 0531111857 (lib. bdg.)
Notes: Includes bibliographical references (p. 153-155) and index.
Subjects: Hispanic Americans--Civil rights. Hispanic Americans--Social conditions.
LC Classification: E184.S75 C63 1994
Dewey Class No.: 305.868 20

Cohen, Lucy M.
Culture, disease, and stress among Latino immigrants / Lucy M. Cohen.
Published/Created: Washington, D.C.: Research Institute on Immigration and Ethnic Studies, Smithsonian Institution, 1979.
Description: xxvii, 314 p.; 23 cm.
Notes: Bibliography: p. [304]-314.
Subjects: Hispanic Americans--Health and hygiene--Washington (D.C.) Hispanic Americans--Diseases--Washington (D.C.) Health attitudes--Washington (D.C.) Hispanic Americans--Washington (D.C.)--Social conditions.

Hispanic Americans--Mental health--Washington (D.C.) Stress (Psychology) Health surveys--Washington (D.C.)
Series: Smithsonian Institution. Research Institute on Immigration and Ethnic Studies. RIIES special study.
LC Classification: RA448.5.H57 C63
Dewey Class No.: 362.1/08968073 19

Colon-Vila, Lillian.
Salsa / written by /Escrito por Lillian Colon-Vila; and illustrated by /ilustrado por Roberta Collier-Morales.
Published/Created: Houston, TX: Pinata Books, 1998.
Related Authors: Collier-Morales, Roberta.
Description: 1 v. (unpaged): col. ill.; 22 x 29 cm.
ISBN: 1558852204 (hardcover)
Summary: Rita, a young girl living in New York's El Barrio, describes the Afro-Caribbean dance music, salsa, and imagines being a salsa director.
Notes: English and Spanish.
Subjects: Hispanic Americans--Fiction. Salsa (Music)--Fiction. Spanish language materials--Bilingual.
LC Classification: PZ73 .C652 1998
Dewey Class No.: [E] 21

Condition of Hispanics in America today.
Published/Created: Washington, D.C.: U.S. Dept. of Commerce, Bureau of the Census: For sale by the Supt. of Docs., U.S. G.P.O., [1983]
Related Authors: United States. Bureau of the Census. Population Division. United States. Congress. House. Committee on Post Office and Civil Service. Subcommittee on Census and Population.
Description: 28 p.: col. ill.; 22 x 28 cm.
Notes: "Presented at the hearings of the Subcommittee on Census and Population, House Committee on Post

Office and Civil Service"--Cover.
"Population Division"--T.p. verso. S/N
003-024-05700-0 Item 146
Bibliography: p. 17-28.
Subjects: Hispanic Americans--Census.
LC Classification: E184.S75 C656 1983
Dewey Class No.: 305.8/6873 19
Govt. Doc. No.: C 3.2:H 62

Copley, Robert E.
The tall Mexican: the life of Hank
Aguirre, all-star pitcher, businessman,
humanitarian / Robert E. Copley; with a
foreword by José F. Niño.
Published/Created: Houston, Tex.: Piñata
Books, 1998.
Description: xv, 159 p.: ill.; 23 cm.
ISBN: 1558852255 (clothbound: alk.
paper)
Summary: A biography of the All-Star
major-league pitcher whose commitment
to his Hispanic heritage led him to found
Mexican Industries to help provide
economic opportunities to the inner-city
Detroit community.
Notes: Includes index.
Subjects: Aguirre, Hank, 1931-1994 --
Juvenile literature. Aguirre, Hank, 1931-
1994. Baseball players--United States--
Biography--Juvenile literature.
Businessmen--United States--Biography-
-Juvenile literature. Baseball players.
Businessmen. Mexican Americans--
Biography.
LC Classification: GV865.A29 C66
1998
Dewey Class No.: 796.357/092 B 21

Criminal justice and Latino communities /
edited with an introduction by Antoinette
Sedillo López.
Published/Created: New York: Garland,
1995.
Related Authors: López, Antoinette
Sedillo.
Description: xiii, 293 p.: ill.; 24 cm.

ISBN: 0815317727 (acid-free paper)
Notes: Includes bibliographical
references.
Subjects: Criminal justice,
Administration of--United States.
Discrimination in criminal justice
administration--United States. Hispanic
Americans. Latin Americans--United
States.
Series: Latinos in the United States; v. 3
LC Classification: HV9950 .C7435 1995
Dewey Class No.: 364/.089/68073 21

Cubillos, Herminia L.
The Hispanic elderly: a demographic
profile / prepared by Herminia L.
Cubillos with Margarita M. Prieto.
Published/Created: Washington, D.C.:
Policy Analysis Center, Office of
Research, Advocacy, and Legislation,
National Council of La Raza, [1987]
Related Authors: Prieto, Margarita.
Yzaguirre, Raúl. National Council of La
Raza. Policy Anlysis Center.
Description: 31 p.: ill.; 28 cm.
Notes: "Raúl Yzaguirre, president."
"October 1987." Includes bibliographical
references (p. 29-31).
Subjects: Hispanic American aged--
Statistics. Hispanic Americans--
Statistics.
LC Classification: E184.S75 C83 1987
Dewey Class No.: 305.26 21

Cullison, Alan.
The South Americans / Alan Cullison.
Published/Created: New York: Chelsea
House Publishers, c1991.
Description: 110 p.: ill. (some col.); 25
cm.
ISBN: 0877548633 0791003051 (pbk.)
Summary: Discusses the history, culture,
and religion of the South Americans,
their place in American society, and the
problems they face as an ethnic group in
North America.

Notes: Includes bibliographical references (p. 107) and index.
Subjects: Hispanic Americans--Juvenile literature. Hispanic Americans.
Series: The Peoples of North America
LC Classification: E184.S75 C85 1991
Dewey Class No.: 973/.0468 20

Cultural factors among hispanics: perception and prevention of HIV infection / produced by Culturelinc Corporation.
Published/Created: New York: The Corporation, 1991.
Related Authors: Culturelinc Corporation. New York (State). AIDS Institute.
Description: 26 p.: col ill., a col. map; 28 cm.
Notes: "Funded by: AIDS Institute, New York State Department of Health".
Includes bibliogrpahical references (p. 22-23).
Subjects: AIDS (Disease)--United States. Hispanic Americans--Diseases. Latin Americans--Diseases--United States.
LC Classification: RC607.A26 C85 1991

Cumpián, Carlos.
Latino rainbow: poems about Latino Americans / Carlos Cumpián; illustrated by Richard Leonard.
Published/Created: Chicago: Childrens Press, 1994.
Related Authors: Leonard, Richard, ill.
Description: 47 p.: col. ill.; 23 cm.
ISBN: 0516051539
Summary: Poems about Latino Americans such as Cesar Chavez, Linda Ronstadt, Henry Cisneros, and Roberto Clemente.
Subjects: Hispanic Americans--Juvenile poetry. Children's poetry, American. Hispanic Americans--Poetry. American poetry.
Series: Many voices, one song
LC Classification: PS3553.U458 L38

1994
Dewey Class No.: 811/.54 20

Daul, Jennifer.
Spanish Americans in North Dakota, 1980: a statistical portrait / by Jennifer Daul, Richard W. Rathge, Sheila D. Pingree.
Published/Created: Fargo, N.D.: North Dakota Census Data Center, Dept. of Agricultural Economics, North Dakota Agricultural Experiment Station, North Dakota State University, [1986]
Related Authors: Rathge, Richard W. Pingree, Sheila D.
Description: iii leaves, 7 p.: ill.; 28 cm.
Notes: Cover title. "October 1986."
Subjects: Hispanic Americans--North Dakota--Statistics. North Dakota--Population--Statistics.
Series: Report series (North Dakota Census Data Center); no. 7.
LC Classification: F645.S75 D38 1986
Dewey Class No.: 304.6/089680784 19

Dávila, Arlene M., 1965-
Latinos, Inc.: the marketing and making of a people / Arlene Dávila.
Published/Created: Berkeley, CA: University of California Press, c2001.
Description: xv, 287 p.: ill.; 24 cm.
ISBN: 0520226690 (cloth: alk. paper) 0520227247 (paper: alk. paper)
Notes: Includes bibliographical references (p. 259-280) and index.
Subjects: Hispanic American consumers. Market segmentation--United States. Hispanic Americans--Ethnic identity.
LC Classification: HF5415.33.U6 D38 2001
Dewey Class No.: 658.8/34/08968073 21

Davis, Mike, 1946-
Magical urbanism: Latinos reinvent the US city / Mike Davis.
Published/Created: London; New York:

Verso, 2000.
Description: xviii, 172 p.: ill., maps; 20
cm.
ISBN: 1859847714
Notes: Includes bibliographical
references (p. [151]-168) and index.
Subjects: Hispanic Americans--Social
conditions. Hispanic Americans--Politics
and government. Inner cities--United
States. City and town life--United States.
Sociology, Urban--United States. United
States--Civilization--Hispanic influences.
United States--Population. United States-
-Ethnic relations.
Series: Haymarket series
LC Classification: E184.S75 D36 2000
Dewey Class No.: 305.868/073 21

Day, Frances Ann.
Latina and Latino voices in literature for
children and teenagers / Frances Ann
Day.
Published/Created: Portsmouth, NH:
Heinemann, [1997]
Description: xi, 228 p.: ill.; 26 cm.
ISBN: 0435072021 (acid-free paper)
Notes: Includes bibliographical
references and indexes.
Subjects: American literature--Hispanic
American authors Bibliography.
Hispanic American literature (Spanish)--
Bibliography. Children's literature,
American--Hispanic American authors
Bibliography. Young adult literature,
American--Hispanic American authors--
Bibliography. American literature--20th
century--Bibliography. Latin American
literature--20th century--Bibliography.
Children--Books and reading--United
States. Teenagers--Books and reading--
United States. Hispanic Americans--
Books and reading.
LC Classification: Z1229.H57 D3 1997
PS153.H56
Dewey Class No.: 016.8109/9283/08968

20

De Anda, Raul.
Hispanic underemployment in state
government. June 1989 update / Raul De
Anda.
Published/Created: [St. Paul, MN] (506
Rice St., St. Paul 55103): Spanish
Speaking Affairs Council, [1989]
Related Authors: Minnesota. Spanish
Speaking Affairs Council. Hispanic
Research Unit.
Description: 24 leaves: ill.; 28 cm.
Notes: "Critique of State of Minnesota
affirmative action 1988 & 1989 annual
reports"--Cover. "June 15, 1989"--Cover.
Subjects: Hispanic Americans in the civil
service--Minnesota. Civil service--
Minority employment--Minnesota.
Minnesota--Officials and employees.
LC Classification: JK6160.5.M5 D42
1989

De Anda, Raul.
Hispanic underemployment in state
government: 1983 and 1988 / prepared
by Raul De Anda (Hispanic Research
Unit, Spanish Speaking Affairs Council).
Published/Created: [St. Paul, MN]: The
Council, [1989]
Related Authors: Minnesota. Spanish
Speaking Affairs Council. Hispanic
Research Unit.
Description: vi, 28 leaves: ill.; 28 cm.
Notes: "In all agencies and in 18
randomly-selected agencies in 1983 and
1988"--Cover. "May 1, 1989."
Subjects: Hispanic Americans in the civil
service--Minnesota. Civil service--
Minority employment--Minnesota.
LC Classification: JK6160.5.M5 D4
1989
Dewey Class No.:
353.9776006/08968073 20

De la Rosa, Mario.
    Status of employment of Hispanics in
    Ohio / Mario de la Rosa.
    Published/Created: Columbus, Ohio:
    Commission on Spanish Speaking
    Affairs, [1987?]
    Related Authors: Ohio. Commission on
    Spanish Speaking Affairs.
    Description: 20 leaves; 28 cm.
    Notes: Bibliography: leaves 19-20.
    Subjects: Hispanic Americans--
    Employment--Ohio.
    LC Classification: HD8081.H7 D4 1987
    Dewey Class No.: 331.6/2/68730771 19

De León, Arnoldo, 1945-
    Ethnicity in the sunbelt: Mexican
    Americans in Houston / Arnoldo De
    León.
    Edition Information: 1st Texas A&M
    University Press ed.
    Published/Created: College Station:
    Texas A&M University Press, c2001.
    Description: p. cm.
    ISBN: 158544149X (pkb.: alk. paper)
    Notes: This edition includes new preface
    and concluding chapter. Includes
    bibliographical references.
    Subjects: Mexican Americans--Texas--
    Houston--Ethnic identity. Mexican
    Americans--Cultural assimilation--
    Texas--Houston. Mexican Americans--
    Texas--Houston--Politics and
    government 20th century. Hispanic
    American neighborhoods--Texas--
    Houston--History 20th century.
    Ethnicity--Texas--Houston--History--
    20th century. Houston (Tex.)--Ethnic
    relations. Houston (Tex.)--Social
    conditions--20th century.
    Series: University of Houston series in
    Mexican American studies; no. 4
    LC Classification: F394.H89 M5144
    2001
    Dewey Class No.: 976.4/14110046872

21

De Varona, Frank.
    Latino literacy: the complete guide to our
    Hispanic history and culture / Frank de
    Varona.
    Edition Information: 1st Owl book ed.
    Published/Created: New York: Henry
    Holt, 1996.
    Description: xx, 378 p.: maps; 24 cm.
    ISBN: 0805038582 (alk. paper)
    0805038590 (pbk.: alk. paper)
    Notes: "An Owl book." A Round Stone
    Press book." Includes bibliographical
    references (p. 359-363) and index.
    Subjects: Hispanic Americans. Hispanic
    Americans--History. United States--
    Civilization--Hispanic influences.
    LC Classification: E184.S75 D38 1996
    Dewey Class No.: 973/.0468 20

DeFreitas, Gregory.
    Inequality at work: Hispanics in the U.S.
    labor force / Gregory DeFreitas.
    Published/Created: New York: Oxford
    University Press, 1991.
    Description: xvi, 284 p.: ill.; 25 cm.
    ISBN: 0195064216
    Notes: Includes bibliographical
    references (p. [258]-276) and index.
    Subjects: Hispanic Americans--
    Employment. United States--Emigration
    and immigration--Economic aspects.
    LC Classification: HD8081.H7 D44
    1991
    Dewey Class No.: 331.6/368073 20

Delgado, Melvin.
    Social services in Latino communities:
    research and strategies / Melvin Delgado.
    Published/Created: New York: Haworth
    Press, c1998.
    Description: 153 p.; 21 cm.
    ISBN: 0789004283 (hardcover: alk.
    paper) 0789004291 (pbk.: alk. paper)
    Notes: Includes bibliographical

references (p. 131-145) and index.
Subjects: Hispanic Americans--Services
for. Hispanic Americans--Services for--
New England. Puerto Ricans--Services
for--United States. Puerto Ricans--
Services for--New England. Social
service--United States. Social service--
New England.
LC Classification: HV3187.A2 D44
1998
Dewey Class No.: 362.84/68073 21

Delgado, Richard.
Home-grown racism: Colorado's historic
embrace, and denial, of equal
opportunity in higher education / Richard
Delgado, Jean Stefancic.
Published/Created: [Denver, Colo.]:
Latino/a Research & Policy Center,
University of Colorado at Denver,
c1999.
Related Authors: Stefancic, Jean.
Latino/a Research and Policy Center.
Description: iii leaves, 92 p.; 28 cm.
Notes: Cover title. Includes
bibliographical references.
Subjects: Discrimination in higher
education--History--Colorado. Hispanic
Americans--Education (Higher)--
Colorado.
Series: Working paper (Latino/a
Research and Policy Center); 1.
LC Classification: LC212.422.C6 D45
1999
Govt. Doc. No.: UCD6/6.11/1 codocs

Demographic characteristics of the older
Hispanic population: a report / by the
chairman of the Select Committee on
Aging, House of Representatives, One
Hundredth Congress, second session.
Published/Created: Washington: U.S.
G.P.O.: For sale by the Supt. of Docs.,
Congressional Sales Office, U.S. G.P.O.,
1989.
Related Authors: United States.

Congress. House. Select Committee on
Aging.
Description: vi, 20 p.: ill.; 24 cm.
Notes: At head of Committee print.
Distributed to some depository libraries
in microfiche. Shipping list no.: 89-106-
P. "December 1988." "Comm. pub. no.
100-696." Item 1009-B-2, 1009-C-2
(microfiche) Includes bibliographical
references.
Subjects: Hispanic American aged--
Statistics. Hispanic Americans--
Statistics.
LC Classification: E184.S75 D46 1989
Dewey Class No.: 305.26/08968073 20
Govt. Doc. No.: Y 4.Ag 4/2:H 62/2

DeRubertis, Barbara.
Count on Pablo / by Barbara deRubertis;
illustrated by Rebecca Thornburgh.
Published/Created: New York: Kane
Press, c1999.
Related Authors: Thornburgh, Rebecca
McKillip, ill.
Description: 32 p.: col. ill.; 23 cm.
ISBN: 1575650908 (pbk.: alk. paper)
Summary: Pablo demonstrates how good
he is at counting while helping his
grandmother, his "abuela," prepare to sell
vegetables at the market.
Notes: "Grades K-2"--cover.
Subjects: Counting--Fiction. Vegetables-
-Fiction. Markets--Fiction.
Grandmothers--Fiction. Hispanic
Americans--Fiction.
Series: Math matters
LC Classification: PZ7.D4475 Cr 1999
Dewey Class No.: [E] 21

DeSipio, Louis.
Counting on the Latino vote: Latinos as a
new electorate / Louis DeSipio.
Published/Created: Charlottesville, Va.:
University Press of Virginia, 1996.
Description: xii, 221 p.; 24 cm.
ISBN: 0813916607 (cloth: alk. paper)

Notes: Includes bibliographical references and index.
Subjects: Hispanic Americans--Politics and government. Voting--United States.
Series: Race and ethnicity in urban politics
LC Classification: E184.S75 D47 1996
Dewey Class No.: 323.1/168073 20

DeSipio, Louis.
Talking back to television: Latinos discuss how television portrays them and the quality of programming options / Tomás Rivera Policy Institute; [report author, Louis DeSipio; research team, Sarah Banet-Weiser ... [et al.]; editor, Joy Hofer].
Published/Created: Claremont, CA: TRPI, c1998.
Related Authors: Hofer, Joy. Tomás Rivera Policy Institute.
Description: 24 p.: ill.; 28 cm.
Subjects: Hispanic Americans on television.
LC Classification: PN1992.8.H54 D47 1998
Dewey Class No.: 791.45/6520368 21

Dialogue rejoined: theology and ministry in the United States Hispanic reality / with a foreword by Donald Senior; Moíses Sandoval ... [et al.]; edited by Ana María Pineda, Robert Schreiter.
Published/Created: Collegeville, Minn.: Liturgical Press, c1995.
Related Authors: Sandoval, Moises. Pineda, Ana María. Schreiter, Robert J.
Description: viii, 187 p.; 23 cm.
Cancelled ISBN: 0814622062 (pbk.)
Notes: Includes bibliographical references.
Subjects: Church work with Hispanic Americans. Hispanic Americans--Religion. Hispanic Americans--Social conditions. Church and social problems--Catholic Church--History. Sociology,

Christian (Catholic) Hispanic American Catholics--History.
LC Classification: BV4468.2.H57 D52 1995
Dewey Class No.: 277.3/082/08968 20

Diaz-Greenberg, Rosario, 1950-
The emergence of voice in Latino high school students / Rosario Diaz-Greenberg.
Published/Created: New York: P. Lang, 2001.
Description: p. cm.
ISBN: 0820449687 (alk. paper)
Notes: Includes bibliographical references and index.
Subjects: Hispanic Americans--Education (Secondary)--Social aspects. Hispanic American students--Social conditions. Critical pedagogy--United States.
Series: Counterpoints (New York, N.Y.); v. 147.
LC Classification: LC2670.4 .D53 2001
Dewey Class No.: 373.1829/68073 21

Díaz-Stevens, Ana María, 1942-
Recognizing the Latino resurgence in U.S. religion: the Emmaus papadigm / Ana María Díaz-Stevens, Anthony M. Stevens-Arroyo.
Published/Created: Boulder, Colo.: Westview Press, 1998.
Related Authors: Stevens Arroyo, Antonio M.
Description: xxi, 272 p.: ill.; 23 cm.
ISBN: 0813325099 (hardcover: alk. paper) 0813325102 (paperback: alk. paper)
Notes: Includes bibliographical references (p. 239-257) and index.
Subjects: Hispanic Americans--Religion.
Series: Explorations (Boulder, Colo.)
LC Classification: BR563.H57 D53 1998
Dewey Class No.: 277.3/0829/08968 21

Discovering Latino religion: a
comprehensive social science
bibliography / edited by Anthony M.
Stevens-Arroyo, with Segundo Pantoja.
Published/Created: New York: Bildner
Center for Western Hemisphere Studies,
c1995.
Related Authors: Stevens Arroyo,
Antonio M.
Description: 142 p.; 23 cm.
ISBN: 0929972139 0929972147 (pbk.)
Subjects: Hispanic Americans--Religion-
-Bibliography. United States--Religion--
Bibliography.
Series: PARAL studies series; v. 4
Bildner Center series on religion; v. 4
LC Classification: Z7757.U5 D57 1995
BR563.H57
Dewey Class No.: 016.2/0089/68073 20

DISCovering multicultural America
[computer file].
Published/Created: Detroit, MI: Gale
Research, c1996-
Related Authors: Gale Research Inc.
Description: computer laser optical discs;
4 3/4 in. 1.0-
ISSN: 1084-1997
Cancel/Invalid LCCN: sn 95005960
Summary: The culture and history of:
African Americans, Asian Americans,
Hispanic Americans, Native Americans.
Notes: Title from disc label. System
requirements: 80386SX or higher
IBM/IBM compatible (80486 or higher
recommended); DOS 3.3 or higher;
Windows 3.1; SVGA graphics card and
monitor (640x480, 256 colors); 4
megabytes (or more) of RAM memory;
10 megabytes free hard disk space; ISO
9660 CD-ROM player; Microsoft CD-
ROM Extensions (MSCDEX) 2.2 or
higher; Windows compatible mouse or
pointing device; 8-bit (or higher)
SoundBlaster-compatible sound card.
Accompanied by user's manual and help

card. SERBIB/SERLOC merged record
Subjects: Pluralism (Social sciences)--
United States. Multiculturalism--United
States. Hispanic Americans--History.
Asian Americans--History. African
Americans--History. Indians of North
America--History. United States--Race
relations. United States--Ethnic relations.
LC Classification: E184.A1
Dewey Class No.: 973 12

Drugs in Hispanic communities / edited by
Ronald Glick and Joan Moore.
Published/Created: New Brunswick:
Rutgers University Press, c1990.
Related Authors: Glick, Ronald, 1943-
Moore, Joan W.
Description: viii, 275 p.; 24 cm.
ISBN: 0813515688: 0813515696 :
Notes: Includes bibliographical
references (P. 253-272).
Subjects: Hispanic Americans--Drug use.
Drug abuse--United States.
LC Classification: HV5824.E85 D79
1990
Dewey Class No.: 362.29/12/08968073
20

Duignan, Peter.
The Spanish speakers in the United
States: a history / Peter J. Duignan and
L.H. Gann.
Published/Created: Lanham: University
Press of America, c1998.
Related Authors: Gann, Lewis H., 1924-
Gann, Lewis H., 1924- Hispanics in the
United States.
Description: xvii, 471 p.; 23 cm.
ISBN: 076181258X (pbk.)
Notes: Rev. ed. of: The Hispanics in the
United States / L.H. Gann and Peter J.
Duignan. 1986. Includes bibliographical
references (p. [441]-452) and index.
Subjects: Hispanic Americans--History.
LC Classification: E184.S75 D85 1998

Dewey Class No.: 973/.0468 21

Durán Trujillo, Marie Oralia, 1927-
Autumn memories: my New Mexican
roots and traditions / by Marie Oralia
Durán Trujillo.
Published/Created: Pueblo, Colo.: El
Escritorio, c1999.
Description: vii, 120 p.: ill.; 22 cm.
ISBN: 0962897477
Notes: Includes bibliographical
references (p. 113-115) and index.
Subjects: Durán Trujillo, Marie Oralia,
1927- Gallegos family. Duran family.
Hispanic Americans--New Mexico--
Biography Hispanic American women--
New Mexico--Biography. Hispanic
American women--New Mexico--Social
conditions. New Mexico--Biography.
LC Classification: F805.S75 D87 1999
Dewey Class No.: 978.9/00468073 21

Education in the new Latino diaspora: policy
and the politics of identity / edited by
Stanton Wortham, Enrique G. Murillo,
Jr., and Edmund T. Hamann.
Published/Created: Westport, Conn.:
Ablex Pub., 2001.
Related Authors: Wortham, Stanton
Emerson Fisher, 1963- Murillo, Enrique
G. Hamann, Edmund T.
Description: p. cm.
ISBN: 1567506305 (alk. paper)
1567506313 (pbk.: alk. paper)
Notes: Includes bibliographical
references and index.
Subjects: Hispanic Americans--
Education.
Series: Sociocultural studies in
educational policy formation and
appropriation, 1530-5473; v. 2
LC Classification: LC2669 .E39 2001
Dewey Class No.: 371.829/68073 21

Educational pathways.
Published/Created: Fort Washington,

MD: Educational Pathways, c1997-
Description: v.: ill.; 28 cm. Vol. 1, issue
1 (spring 1997)-
ISSN: 1092-9916
Cancel/Invalid LCCN: sn 97003643
Notes: Title from cover.
SERBIB/SERLOC merged record
Subjects: African Americans--Education
(Higher)--Virginia Periodicals. Hispanic
Americans--Education--Virginia--
Periodicals. Minorities--Education--
Virginia--Periodicals.
LC Classification: LC2802.V8 E35

El cuerpo de Cristo: the Hispanic presence in
the U.S. Catholic Church / edited by
Peter Casarella and Raúl Gómez.
Published/Created: New York:
Crossroad Pub. Co., c1998.
Related Authors: Casarella, Peter J.
Gómez, Raúl.
Description: 334 p.: ill.; 23 cm.
ISBN: 0824517415
Notes: Proceedings of a conference held
in 1997 at Catholic University of
America. "A Crossroad Herder book."
Includes bibliographical references.
Subjects: Catholic Church--United
States--Congresses. Hispanic American
Catholics--Congresses. Hispanic
Americans--Religion--Congresses.
LC Classification: BX1407.H55 C84
1998
Dewey Class No.: 282/.73/08968 21

Elizondo, Virgilio P.
Our Hispanic pilgrimage / by Virgil
Elizondo and Angela Erevia.
Published/Created: San Antonio, Tex.
(3000 W. French Pl., San Antonio
78228): Mexican American Cultural
Center, c1980.
Related Authors: Erevia, Angela.
Conference of Major Superiors of Men.
Description: 77 p.: ill.; 21 cm.
Notes: Prepared for Conference of Major

Superiors of Men, National Assembly, San Antonio, Texas, August 11, 1980"-- P. [2] of cover. Texts on covers.
Subjects: Catholic Church--United States. Hispanic Americans--Religion.
LC Classification: BX1407.H55 E44
Dewey Class No.: 282/.08968073 19

Family therapy with Hispanics: toward appreciating diversity / [edited by] Maria T. Flores, Gabrielle Carey.
Published/Created: Boston: Allyn and Bacon, c2000.
Related Authors: Flores, Maria T. Carey, Gabrielle.
Description: xiv, 321 p.: ill.; 23 cm.
ISBN: 0205285325 (pbk.: alk. paper)
Notes: Includes bibliographical references and index.
Subjects: Hispanic American families-- Psychology. Hispanic American families--Social conditions. Family psychotherapy--United States. Hispanic Americans--Cultural assimilation. Hispanic Americans--Ethnic identity.
LC Classification: E184.S75 F35 2000
Dewey Class No.: 616.89/156/08968073 21

Farmer, George L.
Education: the dilemma of the Spanish-surname American; a monograph, by George L. Farmer.
Published/Created: [Los Angeles] School of Education, University of Southern California, 1968.
Description: ii, 55 l. 28 cm.
Notes: Bibliography: leaves 54-55.
Subjects: Hispanic Americans-- Education--Southwest, New. Education-- Southwest, New.
LC Classification: F787 .F3
Dewey Class No.: 301.451/6/09791

Fernandez-Florez, Dario.
The Spanish heritage in the United

States.
Edition Information: 3d corrected and enl. ed.
Published/Created: Madrid, Publicaciones Españolas, 1971.
Description: 376 p. illus. (part col.), map. 22 cm.
Notes: Bibliography: p. [333]-357.
Subjects: Spaniards in the United States--History. Hispanic Americans--History. United States--Civilization--Spanish influences.
LC Classification: E169.1 .F37 1971
Dewey Class No.: 917.3/03

Fernández-Flórez, Darío.
The Spanish heritage in the United States / Dario Fernández-Flórez.
Published/Created: New York: Arno Press, 1980.
Description: 362 p.: ill.; 21 cm.
ISBN: 0405131550
Notes: Reprint of the 1965 ed. published by Publicaciones Españolas, Madrid, which was issued as no. 3 of Claves de España. Bibliography: p. [331]-343.
Subjects: Spaniards in the United States--History. Hispanic Americans--History. United States--Civilization--Spanish influences.
Series: Hispanics in the United States
LC Classification: E169.1 .F37 1980
Dewey Class No.: 973/.0461 19

Fernández-Shaw, Carlos M.
The Hispanic presence in North America from 1492 to today / Carlos M. Fernández-Shaw; updated appendixes by Gerardo Piña Rosales; translated by Alfonso Bertodano Stourton and others.
Edition Information: Updated ed.
Published/Created: New York: Facts On File, 1999.
Description: p. cm.
ISBN: 0816040109
Notes: Includes bibliographical

references (p.) and index.
Subjects: Spaniards--United States--
History. Spanish Americans--History.
Hispanic Americans--History. United
States--Civilization--Spanish influences.
LC Classification: E169.1 .F375 1999
Dewey Class No.: 973/.0468 21

Figueroa, Frank M.
Encyclopedia of Latin American music
in New York / by Frank M. Figueroa.
Published/Created: St. Petersburg, Fla.:
Pillar Publications, c1994.
Description: xiii, 237 p.; 24 cm.
ISBN: 096432010X
Notes: Includes bibliographical
references (p. [205]-213), discography
(p. [193]-204), and index.
Subjects: Hispanic Americans--New
York (State)--New York--Music
Encyclopedias. Latin Americans--New
York (State)--New York--Music
Encyclopedias. Popular music--New
York (State)--New York--Encyclopedias.
Popular music--New York (State)--New
York--History and criticism.
LC Classification: ML101.U6 F54 1994
Dewey Class No.: 780/.89/6807471 20

Fincher, Beatrice.
Funds for Hispanics / compiled by
Beatrice Fincher.
Published/Created: Austin, Tex.: Spanish
Publicity, 1981.
Description: iii, 36 p.; 28 cm.
ISBN: 0960738606 (pbk.)
Subjects: Endowments--United States--
Directories. Hispanic Americans--
Services for--Finance.
LC Classification: HV97.A3 F5
Dewey Class No.: 361.7/632/0973 19

Fisher, Maria.
Latino education: status and prospects /
by Maria Fisher with Sonia M. Pérez ...
[et al.].

Published/Created: Washington, D.C.:
National Council of La Raza, c1998.
Related Authors: Pérez, Sonia M.
National Council of La Raza.
Description: ii, 111 p.: ill.; 28 cm.
Contents: Introduction -- Demographic
profile -- Pre-K through 12 -- Elementary
and secondary school -- Postsecondary
education -- Policy implications.
Notes: Includes bibliographical
references (p. 111).
Subjects: Hispanic Americans--
Education.
Series: State of Hispanic America
(National Council of La Raza); 1998.
LC Classification: E184.S75 S735 1998
LC2669
Dewey Class No.: 371.829/68/073 21

Flores, Norma P.
A beginner's guide to Hispanic
genealogy = Introducción a la
investigación genealógical Latino
Americana / Norma P. Flores & Patsy
Ludwig.
Published/Created: San Mateo, Calif.:
Western Book/Journal Press, 1993.
Related Authors: Ludwig, Patsy.
Related Titles: Introducción a la
investigación genealógical Latino
Americana.
Description: x, 58 p.: ill., maps; 24 cm.
ISBN: 0936029315 (pbk.) :
Notes: Includes bibliographical
references (p. 58).
Subjects: Hispanic Americans--
Genealogy--Handbooks, manuals, etc.
LC Classification: E184.S75 F57 1993
Dewey Class No.: 929/.1/08968 20

Fogel, Walter A.
Mexican Americans in Southwest labor
markets.
Published/Created: Los Angeles,
Mexican-American Study Project,
University of California, 1967.

Description: ix, 222 p. 28 cm.
Notes: Includes bibliographical
references.
Subjects: Hispanic Americans--
Employment--Southwest, New.
Series: University of California, Los
Angeles. Mexican-American Study
Project. Advance report 10
LC Classification: E184.M5 C3 no. 10
Dewey Class No.: 331.6/3/60791

Food and nutrient intakes by individuals in
the United States, 1994-96 / United
States Department of Agriculture,
Agricultural Research Service.
Published/Created: [Washington, D.C.]:
The Service, [2000]
Related Authors: United States.
Agricultural Research Service.
Description: 2 v. (xii, 747 p.); 22 x 28
cm.
Contents: v. 1. -- Income, food stamp
program participation, and race -- v. 2--
Hispanic origin and race, and region.
Notes: "August 2000." Includes
bibliographical references (p. 745-747)
Subjects: Nutrition surveys--United
States--Statistics. Diet--United States--
Statistics. Poor--United States--Statistics.
Food stamps--United States--Statistics.
Hispanic Americans--Statistics.
Series: NFS report; no. 96-3
LC Classification: TX360.U6 F646 2000
Dewey Class No.: 363.8/56/0973021 21

Fox, Geoffrey E.
Hispanic nation: culture, politics, and the
constructing of identity / Geoffrey Fox.
Edition Information: 1st University of
Arizona paperbound ed.
Published/Created: Tucson [Ariz.]:
University of Arizona Press, 1997.
Description: viii, 264 p.; 22 cm.
ISBN: 0816517991 (alk. paper)
Notes: Originally published: New York:
Carol Pub., c1996. Includes

bibliographical references (p. 243-256)
and index.
Subjects: Hispanic Americans--Ethnic
identity. Hispanic Americans--Politics
and government.
LC Classification: E184.S75 F69 1997
Dewey Class No.: 305.868 21

Fox, Geoffrey E.
Hispanic nation: culture, politics, and the
constructing of identity / Geoffrey Fox.
Published/Created: New York: Carol
Pub., c1996.
Description: viii, 264 p.; 24 cm.
ISBN: 1559723114 (hardcover)
Notes: "A Birch Lane Press book."
Includes bibliographical references (p.
243-256) and index.
Subjects: Hispanic Americans--Ethnic
identity. Hispanic Americans--Politics
and government.
LC Classification: E184.S75 F69 1996
Dewey Class No.: 305.868 20

From rhetoric to reality: Latino politics in the
1988 elections / edited by Rodolfo O. de
la Garza and Louis DeSipio.
Published/Created: Boulder, Colo.:
Westview Press, 1992.
Related Authors: De la Garza, Rodolfo
O. DeSipio, Louis.
Description: xvii, 182 p.: maps; 23 cm.
ISBN: 0813384346 (alk. paper)
Notes: Includes bibliographical
references.
Subjects: Hispanic Americans--Politics
and government. Hispanic Americans--
Suffrage. Presidents--United States--
Election--1988. United States--Politics
and government--1981-1989.
LC Classification: E184.S75 F75 1992
Dewey Class No.: 324.973/0927 20

Gann, Lewis H., 1924-
The Hispanics in the United States: a
history / L.H. Gann and Peter J.

Duignan.
Published/Created: Boulder: Westview
Press; Stanford, Calif.: Hoover
Institution on War, Revolution, and
Peace, 1986.
Related Authors: Duignan, Peter.
Description: xv, 392 p.; 24 cm.
ISBN: 0813303354 (alk. paper) :
Notes: Includes index. Bibliography: p.
365-376.
Subjects: Hispanic Americans--History.
LC Classification: E184.S75 G36 1986
Dewey Class No.: 973/.0468 19

García, Eugene E., 1946-
Hispanic education in the United States:
raíces y alas / Eugene E. Garcia.
Published/Created: Lanham: Rowman &
Littlefield, c2001.
Description: v, 298 p.: ill.; 24 cm.
ISBN: 074251076X (cloth: alk. paper)
0742510778 (pbk.: alk. paper)
Notes: Includes bibliographical
references (p. 261-288) and index.
Subjects: Hispanic americans--
Education.
Series: Critical issues in contemporary
American education series
LC Classification: LC2669 .G37 2001
Dewey Class No.: 371.829/68073 21

García, John A.
The success of Hispanic magazine: a
publishing success story / John García;
photographs by Ricardo Vargas.
Published/Created: New York: Walker
and Co., 1996.
Related Authors: Arechavala-Vargas,
Ricardo, ill.
Description: v, 84 p.: ill.; 24 cm.
ISBN: 0802783090 (hardcover)
0802783104 (reinforced)
Summary: Describes the people and
processes involved in the production of
Hispanic, a popular magazine which
focuses primarily on positive news

related to all aspects of Hispanic
American culture.
Notes: Includes bibliographical
references (p. 79) and index.
Subjects: Hispanic. Hispanic. Hispanic
American periodicals--Juvenile
literature. Hispanic Americans--
Periodicals. Periodicals--Publishing.
Series: Success series
LC Classification: PN4900.H57 G37
1996
Dewey Class No.: 051/.08968073 20

Garcia, Kimberly, 1966-
Careers in technology / Kimberly Garcia.
Published/Created: Bear, DE: Mitchell
Lane Publishers, 2001.
Description: p. cm.
ISBN: 1584150874
Notes: Includes bibliographical
references and index.
Subjects: Technology--Vocational
guidance--United States. Hispanic
Americans--Education.
Series: Latinos at work.
LC Classification: T65.3 .G37 2001
Dewey Class No.: 602.3/73 21

García, Nasario.
Pláticas: conversations with Hispano
writers of New Mexico / Nasario García.
Published/Created: Lubbock, TX: Texas
Tech University Press, 2000.
Description: xii, 210 p.: ill.; 24 cm.
ISBN: 089672428X (cloth: alk. paper)
Notes: Includes bibliographical
references (p. 199-200) and index.
Subjects: American literature--New
Mexico--History and criticism Theory,
etc. American literature--Hispanic
American authors--History and criticism-
-Theory, etc. American literature--20th
century--History and criticism Theory,
etc. Authors, American--20th century--
Interviews. Hispanic Americans--New
Mexico--Interviews. Authors, American-

-New Mexico--Interviews. Hispanic Americans in literature. New Mexico--In literature.
LC Classification: PS283.N6 G37 2000
Dewey Class No.: 810.9/8680789 21

Gilbert, Thomas W.
Roberto Clemente / Thomas W. Gilbert; traduccíon por Dolores y Gerard Koch.
Edition Information: 1. ed.
Published/Created: New York: Chelsea House, c1995.
Description: 111 p.: ill.; 25 cm.
ISBN: 0791031055
Notes: Includes bibliographical references (p. 107-108) and index.
Subjects: Clemente, Roberto, 1934-1972 --Juvenile literature. Baseball players-- United States--Biography--Juvenile literature. Hispanic Americans-- Biography--Juvenile literature.
Series: Hispanos notables
LC Classification: GV865.C45 G5518 1994
Dewey Class No.: 796.357/092 B 20

Gillespie, Francis P.
What do current estimates of Hispanic mortality really tell us? / Francis P. Gillespie and Teresa A. Sullivan.
Published/Created: [Austin]: Texas Population Research Center, University of Texas at Austin, [1983]
Related Authors: Sullivan, Teresa A., 1949- University of Texas at Austin. Population Research Center.
Description: 12, [14] p.; 28 cm.
Notes: "Paper presented at the annual meeting, Population Association of America, Pittsburgh, PA, April 14-16, 1983." Bibliography: p. [24]-[26].
Subjects: Hispanic Americans-- Mortality.
Series: Papers (University of Texas at Austin. Population Research Center); paper no. 5.010.

LC Classification: HB1335 .G54 1983
Dewey Class No.: 304.6/4/08968 19

Gomis Hernández, Redis.
Los grupos hispanos y la política de los Estados Unidos hacia América Latina: un análisis bibliográfico / Redis Gomis Hernández.
Published/Created: [Havana]: Centro de Estudios sobre América, [between 1985 and 1989]
Description: 29 p.; 20 cm.
Notes: Includes bibliographical references.
Subjects: Hispanic Americans--Politics and government. Hispanic Americans-- Politics and government--Bibliography. United States--Relations--Latin America. Latin America--Relations--United States--Bibliography.
Series: Avances de investigación (Havana, Cuba)
LC Classification: E184.S75 G64 1985

Gonzales, Sylvia Alicia.
Hispanic American voluntary organizations / Sylvia Alicia Gonzales.
Published/Created: Westport, Conn.: Greenwood Press, 1985.
Description: xx, 267 p.; 24 cm.
ISBN: 0313209499 (lib. bdg.)
Notes: Includes index.
Subjects: Hispanic Americans--Societies, etc.--Directories. Voluntarism--United States.
Series: Ethnic American voluntary organizations
LC Classification: E184.S75 G65 1985
Dewey Class No.: 362.8/468073 19

Gonzalez Meza, Choco.
The Latino vote in the 1980 presidential election: a political research report / by Choco Gonzalez Meza; edited by Pamela Eoff.
Edition Information: 1st ed.

Published/Created: San Antonio, Tex. (210 N. St. Mary's St., Suite 501, San Antonio 78205): Southwest Voter Registration Education Project, 1981. Related Authors: Eoff, Pamela. Southwest Voter Registration Education Project (U.S.)
Description: 41 p.: ill.; 28 cm.
Subjects: Hispanic Americans--Politics and government. Presidents--United States--Election--1980. Voting--United States.
LC Classification: E184.S75 G66
Dewey Class No.: 324.973/0926 19

Gonzalez, Juan.
Harvest of empire: a history of Latinos in America / Juan Gonzalez.
Published/Created: New York: Viking, 2000.
Description: xx, 346 p.: maps; 24 cm.
ISBN: 0670867209 (alk. paper)
Notes: Includes bibliographical references (p. 311-324) and index.
Subjects: Hispanic Americans--History. Immigrants--United States--History. United States--Emigration and immigration--History. Latin America--Emigration and immigration--History. United States--Relations--Latin America. Latin America--Relations--United States. United States--Territorial expansion--History. United States--Ethnic relations.
LC Classification: E184.S75 G655 2000
Dewey Class No.: 973/.0468 21

González, Justo L.
Mañana: Christian theology from a Hispanic perspective / Justo L. González.
Published/Created: Nashville: Abingdon Press, c1990.
Description: 184 p.; 23 cm.
ISBN: 0687230675 (alk. paper)
Notes: Includes bibliographical references (p. 169-184).
Subjects: Theology, Doctrinal--United

States. Hispanic Americans--Religion. Liberation theology.
LC Classification: BT30.U6 G65 1990
Dewey Class No.: 230/.08968073 20

Graham, Joe Stanley.
Hispanic-American material culture: an annotated directory of collections, sites, archives, and festivals in the United States / compiled by Joe S. Graham.
Published/Created: New York: Greenwood Press, 1989.
Description: xxiv, 257 p.; 24 cm.
ISBN: 0313247897 (lib. bdg.: alk. paper)
Notes: Includes index. Bibliography: p. [237]-245.
Subjects: Hispanic Americans--Material culture--Directories. Historical museums--United States--Directories. Historic sites--United States--Directories.
Series: Material culture directories, 0743-7528; no. 2
LC Classification: E184.S75 G69 1989
Dewey Class No.: 306/.4/0896872073 19

Grases, Pedro, 1909-
Britain and Hispanic liberalism, 1800-1830 / by Pedro Grases.
Published/Created: London: Hispanic and Luso Brazilian Council: [distributed by Grant & Cutler], 1975.
Description: 23 p.: ill.; 21 cm.
Notes: The 20th annual lecture delivered at Canning House, London, June 4, 1975.
Subjects: Latin Americans--England--London--History. Latin Americans--England--London--History. Portuguese--England--London--History. Civilization, Hispanic. London (England)--Ethnic relations.
LC Classification: DA676.9.S63 G72
Dewey Class No.: 942.1/004/61

Greenfield, Stuart.
Race and ethnicity: an appropriate

methodology / by Stuart Greenfield.
Published/Created: Austin, Tex.:
Graduate School of Business, University
of Texas at Austin: Distributed by
Bureau of Business Research, University
of Texas at Austin, [1980]
Related Authors: University of Texas at
Austin. Graduate School of Business.
Description: 14 p.; 28 cm.
Notes: "November 1980." Bibliography:
p. 14.
Subjects: Minorities--Texas--Economic
conditions--Statistical methods. Hispanic
Americans--Texas--Economic conditions
Statistical methods. Texas--Population--
Statistical methods.
Series: Working paper (University of
Texas at Austin. Graduate School of
Business); 80-27.
LC Classification: F395.A1 G74 1980
Dewey Class No.: 304.6/09764 19

Grossman, Herbert, 1934-
Educating Hispanic students: cultural
implications for instruction, classroom
management, counseling, and assessment
/ by Herbert Grossman.
Published/Created: Springfield, Ill.,
U.S.A.: C.C. Thomas, c1984.
Description: xvi, 250 p.; 24 cm.
ISBN: 0398050570
Notes: Bibliography: p. 239-250.
Subjects: Hispanic Americans--
Education. Hispanic Americans--
Psychology. National characteristics,
Latin American.
LC Classification: LC2670 .G76 1984
Dewey Class No.: 371.97/6872/073 19

Grossman, Herbert, 1934-
Educating Hispanic students:
implications for instruction, classroom
management, counseling, and assessment
/ by Herbert Grossman.
Edition Information: 2nd ed.
Published/Created: Springfield, Ill.,

U.S.A.: C.C. Thomas, c1995.
Description: xvi, 274 p.; 27 cm.
ISBN: 0398059446 (cloth) 0398059454
(paper)
Notes: Includes bibliographical
references (p. 257-274).
Subjects: Hispanic Americans--
Education. Hispanic Americans--
Psychology. National characteristics,
Latin American.
LC Classification: LC2670 .G76 1995
Dewey Class No.: 371.97/6872/073 20

Growing up Latino: memoirs and stories /
edited with an introduction by Harold
Augenbraum and Ilan Stavans; foreword
by Ilan Stavans.
Published/Created: Boston: Houghton
Mifflin, 1993.
Related Authors: Augenbraum, Harold.
Stavans, Ilan.
Description: xxix, 344 p.; 22 cm.
ISBN: 039562231X :
Notes: "A Marc Jaffe book." Includes
bibliographical references (p. [331]-338).
Subjects: American fiction--Hispanic
American authors. Hispanic American
youth--Fiction. Hispanic Americans--
Biography. Short stories, American.
Autobiography.
LC Classification: PS647.H58 G76 1993
Dewey Class No.: 813/.54080868 20

Guide to Hispanic bibliographic services in
the United States / by the staff of the
Hispanic Information Management
Project and the National Chicano
Research Network.
Published/Created: Ann Arbor, Mich.:
Survey Research Center, University of
Michigan, 1980.
Related Authors: Hispanic Information
Management Project. National Chicano
Research Network (U.S.)
Description: 208 p.: ill.; 28 cm.
Notes: Bibliography: p. 5.

Subjects: Libraries--United States--
Directories. Hispanic studies--United
States--Library resources Directories.
Hispanic Americans and libraries--
Directories.
LC Classification: Z731 .G88
Dewey Class No.: 026/.0025/73 19

Guide to Hispanic cultural world: a
publication of Hispanic Institute for the
Performing Arts, Inc.
Published/Created: Washington, D.C.:
HIFPA, [c1988-
Related Authors: Hispanic Institute for
the Performing Arts (Washington, D.C.)
Description: v.: ill.; 28 cm. 1989 ed.-
ISSN: 1040-6654
Cancel/Invalid LCCN: sn 88008595
Notes: Title from cover.
SERBIB/SERLOC merged record
Subjects: Hispanic Americans--
Washington Region--Societies, etc.
Periodicals. Hispanic American arts--
Washington Region--Directories.
Washington Region--Directories.
LC Classification: F205.S75 G85
Dewey Class No.: 975.3/00468/0025 20

Guthrie, Charles C.
The Indianapolis Hispanic community /
Charles Guthrie, Dan Briere, Mary
Moore.
Published/Created: Indianapolis, Ind.:
University of Indianapolis Press, c1995.
Related Authors: Briere, Dan. Moore,
Mary (Mary Candace)
Description: ii, 44 p.: ill., map; 23 cm.
Cancelled ISBN: 1880938016 (pbk.)
Notes: Includes bibliographical
references (p. 35-44).
Subjects: Hispanic Americans--Indiana--
Indianapolis. Hispanic Americans--
Indiana--Indianapolis--History.
Indianapolis (Ind.)--History.
LC Classification: F534.I39 S754 1995

Dewey Class No.: 977.2/5200468 20

Hadley-Garcia, George.
Hispanic Hollywood: the Latins in
motion pictures / by George Hadley-
Garcia.
Published/Created: New York, NY:
Carol Pub. Group, c1990.
Description: 256 p.: ill.; 28 cm.
ISBN: 0806511850 (paper: English
language format): 0806512083 (paper:
Spanish language format) :
Notes: "A Citadel Press book." Includes
bibliographical references (p. 252) and
index.
Subjects: Hispanic American motion
picture actors and actresses. Hispanic
Americans in motion pictures. Latin
Americans in motion pictures. Motion
pictures--United States--History.
LC Classification: PN1998.2 .H34 1990
Dewey Class No.: 791.43/028/0922 20

Hagy, Joe E.
A study of Hispanics in the Oklahoma
state system of higher education /
prepared by Joe E. Hagy.
Published/Created: [Oklahoma City]:
Division of Planning and Policy
Research, Oklahoma State Regents for
Higher Education, [1983]
Related Authors: Oklahoma State
Regents for Higher Education.
Description: iii, 30 leaves: ill.; 28 cm.
Subjects: Hispanic Americans--
Education (Higher)--Oklahoma.
Educational surveys--Oklahoma.
LC Classification: LC2674.O5 H34 1983
Dewey Class No.: 378.1/9829680730766
20

Handbook of Hispanic cultures in the United
States / general editors, Nicolás
Kanellos, Claudio Esteva-Fabregat.
Published/Created: Houston, Tex.: Arte
Público Press; Madrid, Spain: Instituto

de Cooperación Iberoamericana, c1993-
c1994.
Related Authors: Kanellos, Nicolás.
Esteva Fabregat, Claudio.
Description: 4 v.: ill., maps; 29 cm.
ISBN: 1558850740 (v. 1-2) 1558851011
(v. 3) 155885102X (v. 4)
Contents: [1]. Literature and art / edited
and introduced by Francisco Lomelí --
[2]. History / edited by Alfredo Jiménez -
- [3]. Sociology / edited by Félix Padilla
-- [4]. Anthropology / edited by Thomas
Weaver.
Notes: Includes bibliographical
references and index.
Subjects: Hispanic Americans.
LC Classification: E184.S75 H365 1993
Dewey Class No.: 973/.0468 20

Hano, Arnold, 1922-
Roberto Clemente, batting king.
Published/Created: New York, Putnam
[1968]
Description: 192 p. 22 cm.
Summary: Traces the baseball career of
the Puerto Rican who, though plagued by
numerous physical ailments from the
beginning of his career, won the National
League's Most Valuable Player Award in
1966.
Subjects: Clemente, Roberto, 1934-1972.
Clemente, Roberto, 1934-1972. Baseball
players. Hispanic Americans--
Biography.
Series: Putnam sports shelf
LC Classification: GV865.C45 H3
Dewey Class No.: 796.357

Hardy-Fanta, Carol, 1948-
Latina politics, Latino politics: gender,
culture, and political participation in
Boston / Carol Hardy-Fanta.
Published/Created: Philadelphia: Temple
University Press, 1993.
Description: p. cm.
ISBN: 1566390311 (alk. paper)

156639032X (pbk.: alk. paper)
Notes: Includes bibliographical
references and index.
Subjects: Hispanic American women--
Massachusetts--Boston--Political
activity. Hispanic Americans--
Massachusetts--Boston--Politics and
government. Political participation--
Massachusetts--Boston. Boston (Mass.)--
Politics and government.
LC Classification: F73.9.S75 H37 1993
Dewey Class No.: 323.1/168074461 20

Harlan, Judith.
Hispanic voters: a voice in American
politics / by Judith Harlan.
Published/Created: New York: F. Watts,
1988.
Description: 112 p.: ill.; 24 cm.
ISBN: 0531105865 (lib. bdg.)
Summary: Examines the increasingly
important impact the nation's fastest
growing minority is making on
American politics. Discusses the
positions and concerns of Cubans,
Mexican Americans, and Puerto Ricans
and profiles prominent Hispanic leaders.
Notes: Includes index. Bibliography: p.
107.
Subjects: Hispanic Americans--Politics
and government--Juvenile literature.
Hispanic Americans--Politics and
government.
LC Classification: E184.S75 H37 1988
Dewey Class No.: 323.1/168 19

Harvard journal of Hispanic policy.
Published/Created: Cambridge, Mass.:
John F. Kennedy School of Government,
Harvard University c1993-
Related Authors: John F. Kennedy
School of Government.
Description: v.; 26 cm. Vol. 6 (1992-
1993)-
Continues: Journal of Hispanic policy
0892-6115 (DLC) 93648922

(OCoLC)15219215
ISSN: 1074-1917
Incorrect ISSN: 0892-6115
Cancel/Invalid LCCN: sn 93031822
Notes: Title from cover.
SERBIB/SERLOC merged record Has
companion newsletter: Journal update.
Journal update (DLC)sn 95031144
(OCoLC)32609569
Subjects: Hispanic Americans--Politics
and government--Periodicals. Hispanic
Americans--Government policy--
Periodicals. United States--Politics and
government--1989- Periodicals.
LC Classification: E184.S75 J68
Dewey Class No.: 305 12

Harvard Latino law review.
    Published/Created: Cambridge, MA:
    Harvard Latino Law Review Committee,
    1994-
    Related Authors: Harvard Latino Law
    Review Committee.
    Description: v.; 26 cm. Vol. 1, no. 1 (fall
    1994)-
    Notes: Title from cover.
    Additional Form Avail.: Also available
    online.
    Subjects: Hispanic-Americans--Legal
    status, laws, etc.--Periodicals. Mexican
    Americans--Legal status, laws, etc.--
    Periodicals.
    LC Classification: IN PROCESS K8
    .A749

Health policy and the Hispanic / edited by
    Antonio Furino.
    Published/Created: Boulder: Westview
    Press, 1992.
    Related Authors: Furino, Antonio.
    Description: viii, 240 p.: ill.; 24 cm.
    ISBN: 0813314569 (alk. paper)
    Notes: Includes bibliographical
    references.
    Subjects: Hispanic Americans--Medical
    care--Congresses. Hispanic Americans--

Health and hygiene--Congresses. Health
Policy--United States--congresses.
Health Services--organization &
administration--United States--
congresses. Hispanic Americans.
LC Classification: RA448.5.H57 H42
1992
Dewey Class No.: 362.1/089/68073 20

Health practices of Hispanics & Blacks: a
    new view: [survey / conducted by Louis
    Harris & Associates].
    Published/Created: [Emmaus, Pa.]:
    Rodale Press, c1986.
    Related Authors: Louis Harris and
    Associates.
    Related Titles: Health practices of
    Hispanics and Blacks.
    Description: 10 leaves; 28 cm.
    Notes: "December 1986."
    Subjects: Hispanic Americans--Health
    and hygiene--Statistics. Afro-Americans-
    -Health and hygiene--Statistics. Health
    status indicators--United States. Health
    surveys--United States.
    Series: A Prevention index report
    LC Classification: RA448.5.H57 H43
    1986
    Dewey Class No.: 362.1/08996/073 19

Hecho en Utah: a cultural history of Utah's
    Spanish-speaking communities = una
    historia cultural de las comunidades
    hispanas de Utah / edited by Carol A.
    Edison, Anne F. Hatch, Craig R. Miller.
    Published/Created: Salt Lake City, Utah
    (617 E. South Temple, Salt Lake City
    84102): Utah Arts Council, c1992.
    Related Authors: Edison, Carol A.
    Hatch, Anne F. Miller, Craig R. (Craig
    Robb)
    Description: 56 p.: ill., maps; 28 cm. + 3
    sound cassettes (analog)
    Notes: Includes bibliographical
    references.
    Subjects: Hispanic Americans--Utah--

Social life and customs. Hispanic Americans--Utah--History. Utah--Social life and customs. Utah--History.
LC Classification: F835.S75 H43 1992
Dewey Class No.: 979.2/00468 20

Here is my kingdom: Hispanic-American literature and art for young people / edited by Charles Sullivan; foreword by Luis R. Cancel.
Published/Created: New York: H.N. Abrams, 1994.
Related Authors: Sullivan, Charles, 1933-
Description: 119 p.: ill. (some col.); 27 cm.
ISBN: 0810934221
Notes: Includes index.
Subjects: Children's literature, American--Hispanic American authors. Hispanic Americans in art--Juvenile literature. Hispanic Americans--Literary collections. Hispanic Americans--Juvenile literature. Hispanic Americans--Literary collections. American literature--Hispanic American authors Collections. Hispanic Americans in art.
LC Classification: PS508.H57 H47 1994

Herencia: the anthology of Hispanic literature of the United States / editor, Nicolás Kanellos; co-editors, Kenya Dworkin y Méndez ... [et al.]; coordinator, Alejandra Balestra.
Published/Created: Oxford; New York: Oxford University Press, 2002.
Related Authors: Kanellos, Nicolás. Dworkin y Méndez, Kenya. Balestra, Alejandra.
Description: xii, 644 p.; 25 cm.
ISBN: 0195138244 (cloth: acid-free paper)
Notes: Includes bibliographical references (p. 643-644) and index.
Subjects: American literature--Hispanic American authors. Hispanic American

literature (Spanish)--Translations into English. Hispanic Americans--Literary collections.
Series: Recovering the U.S. Hispanic Literary Heritage (Oxford University Press)
LC Classification: PS508.H57 H48 2002
Dewey Class No.: 810.8/0868 21

Hispanic alternatives: a city industrial and economic neighborhood development analysis: final report of the HACIENDA project, a study of Rochester's Marketview Heights neighborhood, conducted by the Urban League of Rochester, New York, Inc. in collaboration with the Spanish Action Coalition / Susan L. Costa, project director.
Published/Created: New York: The League, 1980.
Related Authors: Costa, Susan L. Urban League of Rochester, N.Y. Spanish Action Coalition (Rochester, N.Y.)
Description: xix, 219 p.: ill., maps; 28 cm.
Notes: Includes bibliographical references.
Subjects: Community development--New York (State)--Rochester. Neighborhood--New York (State)--Rochester. Hispanic Americans--New York (State)--Rochester. Rochester (N.Y.)--Economic policy.
LC Classification: HN79.N43 C64
Dewey Class No.: 361.8/09747/89 19

Hispanic American almanac / Bryan Ryan and Nicolás Kanellos, editors.
Published/Created: [Detroit]: U X L, c1995.
Related Authors: Ryan, Bryan. Kanellos, Nicolás.
Description: xxi, 213 p.: ill., maps; 24 cm.
ISBN: 0810398230 (acid-free paper)

Notes: Includes bibliographical references (p. 205) and index.
Subjects: Hispanic Americans.
LC Classification: E184.S75 H556 1995
Dewey Class No.: 973/.0468 20

Hispanic American chronology / edited by Nicolás Kanellos and Bryan Ryan.
Published/Created: New York: U X L, c1996.
Related Authors: Kanellos, Nicolás. Ryan, Bryan.
Description: xvii, 195 p.: ill., maps; 25 cm.
ISBN: 0810398265 (alk. paper)
Notes: Includes bibliographical references and index.
Subjects: Hispanic Americans--History--Chronology. Spain--History--Chronology. Latin America--History--Chronology. Portugal--History--Chronology.
LC Classification: E184.S75 H559 1995
Dewey Class No.: 973/.0468 20

Hispanic American communication environments: accounts of Hispanic leaders in six western U.S. communities / Felipe Korzenny ... [et al.].
Published/Created: [East Lansing, Mich.]: Dept. of Communication, Michigan State University, [1980]
Related Authors: Korzenny, Felipe. Michigan State University. Dept. of Communication.
Description: 28 leaves: ill.; 28 cm.
Notes: "October, 1980."
Subjects: Hispanic Americans and mass media--Southwestern States.
Series: CASA (Michigan State University. Dept. of Communication); report no. 3.
LC Classification: P94.5.H582 S684 1980
Dewey Class No.: 302.2/34/08968078 19

Hispanic American genealogical sourcebook / edited by Paula K. Byers.
Published/Created: New York: Gale Research, c1995.
Related Authors: Byers, Paula K. (Paula Kay), 1954-
Description: xix, 224 p.; 29 cm.
ISBN: 0810392275 (alk. paper)
Notes: Includes bibliographical references and indexes.
Subjects: Hispanic Americans--Genealogy--Handbooks, manuals, etc. Hispanic Americans--Genealogy--Bibliography.
Series: Genealogy sourcebook series
LC Classification: E184.S75 H563 1995
Dewey Class No.: 929/.1/08968 20

Hispanic American literature: a brief introduction and anthology / Nicolás Kanellos.
Published/Created: New York: HarperCollins College Publishers, c1995.
Related Authors: Kanellos, Nicolás.
Description: xii, 339 p.; 24 cm.
ISBN: 0673469565
Notes: Includes bibliographical references (p. [328]-332) and index.
Subjects: American literature--Hispanic American authors. American literature--Hispanic American authors--History and criticism. Hispanic Americans--Literary collections. Hispanic Americans--Intellectual life. Hispanic Americans in literature.
Series: The HarperCollins literary mosaic series
LC Classification: PS508.H57 H55 1995
Dewey Class No.: 810.8/0868 20

Hispanic American literature: an anthology / [compiled by] Rodolfo Cortina.
Published/Created: Lincolnwood, IL: NTC Pub. Group, c1998.
Related Authors: Cortina, Rodolfo J.

Description: xx, 414 p.; 23 cm.
ISBN: 0844257303 (student edition)
0844257311 (insructor's edition)
Notes: Includes index.
Subjects: American literature--Hispanic American authors. American literature--Hispanic American authors--Problems, exercises, etc. Hispanic Americans--Literary collections.
LC Classification: PS508.H57 H554 1998
Dewey Class No.: 810.8/0868 21

Hispanic American reference library: cumulative index / Sonia Benson, index coordinator.
Published/Created: [Detroit, Mich.]: U-X-L, c1997.
Related Authors: Benson, Sonia.
Description: 31 p.; 24 cm.
ISBN: 0787618829 (pbk.)
Notes: "Includes indexes for: Hispanic American almanac, Hispanic American biography, Hispanic American chronology, and Hispanic American voices."
Subjects: Hispanic Americans--Indexes.
LC Classification: Z1361.S7 H57 1997 E184.S75
Dewey Class No.: 016.973/0468 21

Hispanic American voices / Deborah Gillan Straub, editor.
Published/Created: Detroit: UXL, c1997.
Related Authors: Straub, Deborah Gillan.
Description: xx, 244 p.: ill.; 25 cm.
ISBN: 0810398273 (acid-free paper)
Notes: Includes bibliographical references and index.
Subjects: Hispanic Americans--Biography. Hispanic Americans--History. Speeches, addresses, etc., American--Hispanic American authors.
LC Classification: E184.S75 H564 1997
Dewey Class No.: 973/.0468 20

Hispanic Americans information directory.
Published/Created: Detroit, MI: Gale Research, c1990-c1994.
Related Authors: Gale Research Inc.
Description: 3 v.; 29 cm. 1st ed. (1990-1991)-3rd ed. (1994-1995).
ISSN: 1046-3933
Cancel/Invalid LCCN: sn 89008473
Notes: "A guide to ... organizations, agencies, institutions, programs, and publications concerned with Hispanic American life and culture."
SERBIB/SERLOC merged record
Subjects: Hispanic Americans--Directories. Hispanic Americans--Societies, etc.--Directories.
LC Classification: E184.S75 H566
Dewey Class No.: 973/.0468/0025 20

Hispanic Americans: a statistical sourcebook.
Published/Created: Boulder, Colo.: Numbers & Concepts, c1991-
Related Authors: Numbers & Concepts (Firm) Information Publications (Firm)
Description: v.; 20-23 cm. 1991 ed.-
ISSN: 1056-7992
Notes: Published: <1995-1997>- Palo Alto, CA: Information Publications.
SERBIB/SERLOC merged record
Subjects: Hispanic Americans--Statistics--Periodicals. Hispanic Americans--statistics.
LC Classification: E184.S75 H5655
Dewey Class No.: 305.868/0021 20

Hispanic arts and ethnohistory in the Southwest: new papers inspired by the work of E. Boyd / edited by Marta Weigle with Claudia Larcombe, Samuel Larcombe.
Published/Created: Santa Fe, N.M.: Ancient City Press, c1983.
Related Authors: Boyd, E. (Elizabeth), 1903-1974. Weigle, Marta. Larcombe, Claudia. Larcombe, Samuel.
Description: x, 413 p.: ill.; 26 cm.

ISBN: 0941270149 (case bound): 0941270130 (pbk.)
Notes: "A Spanish Colonial Arts Society book." Includes index. Bibliography: p. [391]-408.
Subjects: Hispanic American arts-- Southwest, New. Hispanic Americans-- Southwest, New.
LC Classification: NX508.6 .H57 1983
Dewey Class No.: 700/.89680789 19

Hispanic Colorado: a sourcebook for policymaking / compiled for the Tomás Rivera Center by the Latin American Research and Service Agency.
Published/Created: Claremont, Calif.: Tomás Rivera Center, c1989.
Related Authors: Tomás Rivera Center. Latin American Research and Service Agency.
Description: xi, 93 p.: ill.; 28 cm.
ISBN: 0942177010
Subjects: Hispanic Americans-- Colorado--Population--Statistics. Hispanic Americans--Colorado-- Population. Colorado--Population-- Statistics. Colorado--Population.
LC Classification: F785.S75 H565 1989
Dewey Class No.: 305.868/0788 20

Hispanic employment: a recruitment sources booklet: including recruitment sources in Puerto Rico.
Published/Created: [Washington, D.C.?]: U.S. Office of Personnel Management, Hispanic Employment Program: For sale by the Supt. of Docs., U.S. G.P.O., 1980 [i.e. 1981]
Related Authors: United States. Office of Personnel Management. Hispanic Employment Program.
Description: 136 p.: 1 map; 27 cm.
Notes: "September 1980"--Cover. "HEP-80-1"--Cover. S/N 006-000-01192-6
Item 269-B
Subjects: Hispanic Americans--

Employment. Puerto Ricans-- Employment. United States--Officials and employees--Recruiting.
LC Classification: JK723.M54 H57
Dewey Class No.: 353.001/04 19
Govt. Doc. No.: PM 1.8:H62

Hispanic genealogical journal.
Published/Created: [Houston, Tex.]: Hispanic Genealogical Society of Houston,
Related Authors: Hispanic Genealogical Society of Houston.
Description: v.; 28 cm.
Former Frequency: Twice a year, -<1987
Continues: Hispanic Genealogical Society bulletin (DLC) 00240190 (OCoLC)43555767
Notes: Description based on: Vol. 5, no. 1, copyrighted in 1987; title from cover. SERBIB/SERLOC merged record
Subjects: Hispanic Americans--Texas-- Houston--Genealogy Periodicals. Mexican Americans--Texas--Houston-- Genealogy--Periodicals. Registers of births, etc.--Texas--Houston-- Periodicals. Houston (Tex.)--Genealogy--Periodicals.
LC Classification: F394.H89 S754
Dewey Class No.: 929/.1/0896807641411 19

Hispanic health care: today's shame, tomorrow's crisis: joint hearing before the Select Committee on Aging and the Congressional Hispanic Caucus, House of Representatives, One Hundred Second Congress, first session, September 19, 1991.
Published/Created: Washington: U.S. G.P.O.: For sale by the U.S. G.P.O., Supt. of Docs., Congressional Sales Office, 1992.
Related Authors: Congressional Hispanic Caucus (U.S.)
Description: iii, 275 p.: ill.; 24 cm.

ISBN: 0160374456
Notes: Item 1009-B-2, 1009-C-2 (MF)
Distributed to some depository libraries
in microfiche. Shipping list no.: 92-161-
P. "Comm. pub. no. 102-842." Includes
bibliographical references.
Subjects: Hispanic Americans--Medical
care. Hispanic American aged--Medical
care.
LC Classification: KF27.5 .A3 1991b
Dewey Class No.: 362.1/089/68073 20
Govt. Doc. No.: Y 4.Ag 4/2:H 62/4

Hispanic heroes: portraits of New Mexicans
who have made a difference / [editors-in-
chief Rose Diaz, Jan Dodson Barnhart].
Published/Created: Albuquerque, NM
(8005 Pennsylvania Circle N.E.,
Albuquerque, New Mexico 87110):
Starlight Publishing Inc., [1992]
Related Authors: Diaz, Rose. Barnhart,
Jan Dodson. Hispanic Heroes Project.
Description: 23 p.: ill., ports., 1 map; 28
cm.
Notes: Title from cover. "Hispanic
Heroes Project"--Verso t.p.
Subjects: Hispanic Americans--New
Mexico--Biography. New Mexico--
Biography.
LC Classification: F805.S75 H57 1992
Dewey Class No.: 920/.009268 20

Hispanic human service directory.
Published/Created: New York: Raymond
Amalbert, Jr., c1987-
Related Authors: Amalbert, Raymond.
Description: v.: ill.; 23 cm. 1st ed.
(1988)-
ISSN: 1042-7821
Notes: In English and Spanish, with
Spanish text on inverted pages.
SERBIB/SERLOC merged record
Subjects: Hispanic Americans--Services
for--New York (State) Directories.
Hispanic Americans--Services for--New
Jersey--Directories. Hispanic Americans-

-Services for--Connecticut Directories.
Human services--New York (State)--
Directories. Human services--New
Jersey--Directories. Human services--
Connecticut--Directories.
LC Classification: HV3187 .H57
Dewey Class No.: 362.84/68074 20

Hispanic journal of behavioral sciences.
Published/Created: Los Angeles: Spanish
Speaking Mental Health Research
Center, University of California, Los
Angeles, [c1979-
Related Authors: Spanish Speaking
Mental Health Research Center (U.S.)
Description: v.; 23 cm. Vol. 1, no. 1
(Mar. 1979)-
ISSN: 0739-9863
Notes: Published: Newbury Park, Calif.:
Sage Publications, <Feb. 1990->;
Thousand Oaks, CA, <1997- English and
Spanish. SERBIB/SERLOC merged
record
Indx'd selectively by: Current index to
journals in education 0011-3565
Psychological abstracts 0033-2887 1979-
Additional Form Avail.: Also available
via World Wide Web; OCLC FirstSearch
Electronic Collections Online;
Subscription required for access to
abstracts and full text.
Subjects: Hispanic Americans--Mental
health--Periodicals. Hispanic Americans-
-Psychology--Periodicals. Latin
Americans--Mental health--United States
Periodicals. Latin Americans--United
States--Psychology--Periodicals.
Anthropology--United States--
periodicals. Hispanic Americans--
psychology--periodicals. Hispanic
Americans--United States--periodicals.
Socioeconomic Factors--periodicals.
Sociology--United States--periodicals.
LC Classification: RC451.5.H57 H58
Dewey Class No.: 362.2/08968073

Hispanic law journal / the University of
    Texas School of Law.
    Published/Created: Austin, Tex.:
    Hispanic Law Journal, c1994-c1998.
    Related Authors: University of Texas at
    Austin. School of Law.
    Description: 3 v.; 26 cm. Vol. 2, no. 1
    (1996) and vol. 3, no. 1 (1997) issued
    together and called also spring 1997.
    Vol. 1, no. 1 (1994)-v. 3, no. 1 (1997).
    Continued by: Texas Hispanic journal of
    law and policy (DLC) 00240920
    (OCoLC)44990124
    ISSN: 1075-8461
    Cancel/Invalid LCCN: sn 94004470
    Notes: Title from cover.
    SERBIB/SERLOC merged record
    Subjects: Hispanic Americans--Legal
    status, laws, etc.--Periodicals.
    LC Classification: K8 .I48
    Dewey Class No.: 346.7301/3 347.30613
    20

Hispanic legends from New Mexico:
    narratives from the R.D. Jameson
    Collection / edited with an introduction
    and notes by Stanley L. Robe.
    Published/Created: Berkeley: University
    of California Press, 1980.
    Related Authors: Jameson, R. D.
    (Raymond De Loy), 1896-1959. Robe,
    Stanley Linn, 1915-
    Description: xi, 548 p.; 29 cm.
    ISBN: 0520096142 (pbk.)
    Notes: Bibliography: p. 31-41.
    Subjects: Hispanic Americans--New
    Mexico--Folklore. Legends--New
    Mexico. Legends--New Mexico--
    Classification.
    Series: University of California
    publications. Folklore and mythology
    studies; 31
    LC Classification: GR111.H57 H57
    Dewey Class No.: 398.2/088036872073
    19

Hispanic ministry: three major documents /
    [text preparation and design by Marina
    Herrerra].
    Edition Information: Bilingual ed.
    Published/Created: Washington, DC:
    Secretariat for Hispanic Affairs, National
    Conference of Catholic Bishops, c1995.
    Related Authors: Herrera, Marina.
    Secretariat for Hispanic Affairs.
    Description: 1 v. (various pagings): ill.;
    29 cm.
    ISBN: 1555861970 (pbk.)
    Contents: The Hispanic presence --
    Prophetic voices -- National pastoral
    plan for Hispanic ministry.
    Notes: Includes bibliographical
    references. English and Spanish.
    Subjects: Church work with Hispanic
    Americans. Hispanic American
    Catholics.
    LC Classification: BV4468.2.H57 H55
    1995
    Dewey Class No.: 282/.73/08968 20

Hispanic mosaic: a forum on Hispanic health
    concerns.
    Published/Created: Rockville, Md.: Dept.
    of Health, Education, and Welfare,
    Public Health Service, Parklawn
    Building, [1979?]
    Related Authors: United States. Public
    Health Service. United States. Food and
    Drug Administration.
    Description: i, 147 p.; 28 cm.
    Notes: "Paquita Vivo', Editor"--Prelim.
    p. "Presented by the Public Health
    Service in commemoration of Hispanic
    Heritage Week, September 7-8, 1978."
    "This publication was edited for the Food
    and Drug Administration"--Prelim. p.
    Includes bibliographies.
    Subjects: Hispanic Americans--Health
    and hygiene--Congresses. Hispanic
    Americans--Medical care--Congresses.
    LC Classification: RA448.5.H57 F67
    1979

Dewey Class No.: 362.1/08968073 19
Govt. Doc. No.: HE 20.2:H 62/3

Hispanic Network magazine.
Published/Created: Yorba Linda, CA:
Olive Tree Publishing, Inc.,
Related Authors: Hispanic Network (San
Antonio, Tex.)
Description: v.: col. ill.; 28 cm.
Notes: Description based on: v. 10, issue
3 (July/Aug./Sept. 1998); title from
cover. Published by Olive Tree
Publishing Inc., <2000-
Subjects: Hispanic Americans--
Employment--Periodicals. Hispanic
Americans--Services for--Periodicals.
Hispanic Americans--Periodicals.
LC Classification: HD8081.H5 H57

Hispanic New Yorkers: education and
employment.
Published/Created: [Albany, N.Y.]:
University of the State of New York, the
State Education Department, Office of
Planning, Research, and Support
Services, [1994]
Related Authors: University of the State
of New York. Office for Planning,
Research, and Support Services.
Description: vii, 32 p.: ill.; 28 cm.
Notes: "June 1994" Includes
bibliographical references (p. 30-31).
Subjects: Hispanic Americans--
Education--New York (State) Statistics.
Hispanic Americans--Employment--New
York (State) Statistics.
LC Classification: LC2675.N7 H57 1994
Dewey Class No.: 371.9768/0747 20
Govt. Doc. No.: UNI,617-4,HISNY,94-
28404 nydocs

Hispanic notables in the United States of
North America.
Published/Created: Albuquerque, N.M.,
Saguaro Publications.
Description: v. ill. 26 cm.

ISSN: 0191-6297
Notes: English or Spanish.
SERBIB/SERLOC merged record
Subjects: Hispanic Americans--
Biography--Periodicals. Hispanic
Americans--Periodicals.
LC Classification: E184.S75 H58
Dewey Class No.: 920/.0092/6873

Hispanic poverty: how much does
immigration explain? / [prepared by Julie
Quiroz].
Published/Created: Washington, D.C.:
National Council of La Raza, Poverty
Project, [1990]
Related Authors: Quiroz, Julia Teresa.
National Council of La Raza. Poverty
Project.
Description: 33 p.: ill.; 28 cm.
Notes: "Proceedings from the National
Council of La Raza's Poverty Project
roundtable, Nov. 27, 1989." Includes
bibliographical references (p. 18-22).
Subjects: Hispanic Americans--
Economic conditions. Poor--United
States. Immigrants--United States.
LC Classification: E184.S75 H5832
1990

Hispanic presence in the United States:
historical beginnings / Frank de Varona,
editor.
Published/Created: Miami: National
Hispanic Quincentennial Commission:
Mnemosyne Pub. Co., 1993.
Related Authors: De Varona, Frank.
National Hispanic Quincentennial
Commission.
Description: xii, 253 p.: maps; 23 cm.
ISBN: 1566750296
Notes: Includes bibliographical
references (p. [245]-253).
Subjects: Hispanic Americans--History.
LC Classification: E184.S75 H5834
1993

Dewey Class No.: 973/.0468 20

Hispanic professional.
Published/Created: Baltimore, MD:
Career Communications Group, Inc.,
c1993-
Related Authors: Career
Communications Group.
Description: v.: ill.; 28 cm. Vol. 1, no. 1
(spring 1993)-
Continues in part: Professional
(Baltimore, Md.) (OCoLC)38033914
ISSN: 1098-4666
Notes: Title from cover.
SERBIB/SERLOC merged record
Subjects: Hispanic Americans in the
professions--Periodicals.
LC Classification: HD8081.H7 A24
Dewey Class No.: 305 13

Hispanic psychology: critical issues in theory
and research / Amado M. Padilla, editor.
Published/Created: Thousand Oaks: Sage
Publications, c1995.
Related Authors: Padilla, Amado M.
Description: xxi, 381 p.: ill.; 24 cm.
ISBN: 0803955529 (cl) 0803955537 (pb)
Notes: Includes bibliographical
references (p. 326-361) and index.
Subjects: Hispanic Americans--
Psychology.
LC Classification: E184.S75 H5836
1995
Dewey Class No.: 155.8/468 20

Hispanic resource directory.
Published/Created: Juneau, Alaska:
Denali Press, c1988-
Related Authors: Schorr, Alan Edward.
Description: v.: ill.; 28 cm. First issue
lacks designation. [1988]- Ceased in
1996.
ISSN: 1085-276X
Cancel/Invalid LCCN: sn 92024025
Notes: Editor: 1988- Alan Edward
Schorr. SERBIB/SERLOC merged

record
Subjects: Hispanic Americans--Societies,
etc.--Directories. Associations,
institutions, etc.--United States
Directories.
LC Classification: E184.S75 H584
Dewey Class No.: 305 12

Hispanic review of business.
Published/Created: New York, N.Y.:
Americana Communications Corp.,
Description: v.: ill.; 28 cm. Began in
1983.
Continues: Hispanic business monthly
(DLC)sn 84011334 (OCoLC)10121129
ISSN: 1046-0942
Cancel/Invalid LCCN: sn 85012185
Notes: Published by: Latin National
Publishing Corporation, Dec. 1986-
Description based on: Vol. 4, no. 3 (Apr.
1983); title from cover.
SERBIB/SERLOC merged record
Subjects: Hispanic American business
enterprises--Periodicals. Hispanic
Americans in business--Periodicals.
LC Classification: HD2346.U5 H57
Dewey Class No.: 650 11

Hispanic Texas: a historical guide / edited by
Helen Simons and Cathryn A. Hoyt.
Edition Information: 1st ed.
Published/Created: Austin: University of
Texas Press, 1992.
Related Authors: Simons, Helen, 1939-
Hoyt, Cathryn A. (Cathryn Ann), 1958-
Description: xviii, 502 p.: ill. (some
col.), maps; 29 cm.
ISBN: 0292776624 (alk. paper)
Notes: Includes bibliographical
references (p. [475]-486) and index.
Subjects: Historic sites--Texas--
Guidebooks. Hispanic Americans--
Texas--History. Texas--Guidebooks.
Texas--History, Local.
LC Classification: F387 .H56 1992

Dewey Class No.: 917.6404/63 20

Hispanic times.
Published/Created: Woodland, Hills,
CA: Hispanic Times Enterprises, -1981.
Description: 2 v.: ill.; 28 cm. Began with
Mar./Apr. 1980 issue. -v. 2, no. 3
(Aug./Sept. 1981).
Continues: Adelante con vida nueva
0195-2757 (OCoLC)5459462 (DLC)sn
79019401
Continued by: Hispanic times magazine
0892-1369 (DLC)sn 87002167
(OCoLC)15100479
ISSN: 0199-770X
Incorrect ISSN: 0195-2757
Cancel/Invalid LCCN: sn 80011076
Notes: Description based on: Vol. 1, no.
2 (May/June 1980); title from cover.
English and Spanish. SERBIB/SERLOC
merged record
Subjects: Hispanic Americans--
Employment--Periodicals.
Discrimination in employment--United
States--Periodicals. Indians of North
America--Employment--Periodicals.
Hispanic Americans--Periodicals.
LC Classification: HD8081 .A27
Dewey Class No.: 331.6/3/6873 19

Hispanic voices: Hispanic health educators
speak out / edited by Sara Torres.
Published/Created: New York: National
League for Nursing Press, c1996.
Related Authors: Torres, Sara.
Description: xviii, 238 p.: ill.; 23 cm.
ISBN: 0887376533
Notes: Includes bibliographical
references and index.
Subjects: Hispanic Americans--Health
and hygiene. Hispanic Americans--
Diseases. Hispanic Americans--Medical
care.
LC Classification: RA448.5.H57 H574
1996

Dewey Class No.: 362.1/089/68073 20

Hispanic young people and the church's
pastoral response / Prophets of Hope
Editorial Team.
Published/Created: Winona, Minn.: Saint
Mary's Press, c1994.
Related Authors: Prophets of Hope
Editorial Team.
Description: 291 p.: ill.; 23 cm.
ISBN: 0884893251 :
Notes: Includes bibliographical
references (p. 249-262) and index.
Subjects: Church work with Hispanic
Americans. Hispanic American youth.
Church work with youth--Catholic
Church.
Series: Prophets of hope; v. 1
LC Classification: BV4468.2.H57 H57
1994
Dewey Class No.:
261.8/34235/08968073 21

Hispanic.
Published/Created: [Washington, D.C.:
Hispanic Pub. Corp., c1988-
Description: v.: ill.; 28 cm. First issue
preceded by a prototype issue dated Jan.
1988. Apr. 1988-
Former Frequency: Monthly, Apr. 1988-
ISSN: 0898-3097
Cancel/Invalid LCCN: sn 88027761
Notes: Title from cover.
SERBIB/SERLOC merged record Has
supplement: Guide to the top 25 colleges
for Hispanics.
Additional Form Avail.: Also available
by subscription via the World Wide
Web.
Subjects: Hispanic Americans--
Periodicals. Latin Americans--United
States--Periodicals.
LC Classification: E184.S75 H54
Dewey Class No.: 973/.0468/005 20

Hispanic-American experience on file /
[edited by] Carter Smith III and David
Lindroth.
Published/Created: New York: Facts On
File, 1999.
Related Authors: Smith, Carter, 1962-
Lindroth, David.
Description: 1 v. (various pagings): ill.,
maps; 30 cm.
ISBN: 0816036950 (alk. paper)
Notes: Includes bibliographical
references and index.
Subjects: Hispanic Americans--History.
Hispanic Americans--Statistics. Hispanic
Americans--Maps. Hispanic Americans--
Pictorial works.
LC Classification: E184.S75 H562 1999
Dewey Class No.: 980 21

Hispanic-American writers / edited and with
an introduction by Harold Bloom.
Published/Created: Philadelphia: Chelsea
House Publishers, c1998.
Related Authors: Bloom, Harold.
Description: x, 230 p.; 25 cm.
ISBN: 0791047865 (hc: alk. paper)
Notes: Includes bibliographical
references (p. 215-221) and index.
Subjects: American literature--Hispanic
American authors--History and criticism.
Hispanic Americans in literature.
Series: Modern critical views
LC Classification: PS153.H56 H56 1998
Dewey Class No.: 810.9/868 21

Hispanics and jobs: barriers to progress.
Published/Created: Washington, D.C.:
National Commission for Employment
Policy, 1982.
Related Authors: United States. National
Commission for Employment Policy.
Description: ii, 86 p.: ill.; 28 cm.
Notes: "September 1982." Item 1089
Subjects: Hispanic Americans--
Employment.
Series: United States. National

Commission for Employment Policy.
Report; no. 14.
LC Classification: HD8081.H7 H57
1982
Dewey Class No.: 331.6/3/68073 19
Govt. Doc. No.: Y 3.Em 7/3:10/14

Hispanics and the humanities in the
Southwest: a directory of resources /
edited by F. Arturo Rosales, David
William Foster; editorial assistant,
Carmen de Novais.
Published/Created: Tempe: Center for
Latin American Studies, Arizona State
University, c1983.
Related Authors: Rosales, Francisco A.
(Francisco Arturo) Foster, David
William. De Novais, Carmen.
Association of Southwestern Humanities
Councils.
Description: xxv, 327 p.: ill.; 23 cm.
ISBN: 0879180552 :
Notes: "Result of two years of research
conducted by the staff of the Association
of Southwestern Humanities Councils"--
Introd. Includes index.
Subjects: Hispanic Americans--
Research--Southwest, New--Directories.
Hispanic Americans--Study and
teaching--Southwest, New Directories.
Hispanic Americans--Southwest, New--
Library resources. Hispanic Americans--
Southwest, New--Archival resources.
Hispanic Americans--Southwest, New.
Humanities--Research grants--United
States--Handbooks, manuals, etc.
LC Classification: F790.S75 H57 1983
Dewey Class No.: 979/.00468073 19

Hispanics and the nonprofit sector / Herman
E. Gallegos and Michael O'Neill, eds.
Published/Created: New York:
Foundation Center, 1991.
Related Authors: Gallegos, Herman E.
O'Neill, Michael, 1938-
Description: vi, 209 p.; 23 cm.

ISBN: 0879543981 :
Notes: Includes bibliographical
references (p. 183-195) and index.
Subjects: Hispanic Americans--Societies,
etc. Charities--United States.
Voluntarism--United States.
LC Classification: HS1721 .H57 1991
Dewey Class No.: 361.7/63/08968073 20

Hispanics and the scholastic aptitude test in
Texas / project directors, Jorge Chapa,
Lodis Rhodes; project researchers Carlos
Contreras ... [et al.].
Published/Created: [Austin]: L.B.
Johnson School of Public Affairs,
University of Texas at Austin, 1992.
Related Authors: Chapa, Jorge, 1953-
Rhodes, Lodis.
Description: 1 v. (various pagings): ill.;
28 cm.
Subjects: Hispanic Americans--
Education (Secondary)--Texas. Hispanic
American students--Texas. Scholastic
Aptitude Test. Academic achievement--
Texas.
Series: Working paper series (Lyndon B.
Johnson School of Public Affairs); no.
60.
LC Classification: LC2674.T4 H57 1992
Dewey Class No.: 371.97/68/073 20

Hispanics in Montana: report to the 47th
Montana Legislative Assembly as
mandated by House Joint Resolution no.
19, October 31, 1980 / prepared by the
Department of Community Affairs,
Community Services Division, the
Hispanic Task Force.
Published/Created: [Helena]: The Task
Force, [1980]
Description: 46, [22] p.: forms; 28 cm.
Notes: Cover title. Bibliography: p. 41-
43.
Subjects: Hispanic Americans--Montana-
-Social conditions. Hispanic Americans--
Montana--Economic conditions.

Hispanic Americans--Education--
Montana. Montana--Social conditions.
Montana--Economic conditions.
LC Classification: F740.S75 M66 1980
Dewey Class No.: 305.8/68/0786 19

Hispanics in the U.S. economy / edited by
George J. Borjas, Marta Tienda.
Published/Created: Orlando: Academic
Press, 1985.
Related Authors: Borjas, George J.
Tienda, Marta.
Description: xx, 374 p.; 24 cm.
ISBN: 0121186407 (alk. paper)
Notes: Includes index. Bibliography: p.
351-367.
Subjects: Hispanic Americans--
Employment. Wages--Hispanic
Americans. Hispanic Americans--
Economic conditions. Hispanic
Americans--Social conditions.
LC Classification: HD8081.H7 H58
1985
Dewey Class No.: 331.6/3/6873 19

Hispanics in the United States: a new social
agenda / edited by Pastora San Juan
Cafferty and William C. McCready.
Published/Created: New Brunswick,
N.J.: Transaction Books, c1985.
Related Authors: Cafferty, Pastora San
Juan. McCready, William C., 1941-
Description: vi, 257 p.; 24 cm.
ISBN: 0887380182 0878559752 (pbk.)
Notes: Includes bibliographies.
Subjects: Hispanic Americans.
LC Classification: E184.S75 H6 1985
Dewey Class No.: 973/.0468 19

Hispanics in the United States: abstracts of
the psychological and behavioral
literature, 1980-1989 / Esteban L.
Olmedo, Verna R. Walker, editors.
Edition Information: 1st ed.
Published/Created: Washington, DC:
American Psychological Association;

Hyattsville, MD: Copies may be ordered from APA Order Dept., c1990.
Related Authors: Olmedo, Esteban L. Walker, Verna R.
Description: xi, 307 p.; 28 cm.
ISBN: 1557981035 (pbk.)
Notes: Includes indexes.
Subjects: Hispanic Americans--Psychology--Abstracts.
Series: Bibliographies in psychology; no. 8
LC Classification: E184.S75 H62 1990
Dewey Class No.: 155.8/468073 20

Hispanics in the United States: an agenda for the twenty-first century / Pastora San Juan Cafferty and David W. Engstrom, editors; with a new preface & introduction by the editors.
Published/Created: New Brunswick, NJ: Transaction Publishers, 2001.
Related Authors: Cafferty, Pastora San Juan. Engstrom, David Wells, 1958-
Description: p. cm.
ISBN: 0765809052 (paper: alk. paper)
Notes: Includes bibliographical references and index.
Subjects: Hispanic Americans--Social conditions. Hispanic Americans--Government policy. Hispanic Americans--Social conditions--Forecasting.
LC Classification: E184.S75 H623 2001
Dewey Class No.: 305.868073 21

Hispanics in the United States: an agenda for the twenty-first century / Pastora San Juan Cafferty, David W. Engstrom, editors.
Published/Created: New Brunswick (U.S.A.): Transaction Publishers, c2000.
Related Authors: Cafferty, Pastora San Juan. Engstrom, David Wells, 1958-
Description: xxii, 363 p.; 24 cm.
ISBN: 1560004150 (cloth: alk. paper) 0765804743 (pbk.: alk. paper)

Notes: Includes bibliographical references and index.
Subjects: Hispanic Americans--Social conditions. Hispanic Americans--Government policy. Hispanic Americans--Social conditions--Forecasting.
LC Classification: E184.S75 H623 2000
Dewey Class No.: 305.868/073 21

Hispanics in the United States: an anthology of creative literature / edited by Francisco Jiménez and Gary D. Keller.
Published/Created: Ypsilanti, Mich.: Bilingual Review/Press, <c1982-
Related Authors: Jiménez, Francisco, 1943- Keller, Gary D.
Description: v. <2 >; 26 cm.
ISBN: 0916950298 (pbk.)
Notes: English and Spanish.
Subjects: American literature--Hispanic American authors. Hispanic American literature (Spanish) Hispanic Americans--Literary collections. American literature--20th century.
Series: Bilingual review (New York, N.Y.); v. 8, no. 2-3.
LC Classification: PS508.H57 H57 1982
Dewey Class No.: 810/.8/086873 19

Hispanics in the workplace / Stephen B. Knouse, Paul Rosenfeld, Amy Culbertson, editors.
Published/Created: Newbury Park, Calif.: Sage Publications, c1992.
Related Authors: Knouse, Stephen B. Rosenfeld, Paul. Culbertson, Amy.
Description: viii, 292 p.; 24 cm.
ISBN: 0803939434 (cl) 0803939442 (pb)
Notes: Includes bibliographical references and indexes.
Subjects: Hispanic Americans--Employment.
LC Classification: HD8081.H7 H59 1992

Dewey Class No.: 331.6/368073 20

Hispanics in transition.
Published/Created: [Phoenix]: Arizona
Dept. of Economic Security, [1986]
Related Authors: Arizona. Dept. of
Economic Security.
Description: iii, 22 p.: ill.; 28 cm.
Notes: Bibliography: p. 22.
Subjects: Hispanic Americans--Arizona--
Economic conditions. Arizona--
Population.
LC Classification: F820.S75 H57 1986

Hispanics/Latinos in the United States:
ethnicity, race, and rights / edited by
Jorge J.E. Gracia & Pablo De Greiff.
Published/Created: New York:
Routledge, 2000.
Related Authors: Gracia, Jorge J. E. De
Greiff, Pablo.
Description: 281 p.; 24 cm.
ISBN: 041592619X (acid-free paper)
0415926203 (pbk.: acid-free paper)
Notes: Includes bibliographical
references (p. [253]-268) and indexes.
Subjects: Hispanic Americans--Ethnic
identity. Hispanic Americans--Race
identity. Hispanic Americans--Civil
rights. United States--Ethnic relations.
United States--Race relations.
LC Classification: E184.S75 H627 2000
Dewey Class No.: 305.8/68073 21

Hispanics-Latinos, diverse people in a
multicultural society: a special report.
Published/Created: Washington, DC:
National Association of Hispanic
Publications: U.S. Bureau of the Census,
Related Authors: National Association of
Hispanic Publications. United States.
Bureau of the Census.
Description: v.; 22 x 28 cm.
Notes: Description based on: 2nd. ed.
(1995). SERBIB/SERLOC merged
record

Subjects: Hispanic Americans--Charts,
diagrams, etc.
LC Classification: E184.S75 H625

Hispano music & culture of the Northern Rio
Grande [computer file]: the Juan B. Rael
Collection / from the American Folklife
Center, Library of Congress.
Edition Information: First release.
Published/Created: [Washington, D.C.]:
Library of Congress, [1998-]
Related Authors: Rael, Juan Bautista.
American Folklife Center. Archive of
Folk Culture (Library of Congress)
Library of Congress. National Digital
Library Program.
Computer File Info.: Computer data.
Summary: Presents ethnographic field
collection documenting religious and
secular music of Spanish-speaking
residents of rural Northern New Mexico
and Southern Colorado. Features
recordings from the Archive of Folk
Culture collection of alabados (hymns),
folk drama, wedding songs, and dance
tunes that were performed by various
artists and recorded by Juan B. Rael.
Includes manuscript materials and
publications by Rael covering the
musical heritage and cultural traditions
of the region.
Notes: Title from home page viewed on
Jan. 20, 1999. Offered as part of the
American Memory online resource
compiled by the National Digital Library
Program of the Library of Congress.
Audio recorded in Alamosa, Manassa,
and Antonito, Colo., and in Cerro and
Arroyo Hondo, N.M. System
requirements: World Wide Web (WWW)
browser software. Mode of access:
Internet. Text in English and Spanish;
audio in Spanish.
Subjects: Hispanic Americans--New
Mexico--Music. Hispanic Americans--
Colorado--Music. Folk music--New

Mexico. Folk music--Colorado. Folk songs, Spanish--New Mexico. Folk songs, Spanish--Colorado. Hispanic Americans--New Mexico. Hispanic Americans--Colorado.
LC Classification: M1668.4
Dewey Class No.: 781.62 13

Hough, Granville W.
California patriots during Spain's 1779-1783 war with England / by Granville W. and N.C. Hough.
Published/Created: Laguna Hills, CA (3438 Bahia Blanca West, Apt. B, Laguna Hills 92653-2830): G.W. & N.C. Hough, c1998-c1999.
Related Authors: Hough, N. C.
Description: 2 v.; 28 cm.
Notes: Title of pt. 2: Spain's California patriots in its 1779-1783 war with England during the American Revolution. Includes bibliographical references and index.
Subjects: Sons of the American Revolution--Membership. Daughters of the American Revolution--Membership. Hispanic Americans--California--Genealogy. Anglo-Spanish War, 1779-1783--Registers. California--Genealogy. United States--History--Revolution, 1775-1783 Participation, Spanish.
LC Classification: F870.S75 H68 1998
Dewey Class No.: 929/.3/089680794 21

Hough, Granville W.
Spain's California patriots in its 1779-1783 war with England during the American Revolution / Granville W. and N.C. Hough.
Published/Created: [Midway City, CA: Society of Hispanic Historical and Ancestral Research], c1998-c1999.
Related Authors: Hough, N. C. Society of Hispanic Historical and Ancestral Research.
Description: 2 v.; 18 cm.

Notes: Includes bibliographic references and index.
Subjects: Sons of the American Revolution--Membership. Daughters of the American Revolution--Membership. Hispanic Americans--California--Genealogy. Anglo-Spanish War, 1779-1783--Registers. California--Genealogy. United States--History--Revolution, 1775-1783 Participation, Spanish.
LC Classification: F870.S75 H68 1998b
Dewey Class No.: 929/3/089680794 21

Hough, Granville W.
Spain's Louisiana patriots in its 1779-1783 war with England during the American Revolution / by Granville W. and N.C. Hough.
Published/Created: [Midway City, CA] (P.O. Box 490, Midway City, 92655-0490): [SHHAR Press, c2000].
Description: iv, 198 p.; 28 cm.
Notes: Includes bibliographical references (p. 193-197) and index.
Subjects: Spaniards--Louisiana--Registers. Hispanic Americans--Louisiana--Genealogy. Anglo-Spanish War, 1779-1783--Registers. Louisiana--Genealogy. United States--History--Revolution, 1775-1783 Participation, Spanish.
Series: Hough, Granville W. Spanish borderlands studies; pt. 6.
LC Classification: F380.S75 H68 2000
Dewey Class No.: 929/.3763 21

Hough, Granville W.
Spain's New Mexico patriots in its 1779-1783 war with England during the American Revolution / by Granville W. and N.C. Hough.
Published/Created: Midway City, CA (P.O. Box 490, Midway City 92655-0490): SHHAR Press c1999.
Related Authors: Hough, N. C.
Description: v, 182 p.; 28 cm.

Notes: Includes bibliographical references (p. 181) and index.
Subjects: Anglo-Spanish War, 1779-1783--Registers. Hispanic Americans--New Mexico--Genealogy. United States--History--Revolution, 1775-1783 Participation, Spanish. New Mexico--Genealogy.
Series: Hough, Granville W. Spanish borderlands studies; pt. 4.
LC Classification: E269.S63 H68 1999
Dewey Class No.: 973.3/46 21

Hough, Granville W.
Spain's Texas patriots in its 1779-1783 War with England during the American Revolution / by Granville W. and N.C. Hough.
Published/Created: Midway City, CA: SHHAR Press, c2000.
Related Authors: Hough, N. C.
Description: vi, 176 p.; 28 cm.
Notes: Includes bibliographical references and index.
Subjects: Spaniards--Texas--Registers. Hispanic Americans--Texas--Genealogy. Texas--Genealogy. Anglo-Spanish War, 1779-1783--Registers. United States--History--Revolution, 1775-1783 Participation, Spanish.
Series: Hough, Granville W. Spanish borderlands studies; pt. 5.
LC Classification: F395.S75 H68 2000
Dewey Class No.: 929/.3/089610764 21

Hoyt-Goldsmith, Diane.
Las Posadas: an Hispanic Christmas celebration / by Diane Hoyt-Goldsmith; photographs by Lawrence Migdale.
Edition Information: 1st ed.
Published/Created: New York: Holiday House, c1999.
Related Authors: Migdale, Lawrence, ill.
Description: 32 p.: col. ill., col. map; 27 cm.
ISBN: 0823414493

Summary: Follows a Hispanic American family in a small New Mexican community as they prepare for and celebrate the nine-day religious festival which occurs just before Christmas.
Notes: Includes index.
Subjects: Posadas (Social custom)--New Mexico--Juvenile literature. Christmas--New Mexico--Juvenile literature. Hispanic Americans--Social life and customs--Juvenile literature. Posadas (Social custom) Christmas--New Mexico. Mexican-Americans--Social life and customs. New Mexico--Social life and customs--Juvenile literature. New Mexico--Social life and customs.
LC Classification: GT4986.N6 H69 1999
Dewey Class No.: 394.266 21

Ibarra, Robert A.
Beyond affirmative action: reframing the context of higher education / Robert A. Ibarra.
Published/Created: Madison, Wis.: University of Wisconsin Press, c2001.
Description: xv, 323 p. 24 cm.
ISBN: 0299169006 (cloth: alk. paper) 0299169049 (pbk.: alk. paper)
Notes: Includes bibliographical references (p. [281]-304) and index.
Subjects: Education, Higher--Social aspects--United States. Affirmative action programs--United States. Hispanic Americans--Education (Higher)--Social aspects. Minorities--Education (Higher)--Social aspects--United States. Education, Higher--Aims and objectives--United States.
LC Classification: LC191.9 .I23 2001
Dewey Class No.: 378.1/9829 21

Iber, Jorge, 1961-
Hispanics in the Mormon Zion, 1912-1999 / Jorge Iber.
Edition Information: 1st ed.
Published/Created: College Station:

Texas A&M University Press, c2000.
Description: xvi, 196 p.: ill., maps; 25
cm.
ISBN: 0890969337 (cloth: alk. paper)
Notes: Includes bibliographical
references (p. 169-182) and index.
Subjects: Hispanic Americans--Cultural
assimilation--Utah. Hispanic Americans-
-Utah--Religion. Utah--Ethnic relations.
LC Classification: F835.S75 I24 2000
Dewey Class No.: 305.8680792 21

Ignored voices: public opinion polls and the
Latino community / edited by Rodolfo
O. de la Garza.
Edition Information: 1st ed.
Published/Created: Austin, Tex.: Center
for Mexican American Studies,
University of Texas at Austin, 1987.
Related Authors: De la Garza, Rodolfo
O. University of Texas at Austin. Center
for Mexican American Studies.
Description: viii, 224 p.: ill.; 23 cm.
ISBN: 0292738447 (pbk.)
Notes: Papers from a conference
organized by the Center for Mexican
American Studies, University of Texas at
Austin; held Oct. 18, 1985, Austin, Tex.
Bibliography: p. [195]-218.
Subjects: Public opinion polls--United
States--Congresses. Public opinion--
United States--Congresses. Hispanic
Americans--Attitudes--Congresses.
Voting research--United States--
Congresses.
Series: CMAS publications
LC Classification: HN90.P8 I34 1987
Dewey Class No.: 303.3/8768073 20

Jaffe, Abram J., 1912-
Spanish Americans in the United States:
changing demographic characteristics /
A. J. Jaffe, Ruth M. Cullen, and Thomas
D. Boswell.
Published/Created: New York: Research
Institute for the Study of Man, 1976.

Related Authors: Cullen, Ruth M., joint
author. Boswell, Thomas D., joint
author.
Description: xiv, 431 p.: ill.; 28 cm.
Notes: Bibliography: p. 423-431.
Subjects: Hispanic Americans. Latin
Americans--United States.
LC Classification: E184.S75 J33
Dewey Class No.: 973/.04/68

Jensen, Jeffry, 1950-
Hispanic American struggle for equality
/ by Jeffry Jensen.
Published/Created: Vero Beach, Fla.:
Rourke Corp., c1992.
Description: v, 103 p.: ill. (some col.); 23
cm.
ISBN: 0865931801
Summary: Identifies discrimination and
discusses how Hispanic Americans have
struggled for their civil rights.
Notes: Includes bibliographical
references and index.
Subjects: Hispanic Americans--Civil
rights--Juvenile literature. Hispanic
Americans--Civil rights. Ethnic relations.
Series: Discrimination
LC Classification: E184.S75 J46 1992
Dewey Class No.: 305.868/073 20

Joge, Carmen T.
The mainstreaming of hate: a report on
Latinos and harassment, hate violence,
and law enforcement abuse in the '90s /
prepared by Carmen T. Joge with Sonia
M. Pérez.
Edition Information: Final ed.
Published/Created: Washington, D.C.:
National Council of La Raza, c1999.
Related Authors: Pérez, Sonia M.
National Council of La Raza.
Description: vii, 54 p.: ill.; 28 cm.
Notes: "November 1999." Includes
bibliographical references.
Subjects: Hispanic Americans--Crimes
against. Mexican Americans--Crimes

against. Hate crimes--United States.
Police brutality--United States.
LC Classification: HV6250.4.E75 J64
1999

Jones, Oscar.
Hippocrene U.S.A. guide to historic
Hispanic America / Oscar and Joy Jones.
Published/Created: New York:
Hippocrene Books, c1993.
Related Authors: Jones, Joy.
Description: 168 p.: ill., maps; 22 cm.
ISBN: 0781801419 :
Notes: Includes index.
Subjects: Hispanic Americans. Spanish
Americans. United States--Civilization--
Spanish influences. United States--
Guidebooks.
LC Classification: E184.S75 J66 1993
Dewey Class No.: 973/.0468 20

Jones-Correa, Michael, 1965-
Between two nations: the political
predicament of Latinos in New York
City / Michael Jones-Correa.
Published/Created: Ithaca: Cornell
University Press, 1998.
Description: xiv, 246 p.: ill., maps; 24
cm.
ISBN: 0801432928 (alk. paper)
0801483646 (pbk.: alk. paper)
Notes: Includes bibliographical
references (p. 209-237) and index.
Subjects: Hispanic Americans--New
York (State)--New York--Politics and
government. Immigrants--New York
(State)--New York--Political activity.
Citizenship--New York (State)--New
York. New York (N.Y.)--Ethnic
relations.
LC Classification: F130.S75 J66 1998
Dewey Class No.: 305.868/07471 21

Journal of Hispanic policy.
Published/Created: Cambridge, MA:
Hispanic Student Caucus of the John F.

Kennedy School of Government at
Harvard University, c1987-c1991.
Related Authors: John F. Kennedy
School of Government. Hispanic Student
Caucus.
Description: 4 v.; 26 cm. Vol. 2 (1986-
1987)-v. 5 (1991).
Continues: Journal of Hispanic politics
0888-2355 (DLC) 93648921
(OCoLC)13540158
Continued by: Harvard journal of
Hispanic policy 1074-1917 (DLC)
94660615 (OCoLC)29355926
ISSN: 0892-6115
Cancel/Invalid LCCN: sn 87000765
Notes: Title from cover.
SERBIB/SERLOC merged record
Subjects: Hispanic Americans--Politics
and government--Periodicals. Hispanic
Americans--Government policy--
Periodicals.
LC Classification: E184.S75 J68

Journal of Hispanic politics.
Published/Created: Cambridge, MA:
Hispanic Student Caucus of the John F.
Kennedy School of Government at
Harvard University, 1985.
Related Authors: John F. Kennedy
School of Government. Hispanic Student
Caucus.
Description: 1 v.: ill.; 26 cm. Vol. 1, no.
1 (1985).
Continued by: Journal of Hispanic policy
0892-6115 (DLC) 93648922
(OCoLC)15219215
ISSN: 0888-2355
Cancel/Invalid LCCN: sn 86001441
Notes: Title from cover.
SERBIB/SERLOC merged record
Subjects: Hispanic Americans--Politics
and government--Periodicals. Hispanic
Americans--Government policy--
Periodicals.
LC Classification: E184.S75 J68

Dewey Class No.: 323 11

Kanellos, Nicolás.
Hispanic firsts: 500 years of
extraordinary achievement / Nicolás
Kanellos.
Published/Created: Detroit: Gale, c1997.
Description: xxvi, 372 p.: ill.; 25 cm.
ISBN: 0787605174 (p. [4] of cover)
Cancelled ISBN: 0781605174 (alk.
paper)
Notes: Includes bibliographical
references (p. 323-327) and index.
Subjects: Hispanic Americans--History--
Miscellanea. World records--United
States.
LC Classification: E184.S75 K36 1997
Dewey Class No.: 973/.0468073 21

Kanellos, Nicolás.
Hispanic periodicals in the United States,
origins to 1960: a brief history and
comprehensive bibliography / by Nicólas
Kanellos and Helvetia Martell.
Published/Created: Houston, TX: Arte
Publico Press, 2000.
Related Authors: Martell, Helvetia.
Description: 359 p.; 24 cm.
ISBN: 1558852530 (alk. paper)
Notes: Includes indexes.
Subjects: Hispanic American
periodicals--Bibliography--Union lists.
Hispanic American newspapers--
Bibliography--Union lists. Hispanic
Americans--Periodicals--Bibliography--
Union lists. Catalogs, Union--United
States.
Series: Recovering the U.S. Hispanic
Literary Heritage Project publication
LC Classification: Z6953.5.S66 K36
2000 PN4885.S75
Dewey Class No.: 015.73/034/08968 21

Kanellos, Nicolás.
Thirty million strong: reclaiming the
Hispanic image in American culture /

Nicolás Kanellos.
Published/Created: Golden, Colo.:
Fulcrum Pub., c1998.
Description: x, 166 p.: ill.; 23 cm.
ISBN: 1555912656 (pbk.)
Notes: Includes bibliographical
references (p. 153-160) and index.
Subjects: Hispanic Americans--History.
Hispanic Americans and mass media.
United States--Civilization--Hispanic
influences.
LC Classification: E184.S75 K38 1998
Dewey Class No.: 973/.0468 21

Keller, Gary D.
A biographical handbook of Hispanics
and United States film / Gary D. Keller
with the assistance of Estela Keller.
Published/Created: Tempe, Ariz.:
Bilingual Press/Editorial Bilingüe,
c1997.
Related Authors: Keller, Gary D.
Hispanics and United States film.
Description: xi, 322 p.: ill.; 28 cm.
ISBN: 0927534568 (pbk.: alk. paper)
0927534657 (cloth: alk. paper)
Notes: Companion volume to: Hispanics
and United States film / Gary D. Keller.
Includes bibliographical references (p.
223-265) and indexes.
Subjects: Hispanic Americans in the
motion picture industry Biography--
Dictionaries. Hispanic American motion
picture actors and actresses Credits.
Hispanic American motion picture
producers and directors Credits.
LC Classification: PN1995.9.H47 K46
1997
Dewey Class No.: 791.43/08968073 20

Keller, Gary D.
Hispanics and United States film: an
overview and handbook / Gary D. Keller.
Published/Created: Tempe, Ariz.:
Bilingual Review/Press, c1994.
Description: 230 p.: ill.; 26 cm.

ISBN: 0927534401 (pbk.)
Notes: Includes bibliographical
references (p. 221-230).
Subjects: Latin Americans in motion
pictures. Hispanic Americans in motion
pictures. Motion pictures--United States-
-History.
LC Classification: PN1995.9.L37 K46
1994
Dewey Class No.: 791.43/08968 20

Kenig, Graciela.
Best careers for bilingual Latinos:
market your fluency in Spanish to get
ahead on the job / Graciela Kenig.
Published/Created: Lincolnwood, Ill.:
VGM Career Horizons, c1999.
Description: xiii, 238 p.; 23 cm.
ISBN: 0844245410
Subjects: Vocational guidance--United
States. Hispanic Americans--
Employment. Bilingualism--United
States. Spanish language--Vocational
guidance--United States.
LC Classification: HF5382.5.U5 K455
1999
Dewey Class No.: 331.7/02/08968073 21

Kevane, Bridget A., 1963-
Latina self-portraits: interviews with
contemporary women writers / Bridget
Kevane & Juanita Heredia.
Edition Information: 1st ed.
Published/Created: Albuquerque:
University of New Mexico Press, c2000.
Related Authors: Heredia, Juanita, 1966-
Description: viii, 166 p.; 24 cm.
ISBN: 0826319718 (alk. paper)
0826319726 (pbk.: alk. paper)
Notes: Includes bibliographical
references (p. [155]-166).
Subjects: American literature--Hispanic
American authors--History and criticism-
-Theory, etc. American literature--
Women authors--History and criticism
Theory, etc. American literature--20th

century--History and criticism Theory,
etc. Authors, American--20th century--
Interviews. Hispanic American women--
Intellectual life. Women authors,
American--Interviews. Hispanic
American women--Interviews. Hispanic
Americans in literature. Authorship.
LC Classification: PS153.H56 K48 2000
Dewey Class No.: 810.9/9287/08968 21

Kuypers-Denlinger, Corinne.
Hispanics in America: the "sleeping
giant" awakens.
Published/Created: Washington, D.C.
(1101 30th St., Washington 20007):
Naisbitt Group, [c1985]
Description: ii, 46 leaves; 28 cm.
Subjects: Hispanic Americans--Ethnic
identity. Hispanic Americans--Economic
conditions. Hispanic Americans--Social
conditions. United States--Economic
conditions--1981-
Series: A Naisbitt Group trend report
LC Classification: E184.S75 K88 1985
Dewey Class No.: 305.8/68073 19

Lachaga, José María de.
El pueblo hispano en USA: minorías
étnicas y la Iglesia Católica / José María
de Lachaga.
Published/Created: Bilboa: Desclée de
Brouwer, c1982.
Description: 269 p.: maps; 21 cm.
ISBN: 8433005952
Notes: Bibliography: p. 267-269.
Subjects: Hispanic Americans. Hispanic
American Catholics. Hispanic
Americans--History--Chronology.
LC Classification: E184.S75 L3 1982
Dewey Class No.: 973/.046873 19

Landes, Ruth, 1908-
Latin Americans of the Southwest.
Published/Created: St. Louis, Webster
Division, McGraw-Hill [1965]
Description: 104 p. illus., maps, ports. 21

cm.
Notes: Bibliography: p. 101-102.
Subjects: Hispanic-Americans--
Southwest, New. Southwest, New--
History.
LC Classification: F786 .L29
Dewey Class No.: 301.45160791

Latino Americans.
Published/Created: New York:
Macmillan Library Reference USA,
1999.
Related Authors: Macmillan Library
Reference USA.
Description: xii, 465 p.: ill.; 26 cm.
ISBN: 0028653734 (hardcover: alk.
paper)
Notes: Includes bibliographical
references (p. 395-417) and index.
Subjects: Hispanic Americans--
Biography. Hispanic Americans--
History.
Series: Macmillan profiles
LC Classification: E184.S75 L3556 1999
Dewey Class No.: 920/.009268073 B 21

Latino college students / edited by Michael
A. Olivas.
Published/Created: New York: Teachers
College Press, c1986.
Related Authors: Olivas, Michael A.
Description: xxi, 360 p.: ill.; 24 cm.
ISBN: 0807727989 (pbk.)
Notes: Includes bibliographies and
index.
Subjects: Hispanic Americans--
Education (Secondary)--Congresses.
Hispanic Americans--Education
(Higher)--Congresses. Educational
equalization--United States--Congresses.
Universities and colleges--United States-
-Entrance examinations--Congresses.
Series: Bilingual education series
(Columbia University. Teachers College)
LC Classification: LC2670.4 .L37 1986

Dewey Class No.: 378/.1982 19

Latino cultural citizenship: claiming identity,
space, and rights / edited by William V.
Flores and Rina Benmayor.
Published/Created: Boston: Beacon
Press, c1997.
Related Authors: Flores, William
Vincent. Benmayor, Rina.
Description: 322 p.; 24 cm.
ISBN: 0807046345 (cloth)
Notes: Includes bibliographical
references (p. 291-305) and index.
Subjects: Hispanic Americans--Ethnic
identity. Hispanic Americans--Social life
and customs. Hispanic Americans--
Cultural assimilation. Citizenship--
United States.
LC Classification: E184.S75 L356 1997
Dewey Class No.: 305.868 21

Latino heretics / edited by Tony Diaz.
Published/Created: Normal, IL: Fiction
Collective Two, 1999.
Related Authors: Diaz, Tony, 1968-
Description: p. cm.
ISBN: 1573660779 (alk. paper)
Subjects: American fiction--Hispanic
American authors. Hispanic Americans--
Fiction.
LC Classification: PS647.H58 L38 1999
Dewey Class No.: 813/.54080868 21

Latino language and communicative behavior
/ edited by Richard P. Durán.
Published/Created: Norwood, N.J.:
Ablex Pub. Corp., c1981.
Related Authors: Durán, Richard P.
Educational Testing Service. National
Conference on Chicano and Latino
Discourse Behavior (1978: Princeton,
N.J.)
Description: xiv, 363 p.: ill.; 24 cm.
ISBN: 0893910384
Notes: "Proceedings from the National
Conference on Chicano and Latino

Discourse Behavior sponsored by
Educational Testing Service in 1978"--P.
vii. Includes bibliographies and indexes.
Subjects: Hispanic Americans--
Language--Congresses. Hispanic
Americans--Communication--
Congresses. Bilingualism--United States-
-Congresses.
Series: Advances in discourse processes;
v. 6
LC Classification: P94.5.H58 L37 1981
Dewey Class No.: 420/.4261 19

Latino language and education:
communication and the dream deferred /
edited, with an introduction by
Antoinette Sedillo López.
Published/Created: New York: Garland
Pub., 1995.
Related Authors: López, Antoinette
Sedillo.
Description: xv, 423 p.: ill., map; 24 cm.
ISBN: 0815317743 (alk. paper)
Notes: Includes bibliographical
references.
Subjects: Hispanic Americans--
Education. Language policy--United
States. Education, Bilingual--United
States.
Series: Latinos in the United States; v. 5
LC Classification: LC2669 .L38 1995
Dewey Class No.: 371.97/68/073 20

Latino leaders.
Published/Created: Houston, Tex.:
Ferráez Publications of America, 2000-
Description: v.: ill. (some col.); 27 cm.
Feb./Mar. 2000 issue also called premier
issue. Vol. 1, no. 1 (Feb./Mar. 2000)-
ISSN: 1529-3998
Notes: Title from cover.
Subjects: Hispanic Americans--
Periodicals. Success--United States--
Periodicals.
LC Classification: E184.S75 L3623

Dewey Class No.: 305 13

Latino librarianship: a handbook for
professionals / Salvador Güereña, editor.
Published/Created: Jefferson, N.C.:
McFarland & Co., c1990.
Related Authors: Güereña, Salvador.
Description: xiii, 192 p.; 24 cm.
ISBN: 0899505325 (lib. bdg.: alk. paper)
Notes: Includes bibliographical
references and index.
Subjects: Libraries--Special collections--
Hispanic Americans. Hispanic
Americans--Bibliography--Methodology.
Hispanic Americans--Information
services. Hispanic Americans--Archival
resources. Hispanic Americans--Library
resources. Hispanic Americans--
Databases. Hispanic Americans and
libraries.
LC Classification: Z688.H57 L38 1990
Dewey Class No.: 027.6/3089/68 20

Latino poetry.
Published/Created: Paramus, N.J.: Globe
Fearon, c1994.
Description: vii, 120 p.: ill.; 23 cm.
ISBN: 0835907260
Notes: Includes index.
Subjects: Young adult poetry, American-
-Hispanic American authors. Hispanic
Americans--Poetry. Hispanic Americans-
-Poetry. American poetry--Hispanic
American authors--Collections.
LC Classification: PS591.H58 L38 1994

Latino poverty and economic development in
Massachusetts / edited by Edwin
Meléndez and Miren Uriarte.
Published/Created: Boston: Mauricio
Gastón Institute for Latino Community
Development and Public Policy,
University of Massachusetts at Boston;
Amherst, MA, USA: Distributed by
University of Massachusetts Press,
c1993.

Related Authors: Meléndez, Edwin.
Uriarte-Gastón, Miren.
Description: xi, 200 p.; 23 cm.
ISBN: 0870238949 (pbk.)
Notes: Includes bibliographical
references.
Subjects: Hispanic Americans--
Massachusetts--Economic conditions.
Massachusetts--Economic conditions.
LC Classification: F75.S75 L38 1993
Dewey Class No.: 330.9744/0089/68 20

Latino poverty in the new century:
inequalities, challenges, and barriers /
Maria Vidal de Haymes, Keith M. Kilty,
Elizabeth A. Segal, editors.
Published/Created: New York: Haworth
Press, c2000.
Related Authors: De Haymes, Maria
Vidal. Kilty, Keith M. (Keith Michael),
1946- Segal, Elizabeth A.
Related Titles: Journal of poverty.
Description: xv, 183 p.: ill.; 22 cm.
ISBN: 0789011603 (alk. paper)
0789011611 (pbk.: alk. paper)
Notes: "Has been co-published
simultaneously as Journal of poverty,
Volume 4, Number 1/2, 2000." Includes
bibliographical references and index.
Subjects: Hispanic Americans--
Economic conditions--21st century.
Hispanic Americans--Social conditions--
21st century. Hispanic Americans--
Politics and government--21st century.
Poverty--United States. United States--
Economic policy--21st century. United
States--Ethnic relations.
LC Classification: E184.S75 L3625 2000
Dewey Class No.: 305.868073 21

Latino social movements: historical and
theoretical perspectives: a new political
science reader / Rodolfo D. Torres and
George Katsiaficas, editors.
Published/Created: New York:
Routledge, 1999.

Related Authors: Torres, Rodolfo D.,
1949- Katsiaficas, George N., 1949-
Description: v, 209 p.; 23 cm.
ISBN: 0415922992 (pbk.: acid-free
paper)
Notes: Includes bibliographical
references.
Subjects: Hispanic Americans--Politics
and government. Hispanic Americans--
Social conditions. Hispanic Americans--
Economic conditions.
LC Classification: E184.S75 L3636 1999
Dewey Class No.: 305.868 21

Latino socio/economic study: prepared for
the Latino and Puerto Rican Affairs
Commission, Hartford, Connecticut /
submitted by the Center for Research &
Public Policy.
Published/Created: New Haven, Conn.
(35 Elm St., New Haven 06510): The
Center, [1996]
Related Authors: Center for Research &
Public Policy (New Haven, Conn.)
Connecticut. Latino and Puerto Rican
Affairs Commission.
Description: 55 p.; 28 cm.
Notes: "June 1996." Errata slip inserted.
Subjects: Hispanic Americans--
Connecticut--Statistics. Quality of life--
Connecticut--Statistics.
LC Classification: F105.S75 L38 1996

Latino studies / compiled by the Choice
editorial staff; editor & publisher,
Patricia E. Sabosik.
Published/Created: Middletown, CT:
Choice, c1992.
Related Authors: Sabosik, Patricia E.
Related Titles: Choice (Chicago, Ill.)
Description: ii, 100 p.; 28 cm.
ISBN: 083897631X
Notes: Includes indexes.
Subjects: Hispanic Americans--Book
reviews. Hispanic Americans--
Bibliography. Latin America--Book

reviews. Latin America--Bibliography.
Series: Choice ethnic studies reviews
LC Classification: E184.S75 L364 1992

Latino studies journal / DePaul University.
Published/Created: Chicago, IL: DePaul
University, Center for Latino Research,
c1990-
Related Authors: DePaul University.
DePaul University. Center for Latino
Research. Northeastern University
(Boston, Mass.) Herbert H. Lehman
College. Long Island University. C.W.
Post Campus. Dept. of Sociology and
Anthropology.
Description: v.; 26 cm. Issue for Jan.
1994 called v. 1, issue 1 but constitutes
v. 5, issue 1. Vol. 1, issue 1 (Jan. 1990)-
ISSN: 1066-1344
Cancel/Invalid LCCN: sn 91030196
Notes: Title from cover. Issued by:
Northeastern University, 1994-1996; by:
Lehman College, CUNY, Winter 1996-;
by: Dept. of Sociology and
Anthropology, C.W. Post Campus, Long
Island University, Winter 1998-
SERBIB/SERLOC merged record
Subjects: Hispanic Americans--
Periodicals.
LC Classification: E184.S75 L38
Dewey Class No.: 973/.0468 20

Latino voices / edited by Frances R.
Aparicio.
Published/Created: Brookfield, Conn.:
Millbrook Press, c1994.
Related Authors: Aparicio, Frances R.
Description: 143 p.: ill.; 24 cm.
ISBN: 156294388X (lib. bdg.)
Summary: An anthology of Latino
fiction, poetry, biography, and other
writings which describe the experiences
of Hispanic Americans.
Notes: Includes bibliographical
references and index
Subjects: Hispanic Americans--Literary

collections. Hispanic Americans--
Literary collections.
Series: Writers of America
LC Classification: PZ5 .L47 1994
Dewey Class No.: 860.8/098 20

Latino voices: Mexican, Puerto Rican, and
Cuban perspectives on American politics
/ Rodolfo O. de la Garza ... [et al.].
Published/Created: Boulder: Westview
Press, 1992.
Related Authors: De la Garza, Rodolfo
O.
Description: vii, 232 p.; 23 cm.
ISBN: 0813387248
Notes: Includes bibliographical
references.
Subjects: Hispanic Americans--Politics
and government. Mexican Americans--
Politics and government. Puerto Ricans--
United States--Politics and government.
Cuban Americans--Politics and
government. United States--Politics and
government--1989-1993.
LC Classification: E184.S75 L365 1992
Dewey Class No.: 323.1/168 20

Latino workers in the contemporary South /
edited by Arthur D. Murphy, Colleen
Blanchard, and Jennifer A. Hill.
Published/Created: Athens, Ga.:
University of Georgia Press, c2001.
Related Authors: Murphy, Arthur D.
Blanchard, Colleen. Hill, Jennifer A.
Description: vi, 139 p.; 24 cm.
ISBN: 0820322784 (alk. paper)
0820322792 (pbk.: alk. paper)
Notes: Includes bibliographical
references.
Subjects: Hispanic Americans--
Employment--Southern States. Mexican
Americans--Employment--Southern
States. Alien labor, Mexican--
Employment--Southern States. Southern
States--Emigration and immigration.
Southern States--Social conditions.

Southern States--Race relations.
Series: Southern Anthropological
Society proceedings; no. 34
LC Classification: GN2 .S9243 no. 34
HD8081.H7
Dewey Class No.: 305.868/075 21

Latinos and education: a critical reader /
Antonia Darder, Rodolfo D. Torres, and
Henry Gutíerrez, editors.
Published/Created: New York:
Routledge, 1997.
Related Authors: Darder, Antonia.
Torres, Rodolfo D., 1949- Gutíerrez,
Henry.
Description: xxii, 488 p.: ill.; 24 cm.
ISBN: 0415911818 0415911826 (pbk.)
Notes: Includes bibliographical
references.
Subjects: Hispanic Americans--
Education--Social aspects. Hispanic
Americans--Education--Economic
aspects. Hispanic Americans--Education-
-History. Language and education--
United States. Educational anthropology-
-United States.
LC Classification: LC2669 .L39 1997
Dewey Class No.: 371.97/68/073 20

Latinos and political coalitions: political
empowerment for the 1990s / edited by
Roberto E. Villarreal and Norma G.
Hernandez.
Published/Created: New York:
Greenwood Press, 1991.
Related Authors: Villarreal, Roberto E.
Hernandez, Norma G.
Related Titles: Latino empowerment.
Description: xxvi, 221 p.; 25 cm.
ISBN: 0313278342 (alk. paper)
Notes: Continues: Latino empowerment.
Includes bibliographical references (p.
[193]-208) and index.
Subjects: Mexican Americans--Politics
and government. Mexican Americans--
Texas--Politics and government.

Hispanic Americans--Politics and
government. Coalition (Social sciences)
United States--Politics and government--
1989-1993. Texas--Politics and
government--1951-
Series: Contributions in ethnic studies,
0196-7088; no. 27
LC Classification: E184.M5 L35 1991
Dewey Class No.: 323.1/168720764 20

Latinos and political coalitions: political
empowerment for the 1990s / edited by
Roberto E. Villarreal and Norma G.
Hernandez.
Published/Created: New York: Praeger,
1991.
Related Authors: Villarreal, Roberto E.
Hernandez, Norma G.
Related Titles: Latino empowerment.
Description: xxvi, 221 p.; 24 cm.
ISBN: 0275940926 (pbk.: alk. paper)
Notes: Based on an earlier collection by
the same editors: Latino empowerment,
1988. Includes bibliographical references
(p. [193]-208) and index.
Subjects: Mexican Americans--Politics
and government. Mexican Americans--
Texas--Politics and government.
Hispanic Americans--Politics and
government. Coalition (Social sciences)
United States--Politics and government--
1989-1993. Texas--Politics and
government--1951-
LC Classification: E184.M5 L35 1991b
Dewey Class No.: 323.1/168720764 20

Latinos and politics: a select research
bibliography / compiled by F. Chris
García ... [et al.]; with the research
assistance of Patti Constantakis ... [et
al.].
Edition Information: 1st ed.
Published/Created: Austin: Center for
Mexican American Studies, University
of Texas at Austin: Distributed by
University of Texas Press, 1991.

Related Authors: Garcia, F. Chris.
Description: xvi, 239 p.; 24 cm.
ISBN: 0292746547 (acid-free paper) :
Notes: Includes indexes.
Subjects: Hispanic Americans--Politics
and government--Bibliography.
LC Classification: Z1361.S7 L365 1991
E184.S75
Dewey Class No.: 016.973/0468 20

Latinos and the political system / F. Chris
Garcia, editor.
Published/Created: Notre Dame, Ind.:
University of Notre Dame Press, c1988.
Related Authors: Garcia, F. Chris.
Description: x, 501 p.; 24 cm.
ISBN: 0268012857 :
Notes: Includes bibliographies.
Subjects: Hispanic Americans--Politics
and government. United States--Politics
and government--1981-1989.
LC Classification: E184.S75 L368 1988
Dewey Class No.: 323.1/168/073 19

Latinos and U.S. foreign policy: representing
the "homeland"? / edited by Rodolfo O.
de la Garza and Harry P. Pachon.
Published/Created: Lanham, Md.:
Rowman & Littlefield Publishers, c2000.
Related Authors: De la Garza, Rodolfo
O. Pachon, Harry.
Description: ix, 172 p.: ill.; 24 cm.
ISBN: 0742501361 (alk. paper)
074250137X (pbk.: alk. paper)
Notes: Includes bibliographical
references and index.
Subjects: Hispanic Americans--Politics
and government. Political participation--
United States. United States--Foreign
relations--1989- United States--
Relations--Latin America. Latin
America--Relations--United states.
LC Classification: E184.S75 L3685 2000
Dewey Class No.: 327.7308 21

Latinos in a changing U.S. economy:
comparative perspectives on growing
inequality / Rebecca Morales, Frank
Bonilla, editors.
Published/Created: Newbury Park, CA:
Sage Publications, c1993.
Related Authors: Morales, Rebecca.
Bonilla, Frank.
Related Titles: Latinos in a changing US
economy.
Description: vii, 272 p.: ill.; 23 cm.
ISBN: 0803949235 0803949243 (pbk.)
Notes: Includes bibliographical
references (p. 241-257) and indexes.
Subjects: Hispanic Americans--
Economic conditions.
Series: Sage series on race and ethnic
relations; v. 7
LC Classification: E184.S75 L369 1993
Dewey Class No.: 330.973/09/08968 20

Latinos in Massachusetts / The Mauricio
Gastón Institute for Latino Community
Development and Public Policy.
Published/Created: Boston, MA: The
Institute, c1992.
Related Authors: Mauricio Gastón
Institute for Latino Community
Development and Public Policy.
Description: 15 parts; 28 cm.
Contents: Latinos in Boston -- Latinos in
Brockton -- Latinos in Cambridge --
Latinos in Chelsea -- Latinos in
Framingham -- Latinos in Holyoke --
Latinos in Lawrence -- Latinos in
Leominster -- Latinos in Lowell --
Latinos in Lynn -- Latinos in New
Bedford -- Latinos in Somerville --
Latinos in Springfield -- Latinos in
Waltham -- Latinos in Worcester.
Subjects: Hispanic Americans--
Massachusetts--Statistics.
Massachusetts--Population--Statistics.
LC Classification: F75.S75 L39 1992
Dewey Class No.: 305.868/0744 20

Latinos in New York: communities in transition / edited by Gabriel Haslip-Viera, Sherrie L. Baver.
Published/Created: Notre Dame, Ind.: University of Notre Dame Press, c1996.
Related Authors: Haslip-Viera, Gabriel. Baver, Sherrie L.
Description: xxii, 338 p.: ill.; 24 cm.
ISBN: 0268013055
Notes: Includes bibliographical references.
Subjects: Hispanic Americans--New York (State)--New York. Hispanic Americans--New York Region. New York (N.Y.)--Social conditions. New York Region--Social conditions.
LC Classification: F128.9.S75 L37 1996
Dewey Class No.: 974.7/100468 20

Latinos in Pennsylvania: summary report & recommendations / Pennsylvania, Governor's Advisory Commission on Latino Affairs.
Published/Created: [Harrisburg, Pa.]: The Commission, [1991]
Description: iii, 30 p.; 28 cm.
Notes: Cover title. "April 1991."
Subjects: Hispanic Americans--Government policy--Pennsylvania.
LC Classification: F160.S75 P46 1991

Latinos in Texas: a socio-demographic profile / The Tomás Rivera Center.
Published/Created: Austin, TX: The Center, c1995.
Related Authors: Tomás Rivera Center.
Description: 117 p.: ill.; 28 cm.
ISBN: 1572400021
Subjects: Hispanic Americans--Texas--Census, 1990. Texas--Census, 1990. United States--Census, 21st, 1990.
LC Classification: F395.S75 L38 1995
Dewey Class No.: 929/.3/089680764 20

Latinos in the United States / Carlos E. Cortés, editor.
Published/Created: New York: Arno Press, 1980.
Related Authors: Cortés, Carlos E.
Description: 448 p. in various pagings: ill.; 24 cm.
ISBN: 0405131798 :
Notes: Includes bibliographical references.
Subjects: Hispanic Americans. Hispanic Americans--New York (State)--New York. United States--Ethnic relations. New York (N.Y.)--Ethnic relations.
Series: Hispanics in the United States
LC Classification: E184.S75 L37
Dewey Class No.: 973/.0468

Latinos in the United States: a historical bibliography / Albert Camarillo, editor.
Published/Created: Santa Barbara, Calif.: ABC-Clio, c1986.
Related Authors: Camarillo, Albert.
Description: x, 332 p.; 24 cm.
ISBN: 0874364582 (alk. paper)
Notes: Includes indexes.
Subjects: Hispanic Americans--History--Bibliography.
Series: ABC-Clio research guides
LC Classification: Z1361.S7 L37 1986 E184.S75
Dewey Class No.: 016.973/0468 19

Latinos: remaking America / edited by Marcelo M. Suárez-Orozco and Mariela Páez.
Published/Created: Berkeley: University of California Press, 2002.
Related Authors: Suárez-Orozco, Marcelo M., 1956- Páez, Mariela. David Rockefeller Center for Latin American Studies.
Description: p. cm.
ISBN: 0520234863 (alk. paper) 0520234871 (pbk.: alk. paper)
Notes: "David Rockefeller Center for Latin American Studies, Harvard University." Papers originally presented

at the conference entitled Latinos in the 21st century: mapping the research agenda, held in April 2000 at Harvard University. Includes bibliographical references and index.
Subjects: Hispanic Americans--Social conditions--21st century Congresses. Hispanic Americans--Politics and government--21st century Congresses. Hispanic Americans--Economic conditions--21st century Congresses. United States--Social conditions--1980---Congresses. United States--Ethnic relations--Congresses.
LC Classification: E184.S75 L37 2002
Dewey Class No.: 305.868073 21

Latins anonymous: two plays.
Published/Created: Houston, Tex: Arte Público Press, 1996.
Related Authors: Latins Anonymous.
Related Titles: LA LA awards.
Description: 103 p.; 22 cm.
ISBN: 1558851720 (trade pbk.: alk. paper)
Notes: "Latins Anonymous"--T.p. verso. Includes LA LA awards / by Cris Franco ... [et al.] (p. [11]-52).
Subjects: American drama--Hispanic American authors. American drama--20th century. Hispanic Americans--Drama. American drama (Comedy)
LC Classification: PS628.H57 L38 1996
Dewey Class No.: 812/.5408086872 20

Lauenstein, Gary.
Fully devoted: the Hispanic apostolate in the St. Louis Province of Redemptorists / Gary Lauenstein.
Published/Created: [S.l.]: Redemptorists of the Denver Province, 1996.
Description: ix, 417 p.: ill.; 24 cm.
Notes: Includes bibliographical references (p. 401-417) and index.
Subjects: Redemptorists--St. Louis Province--History. Redemptorists--

Texas--San Antonio--History. Redemptorists--Texas--San Antonio--Biography. Hispanic Americans--Missions--Texas--San Antonio.
LC Classification: BX4020.Z6 S75 1996
Dewey Class No.: 271/.64073/08968 21

Lederman, Ruth I.
Hispanic births in Massachusetts / Commonwealth of Massachusetts, Executive Office of Human Services, Department of Public Health.; [prepared by Ruth I. Lederman, Bruce B. Cohen, Daniel J. Friedman].
Published/Created: Boston, Mass. (150 Tremont St., Boston 02111): Bureau of Health Statistics, Research and Evaluation, the Dept., [1989-
Related Authors: Cohen, Bruce B. Friedman, Daniel J. Massachusetts. Bureau of Health Statistics, Research and Evaluation.
Description: v. <1 >: ill.; 28 cm.
Incomplete Contents: v. 1. Facts and figures.
Notes: "April 1989." Includes bibliographical references (v. 1, p. 46-48).
Subjects: Fertility, Human--Massachusetts--Statistics. Hispanic Americans--Massachusetts--Statistics.
LC Classification: HB935.M4 L44 1989
Dewey Class No.: 304.6/32/08968073 20

Lemus, Frank C.
National roster of Spanish surnamed elected officials / [compiled by Frank C. Lemus].
Published/Created: Los Angeles: Aztlán Publications, c1973, 1974 printing.
Description: vii p., p. 313-410; 24 cm.
Notes: "Reprinted from Aztlán-Chicano journal of the social sciences and the arts, vol. 5, no. 1 and no. 2."
Subjects: Local officials and employees--United States--Directories. State

governments--United States--Officials and employees Directories. Hispanic American legislators--United States--Directories. Hispanic Americans--Politics and government--Directories.
Series: Bibliographic series (Los Angeles)
LC Classification: JS363 .L44
Dewey Class No.: 352/.005/20973

Library services to Latinos: an anthology / edited by Salvador Güereña.
Published/Created: Jefferson, N.C.: McFarland, c2000.
Related Authors: Güereña, Salvador.
Description: xi, 249 p.: ill.; 26 cm.
ISBN: 0786409118 (soft: alk. paper)
Notes: Includes bibliographical references and index.
Subjects: Hispanic Americans and libraries.
LC Classification: Z711.8 .L53 2000
Dewey Class No.: 027.6/3 21

Library services to youth of Hispanic heritage / Barbara Immroth and Kathleen de la Peña McCook, editors; assisted by Catherine Jasper.
Published/Created: Jefferson, N.C.: McFarland, 2000.
Related Authors: Immroth, Barbara Froling. McCook, Kathleen de la Peña.
Description: ix, 197 p.: ill.; 26 cm.
ISBN: 0786407905 (softcover: alk. paper)
Notes: Includes bibliographical references and index.
Subjects: Hispanic Americans and libraries. Hispanic American children--Books and reading. Hispanic American youth--Books and reading. Hispanic American children--Education. Hispanic American youth--Education. Children's libraries--United States. School libraries--United States.
LC Classification: Z711.8 .L54 2000

Dewey Class No.: 027.6/3 21

Lopez, D. A. (David Anthony)
The Latino experience in Omaha: a visual essay / D.A. Lopez.
Published/Created: Lewiston, N.Y.: E. Mellen Press, c2001.
Description: ix, 155 p.: ill., maps; 24 cm.
ISBN: 0773475613 (v. 29) 0889466300 (MSS series)
Notes: Includes bibliographical references (p. 133-146) and index.
Subjects: Hispanic Americans--Nebraska--Omaha--Social conditions. Hispanic Americans--Nebraska--Omaha--Social conditions Pictorial works. Hispanic Americans--Nebraska--Omaha--Interviews. Omaha (Neb.)--Ethnic relations. Omaha (Neb.)--Social conditions.
Series: Mellen studies in sociology; v. 29
LC Classification: F674.O59 S755 2001
Dewey Class No.: 305.8680782254 21

Lopez, Elias.
Latinos and economic development in California / Elias Lopez, Enrique Ramirez, Refugio I. Rochin.
Published/Created: Sacramento, CA: California Research Bureau, California State Library, [1999]
Related Authors: Ramirez, Enrique. Rochin, Refugio I. Polanco, Richard G. California State Library. California Research Bureau.
Description: 54 p.: ill.; 28 cm.
Partial Contents: Do Latinos earn less than other ethnic-racial groups? -- Explaining the lower wages of Latinos -- What about the native-born Latinos?: what is their wage & educational attainment? -- A demographic profile of California: 2025 -- The economic benefits of raising the educational attainment of Latinos.
Notes: "prepared at the request of

Richard Polanco, Senate Majority Leader and Chair of the Latino Legislative Caucus." "June 1999." "CRB-99-008." Includes bibliographical references (p. 54-54).
Additional Form Avail.: Also available via the World Wide Web at the CRB web site.
Subjects: Hispanic Americans--California--Economic conditions. Latin Americans--California--Economic conditions. Population forecasting--California. California--Economic conditions.
LC Classification: HC107.C2 L597 1999
Dewey Class No.: 331.6/3680794 21
Govt. Doc. No.: L960.L27 cadocs

Mabbutt, Richard.
Hispanics in Idaho: concerns and challenges / Richard Mabbutt.
Published/Created: [Idaho: Idaho Human Rights Commission, 1990]
Description: 16 leaves; 28 cm.
Notes: Cover title. "Spring 1990." Includes bibliographical references.
Subjects: Hispanic Americans--Idaho.
Series: Research report (Idaho. Human Rights Commission)
LC Classification: F755.S75 M33 1990
Dewey Class No.: 305.868/0796 20

Machalski, Andrew.
Hispanic writers in Canada: a preliminary survey of the activities of Spanish and Latin-American writers in Canada / by Andrew Machalski; edited by Michael S. Batts.
Published/Created: Canada: Dept. of the Secretary of State of Canada, [1988]
Related Authors: Batts, Michael S.
Description: 51 p.; 29 cm.
ISBN: 0662160312
Notes: "January, 1988." "Catalogue no. Ci96-36/4-1988E."
Subjects: Canadian literature--Hispanic authors--Bio-bibliography. French-Canadian literature--Hispanic authors Bio-bibliography. Hispanic Americans--Canada--Intellectual life. Canadian literature (Spanish)--Bio-bibliography. Spaniards--Canada--Intellectual life.
LC Classification: PR9188.2.H56 M33 1988
Dewey Class No.: 810.9/86871 20

Machamer, Gene.
Hispanic American profiles / Gene Machamer; illustrations by Gene Machamer.
Edition Information: 1st Ballentine Books ed.
Published/Created: New York: One World, 1996.
Related Authors: Machamer, Gene. Illustrated Hispanic American profiles.
Description: 182, [1] p.: ill.; 21 cm.
ISBN: 0345404238
Notes: "Formerly entitled The illustrated Hispanic American profiles." Includes bibliographical references (p. [183]) and indexes.
Subjects: Hispanic Americans--Biography.
LC Classification: E184.S75 M325 1996
Dewey Class No.: 920/.009268073 B 21

Mañana is now; the Spanish-speaking in the United States. Illustrated with photos.
Edition Information: [1st ed.]
Published/Created: New York, Atheneum, 1973.
Description: 184 p. illus. 25 cm.
Notes: Bibliography: p. 175-177.
Subjects: Hispanic-Americans--Juvenile literature.
LC Classification: E184.S75 E37
Dewey Class No.: 301.45/16/8073

Manrique, Jaime, 1949-
Latin moon in Manhattan / Jaime Manrique.

Edition Information: 1st ed.
Published/Created: New York: St.
Martin's Press, c1992.
Description: 212 p.; 22 cm.
ISBN: 0312071000 :
Subjects: Hispanic Americans--Fiction.
New York (N.Y.)--Fiction. Manhattan
(New York, N.Y.)--Fiction.
Genre/Form: Humorous stories.
LC Classification: PS3563.A573 L38
1992
Dewey Class No.: 813/.54 20

Manuel, Herschel Thurman, b. 1887.
Spanish-speaking children of the
Southwest: their education and the public
welfare, by Herschel T. Manuel.
Published/Created: Austin, University of
Texas Press [1965]
Description: viii, 222 p. illus., maps. 24
cm.
Notes: Bibliography: p. [209]-216.
Subjects: Hispanic Americans--
Education--Southwest, New. Children--
Southwest, New. Education--Southwest,
New. English language--Study and
teaching--Spanish speakers. Southwest,
New--Social conditions.
LC Classification: F787 .M3
Dewey Class No.: 371.98

Mardenborough, Teresa.
Hispanic heroes of the U.S.A.: teacher's
guide and black line masters for student
activity sheets / by Teresa
Mardenborough and Dennis St. Sauver.
Published/Created: St. Paul: EMC Corp.,
1976.
Related Authors: St. Sauver, Dennis,
joint author. Wheelock, Warren.
Hispanic heroes of the U.S.A.
Description: 5 p., [61] leaves: ill.; 28 cm.
Notes: The main work by W. Wheelock.
Subjects: Hispanic Americans.
LC Classification: E184.S75 M37

Dewey Class No.: 973/.04/68

Marek, Sasha Cesar.
An annotated and indexed bibliography
of documents, reports, and published
materials on Hispanics in Michigan /
compiled and annotated by Sasha Cesar
Marek.
Published/Created: [Lansing]: Michigan
Commission on Spanish Speaking
Affairs; [East Lansing]: Julian Samora
Research Institute, Michigan State
University, [1994]
Related Authors: Michigan. Commission
on Spanish Speaking Affairs. Julian
Samora Research Institute.
Description: iv, 63 p.; 28 cm.
Notes: Cover title. "May 1994". Includes
indexes.
Subjects: Hispanic Americans--
Michigan--Bibliography. Latin
Americans--Michigan--Bibliography.
LC Classification: Z1297 .M3 1994
F575.S75
Dewey Class No.: 016.9774004/68 21

Marín, Gerardo.
Research with Hispanic populations /
Gerardo Marín, Barbara VanOss Marín.
Published/Created: Newbury Park: Sage
Publications, c1991.
Related Authors: Marín, Barbara
VanOss.
Description: ix, 130 p.; 23 cm.
ISBN: 0803937202 (c) 0803937210 (p)
Notes: Includes bibliographical
references (p. 113-123) and index.
Subjects: Hispanic Americans--
Research--Methodology.
Series: Applied social research methods
series; v. 23
LC Classification: E184.S75 M38 1991
Dewey Class No.: 973/.0468 20

Martinez, Elizabeth Coonrod, 1954-
Henry Cisneros: Mexican-American

leader / Elizabeth Coonrod Martinez.
Published/Created: Brookfield, Conn.:
Millbrook Press, c1993.
Description: 32 p.: ill. (some col.); 24
cm.
ISBN: 1562943685 (lib. bdg.)
Summary: A biography of the Mexican-
American mayor of San Antonio, Texas,
who became the first Hispanic mayor of
a major United States city in 1981.
Notes: Includes bibliographical
references (p. 31) and index.
Subjects: Cisneros, Henry--Juvenile
literature. Cisneros, Henry. Mayors--
Texas--San Antonio--Biography--
Juvenile literature. Mexican American
mayors--Texas--San Antonio--Biography
Juvenile literature. Mayors. Mexican
Americans--Biography. San Antonio
(Tex.)--Politics and government--
Juvenile literature.
Series: Hispanic heritage
LC Classification: F394.S2 C565 1993
Dewey Class No.: 976.4/351063/092 B
20

Martinez, Roger D.
The Hispanic population in Colorado:
survey / prepared by Roger D. Martinez.
Published/Created: [Denver]: Colorado
Dept. of Education, 1978.
Description: 19 leaves; 28 cm.
Notes: Based on a survey conducted in
1978 by the Equal Educational Services
Unit, Colorado Dept. of Education.
Photocopy.
Subjects: Hispanic Americans--
Colorado. Hispanic Americans--
Education--Colorado. Mexican
Americans--Colorado. Mexican
Americans--Education--Colorado.
Colorado--Population.
LC Classification: F785.S75 M29 1978
Dewey Class No.: 305.868/0788

Marvis, Barbara J.
Contemporary American success stories:
famous people of Hispanic heritage /
Barbara J. Marvis; [with introduction by
Kathy Escamilla; illustrated by Barbara
Tidman].
Published/Created: [Childs, Md.]:
Mitchell Lane Publishers, c1996-<c1999
Related Authors: Tidman, Barbara.
Description: v. <1-10 >: ill., map; 25 cm.
ISBN: 1883845211 (v. 1: hardcover)
1883845203 (v. 1: softcover)
1883845238 (v. 2: hardcover)
188384522X (v. 2: softcover)
1883845254 (v. 3: hardcover)
1883845246 (v. 3: softcover)
1883845300 (v. 4: hardcover)
1883845297 (v. 4: softcover)
1883845327 (v. 5: hardcover)
1883845319 (v. 5: softcover)
1883845343 (v. 6: hardcover)
1883845335 (v. 6: softcover)
1883845408 (v. 7: hardcover)
1883845394 (v. 7: softcover)
1883845424 (v. 8: hardcover)
1883845416 (v. 8: softcover)
1883845440 (v. 9: hardcover)
1883845432 (v. 9: softcover)
1883845688 (v. 10: hardcover)
188384567X (v. 10: softcover)
Notes: Vol. <7 > by Barbara Marvis,
Melanie Cole, Tony Cantu. Vol. <8 > by
Valerie Menard, Melanie Cole Vol. <9 >
by Melanie Cole, Barbara J. Marvis,
Valerie Menard. Vol. <10 > by Barbara
Marvis ... [et al.]. Includes indexes.
Subjects: Hispanic Americans--
Biography--Juvenile literature.
Series: A Mitchell Lane multicultural
biography series
LC Classification: E184.S75 M384 1996
Dewey Class No.: 920/.009268 20

Mass communication and Hispanic
Americans: a literature review / Bradley
S. Greenberg ... [et al.].

Published/Created: [East Lansing]: Dept.
of Communication, Michigan State
University, 1980.
Related Authors: Greenberg, Bradley S.
Description: 47 p.; 28 cm.
Notes: "August, 1980."
Subjects: Hispanic Americans and mass
media.
Series: CASA (Michigan State
University. Dept. of Communication);
report no. 1.
LC Classification: P94.5.H58 M3 1980
Dewey Class No.: 305.8/68073 19

Matiella, Ana Consuelo.
The Latino family life education
curriculum series. Cultural pride
curriculum unit / Ana Consuelo Matiella.
Published/Created: Santa Cruz, CA:
Network Publications, 1988.
Related Titles: Cultural pride curriculum
unit.
Description: 182 p.; 28 cm.
ISBN: 0941816672
Notes: Bibliography: p. 181-182.
Subjects: Hispanic Americans--Ethnic
identity--Study and teaching.
LC Classification: E184.S75 M39 1988
Dewey Class No.: 375/.0084 19

McCluskey, Cynthia Perez.
Understanding latino delinquency: the
applicability of strain theory by ethnicity
/ Cynthia Perez McCluskey.
Published/Created: New York: LFB
Scholarly Publishing, 2002.
Description: vii, 289 p.: ill.; 23 cm.
ISBN: 1931202214 (alk. paper)
Contents: Introduction. Criminology and
ethnicity. Traditional strain theory.
Purpose of study. Latinos in the United
States. Summary of research goals --
Traditional strain theory. Opportunity
theory. Other extensions of strain theory.
Empirical tests of strain theory --
Ethnicity and traditional strain theory.

Ethnic differences in the strain model.
Hypotheses. Minority group differences -
- Data and methods. Sampling.
Measurement. Descriptive statistics --
Univariate and bivariate analyses. Mean
differences by ethnicity. Bivariate
relationships by ethnicity. Site specific
measures -- Testing traditional strain
theory. Structural equation modeling
with LISREL. Estimating the traditional
strain model. Estimating the modified
strain model. Analysis of site specific
measures -- Testing strain theory by
ethnicity. Estimating stacked models in
LISREL. Evaluating model fit.
Comparing models. Other interactions in
strain theory -- Discussion and
conclusion. Exposure to strain by
ethnicity. Traditional strain theory.
Modified strain theory. Site specific
measures. Estimating models by
ethnicity. Theoretical implications.
Notes: Includes bibliographical
references (p. 271-281) and index.
Subjects: Juvenile delinquency--
Research--United States. Juvenile
delinquency--United States--Cross-
cultural studies. Hispanic Americans--
Ethnic identity. Hispanic Americans--
Social conditions.
Series: Criminal justice (LFB Scholarly
Publishing LLC)
LC Classification: HV9104 .M328 2002
Dewey Class No.: 364.36/089/68073 21

McNair, Doug.
Colorado Hispanic leadership profiles:
who's who among Colorado's
outstanding leaders / [Doug and Wallace
Yvonne McNair, publishers].
Edition Information: Premier ed.
Published/Created: [Denver, CO:
Western Images Publications, c1991]
Related Authors: McNair, Wallace
Yvonne.
Description: 115 p.: ill.; 28 cm.

ISBN: 0962760013 :
Notes: Includes index.
Subjects: Hispanic Americans--
Colorado--Biography. Colorado--
Biography.
LC Classification: F785.S75 M37 1991
Dewey Class No.: 920/.0092680788 B
20

Medford, Roberta.
Online information on Hispanics & other
ethnic groups: a survey of state agency
databases / compiled by Roberta
Medford and Eudora Loh.
Published/Created: Berkeley, Calif.:
Floricanto Press, c1986.
Related Authors: Loh, Eudora.
Description: vi, 324 p.; 23 cm.
ISBN: 0915745070 (pbk.) :
Notes: Includes index.
Subjects: Hispanic Americans--
Statistical services--Directories.
LC Classification: E184.S75 M43 1986
Dewey Class No.: 025/.06352941468073
19

Meier, Kenneth J., 1950-
The politics of Hispanic education: un
paso pa'lante y dos pa'tras / Kenneth J.
Meier, Joseph Stewart, Jr.
Published/Created: Albany: State
University of New York Press, c1991.
Related Authors: Stewart, Joseph, 1951-
Description: xix, 275 p.: ill.; 24 cm.
ISBN: 0791405079 (alk. paper)
0791405087 (pbk.: alk. paper)
Notes: Includes bibliographical
references (p. [227]-266) and index.
Subjects: Hispanic Americans--
Education. Discrimination in education--
United States. Educational equalization--
United States. Education and state--
United States.
Series: SUNY series, United States
Hispanic studies
LC Classification: LC2670 .M45 1991

Dewey Class No.: 370/.8968073 20

Meier, Matt S.
Notable Latino Americans: a
biographical dictionary / Matt S. Meier;
with Conchita Franco Serri and Richard
A. Garcia.
Published/Created: Westport, Conn.:
Greenwood Press, 1997.
Related Authors: Franco Serri, Conchita.
Garcia, Richard A., 1941-
Description: xv, 431 p.: ill.; 24 cm.
ISBN: 0313291055 (alk. paper)
Notes: Includes bibliographical
references and index.
Subjects: Hispanic Americans--
Biography--Dictionaries.
LC Classification: E184.S75 M435 1997
Dewey Class No.: 920/.009268 20

Meltzer, Milton, 1915-
The Hispanic Americans / by Milton
Meltzer; illustrated with photographs by
Morrie Camhi & Catherine Noren.
Edition Information: 1st ed.
Published/Created: New York: Crowell,
c1982.
Description: 149 p.: ill.; 24 cm.
ISBN: 0690041101: 069004111X (lib.
bdg.) :
Summary: Discusses the social and
economic problems faced by twelve
million Hispanic Americans who live
and work in the United States today.
Notes: Includes index. Bibliography: p.
141-144.
Subjects: Hispanic Americans--Social
conditions--Juvenile literature. Hispanic
Americans--Economic conditions--
Juvenile literature. Hispanic Americans.
LC Classification: E184.S75 M44 1982
Dewey Class No.: 305.8/68/073 19

Menard, Valerie.
The Latino holiday book: from Cinco de
Mayo to Dia de los Muertos-- the

celebrations and traditions of Hispanic-Americans / Valerie Menard; foreword by Cheech Marin.
Published/Created: New York: Marlowe & Co.; [Emeryville, CA]: Distributed by Publishers Group West, c2000.
Description: xvi, 174 p.: ill.; 21 cm.
ISBN: 1569246467 (pbk.)
Notes: Includes bibliographical references (p. [163]-165).
Subjects: Festivals--United States. Hispanic Americans--Social life and customs.
LC Classification: GT4803 .M45 2000
Dewey Class No.: 394.26/089/68073 21

Meyer, Nicholas E.
Biographical dictionary of Hispanic Americans / Nicholas E. Meyer.
Edition Information: 2nd ed.
Published/Created: New York: Facts on File, c2001.
Description: p. cm.
ISBN: 0816043310 (pbk.) 0816043302 (alk. paper)
Notes: Includes bibliographical references (p.) and index.
Subjects: Hispanic Americans--Biography--Dictionaries.
LC Classification: E184.S75 M49 2001
Dewey Class No.: 920/.009268/073 21

Meyer, Nicholas E.
The biographical dictionary of Hispanic Americans / Nicholas E. Meyer.
Published/Created: New York: Facts on File, c1997.
Description: x, 242 p.: ill.; 25 cm.
ISBN: 0816032807 (alk. paper)
Summary: Profiles over 100 Hispanic Americans who have made major contributions to American culture.
Notes: Includes bibliographical references (p. 237-238) and index.
Subjects: Hispanic Americans--Biography--Dictionaries--Juvenile

literature. Hispanic Americans--Biography--Dictionaries.
LC Classification: E184.S75 M49 1997
Dewey Class No.: 920/.009268073 B 20

Milkman, Ruth, 1954-
Voices from the front lines: organizing immigrant workers in Los Angeles / Ruth Milkman and Kent Wong; translated by Luis Escala Rabadan.
Published/Created: Los Angeles, CA: Center for Labor Research and Education, UCLA, c2000.
Related Authors: Wong, Kent.
Description: 44, 44 p: ill.; 23 cm.
ISBN: 0892151889
Notes: English and Spanish.
Subjects: Alien labor--Labor unions--Organizing--California--Los Angeles. Hispanic Americans--Employment--California--Los Angeles.
LC Classification: HD6490.O72 U653 2000

Minnesota's Hispanic community: a profile.
Published/Created: Saint Paul, MN: Minnesota Spanish Speaking Affairs Counci l, [1989]
Related Authors: Minnesota. Spanish Speaking Affairs Council.
Description: xiv, 60 p.: ill., maps; 28 cm.
Notes: Bibliography: p. 57-60. "May 1989."
Subjects: Hispanic Americans--Minnesota.
LC Classification: E184.S75 M55 1989

Miyares, Marcelino.
Models of political participation of Hispanic-Americans / Marcelino Miyares.
Published/Created: New York: Arno Press, 1980.
Description: 182 p.: ill.; 24 cm.
ISBN: 040513164X
Notes: Originally presented as the

author's thesis, Northwestern University, 1974. Bibliography: p. 163-168.
Subjects: Hispanic Americans--Illinois--Chicago--Politics and government. Mexican Americans--Illinois--Chicago--Politics and government. Puerto Ricans--Illinois--Chicago--Politics and government. Cuban Americans--Illinois--Chicago--Politics and government. Chicago (Ill.)--Politics and government--1951-
Series: Hispanics in the United States
LC Classification: F548.9.S75 M59 1980
Dewey Class No.: 323.1/16872/077311

Molino, Robert A.
The Hispanic, consumer--employee--contributor / by Robert A. Molino.
Published/Created: [Pico Rivera, Calif.] (7700 Serapis Ave., Los Angeles 90660): [Linda's Mexican Food Products, c1982]
Description: 63 p.: ill.; 28 cm.
Subjects: Hispanic American consumers. Hispanic Americans.
LC Classification: HC110.C6 M58 1982
Dewey Class No.: 658.8/348 19

Moller, Sharon Chickering.
Library service to Spanish speaking patrons: a practical guide / Sharon Chickering Moller.
Published/Created: Englewood, Colo.: Libraries Unlimited, 2001.
Description: xix, 207 p.; 24 cm.
ISBN: 1563087197 (pbk.)
Notes: Includes bibliographical references (p. 191-202) and index.
Subjects: Hispanic Americans and libraries. Libraries--Special collections--Hispanic Americans. Hispanic Americans--Information services. Hispanic Americans--Library resources. Hispanic Americans--Databases.
LC Classification: Z711.8 .M65 2001
Dewey Class No.: 027.6/3 21

Moncada, Alberto, 1931-
Los hispanos en la política norteamericana / Alberto Moncada, Juan Olivas.
Published/Created: Madrid: Instituto de Cooperación Iberoamericana, [1989?]
Related Authors: Olivas, Juan.
Description: 274 p.; 24 cm.
ISBN: 8472325199
Notes: "ICI, Instituto de Cooperación Iberoamericana, Quinto Centenario." Includes bibliographical references p. (264-266) and index.
Subjects: Hispanic Americans--Politics and government. United States--Politics and government--1981-1989.
Series: Colección hispana.
LC Classification: E184.S75 M646 1989

Montes, Fermín S.
Dreams can become a reality / Fermín S. Montes.
Published/Created: Roswell, N.M. (P.O. Box 1915, Roswell 88201): Hall-Poorbaugh Press, c1983.
Description: ix, 184 p.: ill.; 22 cm.
Subjects: Hondo High School. Hondo Fiesta Dancers. Festivals--New Mexico--Hondo. Hispanic Americans--New Mexico--Hondo--Social life and customs. Hispanic Americans--New Mexico--Hondo--Music--History and criticism. Folk dancing--New Mexico--Hondo. Hondo (N.M.)--Social life and customs.
LC Classification: GT2711.H66 M66 1983
Dewey Class No.: 394.2/6978964 19

Montoya, Alex D.
Hispanic ministry in North America / Alex D. Montoya.
Published/Created: Grand Rapids, Mich.: Ministry Resources Library, c1987.
Description: 155 p.; 22 cm.
ISBN: 0310377412 (pbk.)

Notes: "A Zondervan publication."
Bibliography: p. 155.
Subjects: Church work with Hispanic
Americans. Hispanic Americans--
Missions.
LC Classification: BV4468.2.H57 M66
1987
Dewey Class No.: 259/.08968073 19

Moore, Joan W.
Hispanics in the United States / Joan
Moore, Harry Pachon.
Published/Created: Englewood Cliffs,
N.J.: Prentice-Hall, c1985.
Related Authors: Pachon, Harry.
Description: x, 213 p.: ill.; 23 cm.
ISBN: 013388984X (pbk.)
Notes: Includes bibliographical
references and index.
Subjects: Hispanic Americans.
LC Classification: E184.S75 M66 1985
Dewey Class No.: 305.8/68/073 19

Morales, Ed, 1956-
Living in Spanglish: the search for a new
Latino identity in America / Ed Morales.
Edition Information: 1st ed.
Published/Created: New York: St.
Martin's Press, 2002.
Description: p. cm.
ISBN: 0312262329
Subjects: Hispanic Americans--Ethnic
identity. Hispanic Americans--Social
conditions. Racially mixed people--
United States--Social conditions.
Pluralism (Social sciences)--United
States. Pan-Americanism. Ethnicity--
United States. United States--Ethnic
relations. United States--Civilization--
Hispanic influences.
LC Classification: E184.S75 M667 2002
Dewey Class No.: 305.868/073 21

Morey, Janet.
Famous Hispanic Americans / Janet
Nomura Morey and Wendy Dunn.

Edition Information: 1st ed.
Published/Created: New York:
Cobblehill Books, c1996.
Related Authors: Dunn, Wendy.
Description: xviii, 190 p.: ill.; 22 cm.
ISBN: 052565190X
Notes: Includes bibliographical
references (p. 181-186) and index.
Subjects: Hispanic Americans--
Biography--Juvenile literature. Hispanic
Americans--Biography.
LC Classification: E184.S75 M67 1996
Dewey Class No.: 920/.009268073 B 20

Mortality of Hispanic populations: Mexicans,
Puerto Ricans, and Cubans in the United
States and in the home countries / edited
by Ira Rosenwaike.
Published/Created: New York:
Greenwood Press, 1991.
Related Authors: Rosenwaike, Ira, 1936-
Description: xvi, 221 p.; 25 cm.
ISBN: 0313275009 (alk. paper)
Notes: Includes bibliographical
references (p. 203-215) and index.
Subjects: Hispanic Americans--
Mortality. Mortality--United States.
Mortality--Mexico. Mortality--Puerto
Rico. Mortality--Cuba.
Series: Studies in population and urban
demography, 0147-1104; no. 6
LC Classification: HB1335 .M677 1991
Dewey Class No.: 304.6/4/08968 20

Motto, Sytha.
Madrid and Christmas in New Mexico /
Sytha Motto.
Published/Created: Albuquerque, N.M.:
Alpha Printing, c1973 (1981 printing)
Description: x, 76 p.: ill.; 24 cm.
ISBN: 0937268097
Subjects: Christmas--New Mexico--
Madrid. Pueblo dance. Indian dance--
New Mexico. Hispanic Americans--New
Mexico--Madrid--Social life and
customs. Latin Americans--New

Mexico--Madrid--Social life and customs. Madrid (N.M.)--History. Madrid (N.M.)--Social life and customs. LC Classification: GT4986.N6 M67 Dewey Class No.: 394.2/68282/0978956 19

Multicultural theatre II: contemporary Hispanic, Asian, and African-American plays / edited and with a critical introduction by Roger Ellis. Edition Information: 1st ed. Published/Created: Colorado Springs, Colo.: Meriwether Pub., c1998. Related Authors: Ellis, Roger, 1943 May 18- Description: xi, 379 p.; 22 cm. ISBN: 1566080428 Subjects: American drama--Minority authors. Hispanic Americans--Drama. Asian Americans--Drama. Afro-Americans--Drama. Ethnic groups--Drama. Minorities--Drama. LC Classification: PS627.M5 M85 1998 Dewey Class No.: 812/.54080920693 21

Murillo, Louis C. Directory, hispanic resources in Michigan, 81. Published/Created: Grand Rapids, Mich. (P.O. Box 1605, Grand Rapids 49501): Directory, Hispanic Resources, [1982?] Description: 59 p.; 22 cm. Notes: Cover title. Bibliography: p. [41]-54. Subjects: Hispanic Americans--Michigan--Societies, etc. Directories. Michigan--Directories. LC Classification: F575.S75 M87 1982 Dewey Class No.: 977.4/00468/0025 19

Najjar, Matthew F. Anthropometric data and prevalence of overweight for Hispanics, 1982-84. Published/Created: Hyattsville, Md.: U.S. Dept. of Health and Human Services, Public Health Service, Centers for Disease Control, National Center for Health Statistics; Washington, D.C.: For sale by the Supt. of Docs., U.S. G.P.O., [1989] Related Authors: Kuczmarski, Robert J. National Center for Health Statistics (U.S.) Description: iii, 106 p.; 28 cm. ISBN: 0840604033 Notes: Written by Matthew F. Najjar and Robert J. Kuczmarski. "March 1989." Bibliography: p. 8-9. Subjects: Obesity--United States--Statistics. Hispanic Americans--Health and hygiene--Statistics. Hispanic Americans--Anthropometry--Statistics. Nutrition surveys--United States. Anthropometry--United States--statistics. Ethnology--United States. Hispanic Americans. Obesity--occurrence--United States. Series: Vital and health statistics. Series 11, Data from the national health survey; no. 239 DHHS publication; no. (PHS) 89-1689 LC Classification: RA407.3 .A347 no. 239 RA645.O23 Dewey Class No.: 362.1/0973/021 s 362.1/963/98/00973021 19 Govt. Doc. No.: HE 20.6209:11/239

Naylor, Robert K. Wisconsin's population change, 1990-1994, by race and Hispanic origin. Published/Created: Madison, WI: Wisconsin Dept. of Administration, Division of Energy and Intergovernmental Relations, Demographic Services Center, [1997] Related Authors: Wisconsin. Demographic Services Center. Description: [81] p.: ill., maps; 28 cm. Notes: Cover title. "These data formed the basis of a poster presentation by Robert Naylor at the Upper Midwest

Conference on Demographics for Policy Makers held in Minneapolis, Minnesota on April 7-8, 1997"--P. [2] of cover. "May 1997."
Subjects: Minorities--Wisconsin--Population--Statistics. Hispanic Americans--Wisconsin--Population--Statistics. Wisconsin--Population--Statistics.
LC Classification: HA715 .N39 1997
Govt. Doc. No.: A.3/2:R 32/1994 widocs

New directions for Latino public policy research / edited by Harriett Romo.
Published/Created: Austin, Tex. (Student Services Bldg. 4.120, Austin 78712): IUP/SSRC Committee for Public Policy Research on Contemporary Hispanic Issues, Center for Mexican American Studies, University of Texas at Austin, 1990.
Related Authors: Romo, Harriet. IUP/SSRC Committee for Public Policy Research on Contemporary Hispanic Issues. Inter-University Program for Latino Research. Social Science Research Council (U.S.)
Description: iii, 101 p.; 28 cm.
Notes: "Projects funded by the Inter-University Program for Latino Research and the Social Science Research Council." Includes bibliographical references and index.
Subjects: Hispanic Americans--Economic conditions. Hispanic Americans--Government policy.
LC Classification: E184.S75 N48 1990
Dewey Class No.: 320/.6/08968073 20

New Jersey population by race, Spanish origin, and age group, 1980 / State Data Center.
Published/Created: Trenton, N.J.: State of New Jersey, Dept. of Labor, Division of Planning and Research, Office of Demographic and Economic Analysis,

[1982]
Related Authors: New Jersey State Data Center.
Description: 72 p.; 22 x 28 cm.
Notes: "March 1982."
Subjects: Ethnology--New Jersey--Statistics. Hispanic Americans--New Jersey--Statistics. Age distribution (Demography)--New Jersey--Statistics. New Jersey--Population--Statistics. New Jersey--Census, 1980. United States--Census, 20th, 1980.
LC Classification: HA525 .N493 1982
Dewey Class No.: 312/.93/09749 19

New World: young Latino writers / edited and with an introduction by Ilan Stavans.
Published/Created: New York: Delta, 1997.
Related Authors: Stavans, Ilan.
Description: 296 p.; 20 cm.
ISBN: 0385313691
Notes: Includes bibliographical references (p. [294]-296).
Subjects: American literature--Hispanic American authors. Hispanic Americans--Literary collections. American literature--20th century.
LC Classification: PS508.H57 N48 1997
Dewey Class No.: 813/.54080868 20

New York State Hispanics: a challenging minority / Governor's Advisory Committee for Hispanic Affairs.
Published/Created: [New York, N.Y.]: The Committee, [1985?]
Related Authors: New York (State). Governor's Advisory Committee for Hispanic Affairs.
Description: xiii, 433, [25] p.: ill.; 28 cm.
Notes: Cover title. Bibliography: p. 429-432.
Subjects: Hispanic Americans--Government policy--New York (State) New York (State)--Social policy.
LC Classification: F130.S75 N49 1985

Dewey Class No.: 353.97470081/468 19

Newton, Frank (Frank Cota-Robles)
Hispanic mental health research: a
reference guide / Frank Newton, Esteban
L. Olmedo, Amado M. Padilla.
Published/Created: Berkeley: University
of California Press, c1982.
Related Authors: Olmedo, Esteban L.
Padilla, Amado M.
Description: 685 p.; 26 cm.
ISBN: 0520041666
Notes: Includes index.
Subjects: Hispanic Americans--Mental
health--Abstracts. Hispanic Americans--
Mental health services--Abstracts.
LC Classification: RC451.5.H57 N48
1982
Dewey Class No.: 362.2/08968073 19

Nickles, Greg, 1969-
The Hispanics / Greg Nickles.
Edition Information: 1st ed.
Published/Created: New York: Crabtree,
c2001.
Description: 32 p.: ill. (some col.), col.
maps; 28 cm.
ISBN: 0778701867 (RLB) 0778702006
(pbk.)
Notes: Includes index.
Subjects: Hispanic Americans--History--
Juvenile literature. Hispanic Americans--
History. United States--Civilization--
Hispanic influences--Juvenile literature.
North America--Relations--Latin
America--Juvenile literature. Latin
America--Relations--North America--
Juvenile literature. United States--
Civilization--Hispanic influences. North
America--Relations--Latin America.
Latin America--Relations--North
America.
Series: We came to North America
LC Classification: E184.S75 N53 2001
Dewey Class No.: 973/.0468 21

No longer a minority: Latinos and social
policy in California / David E. Hayes-
Bautista ... [et al.].
Published/Created: Los Angeles: UCLA
Chicano Studies Research Center, c1992.
Related Authors: Hayes-Bautista, David
E., 1945- University of California, Los
Angeles. Chicano Studies Research
Center.
Description: xvi, 47 p.: ill.; 29 cm.
ISBN: 0895510928 :
Notes: Includes bibliographical
references (p. 45-47).
Subjects: Hispanic Americans--
California--Social conditions. California-
-Social conditions. California--Social
policy.
LC Classification: F870.S75 N6 1992
Dewey Class No.: 305.868/0794 20

Noche buena: Hispanic American Christmas
stories / edited by Nicolás Kanellos.
Published/Created: Oxford [England];
New York: Oxford University Press,
2000.
Related Authors: Kanellos, Nicolás.
Description: 370 p.: ill.; 22 cm.
ISBN: 019513527X (alk. paper)
0195135288 (pbk.: alk. paper)
Notes: Includes bibliographical
references (p. 365-367) and index. Prose
in English, some translated from
Spanish; poetry in English and Spanish.
Subjects: Christmas--Literary
collections. American literature--
Hispanic American authors. Hispanic
American literature (Spanish)--
Translations into English. Hispanic
Americans--Literary collections.
Christmas--United States.
LC Classification: PS509.C56 N63 2000
Dewey Class No.: 810.8/0334 21

Nosotros: the Hispanic people of Oregon:
essays and recollections / edited by
Erasmo Bamboa and Carolyn M. Buan.

Published/Created: Portland, Ore.:
Oregon Council for the Humanities,
c1995.
Related Authors: Gamboa, Erasmo.
Buan, Carolyn M. Oregon Council for
the Humanities.
Description: 160 p.: ill. (some col.),
maps, ports; 28 cm.
ISBN: 1880377012 :
Contents: What's in a name / Carlos
Blanco -- Hispanics in Oregon / Richard
W. Slatta -- A personal search for
Oregon's Hispanic history / Erasmo
Bamboa -- Spanish explorers in the
Oregon country / Herbert K. Beals --
Vaqueros on the high desert rangeland /
Bob Boyd -- The Bracero Program /
Erasmo Gamboa -- El Movimiento:
Oregon's Mexican-American civil rights
movement / Erasmo Gamboa -- National
and state legislative reforms of the 1980s
/ Daniel P. Santos -- Social policy and
the Oregon Hispanic community /
Antonio Sanchez -- Spanish language
rights and law in Oregon / Steven W.
Bender -- Hispanic businesses in
Oregon: a growing force / Kent Patterson
-- Today's latino university students:
identity, dreams and struggles / Mary
Romero and Donna Wong -- Raiz, rama
y flor: artists of Latin-American descent
in Oregon / Cheryl Hartup --
Celebrations and festivals / Eliza Buch
and Nancy Nusz -- The Mixtecs' annual
3,000-mile journey / Lourdes de León --
Honeymoon in Oregon: reflections on
cultural change / Susan U. Cabello --
Listening to the people, a collection of
oral histories -- Reflections of a Peruvian
immigrant: the letter that was never sent
/ Efrain Diaz-Horna.
Notes: Includes bibliographical
references (p. 158-159).
Subjects: Hispanic Americans--Oregon.
LC Classification: F885.S75 N67 1995

Dewey Class No.: 979.5/00468 21

Novas, Himilce.
Everything you need to know about
Latino history / Himilce Novas.
Edition Information: Rev. ed.
Published/Created: New York: Plume,
c1998.
Description: xv, 352 p.: map; 21 cm.
ISBN: 0452279917
Notes: Includes bibliographical
references (p. 326-338) and index.
Subjects: Hispanic Americans--History.
LC Classification: E184.S75 N69 1998
Dewey Class No.: 973/.0468073 21

Novas, Himilce.
The Hispanic 100: a ranking of the
Latino men and women who have most
influenced American thought and culture
/ Himilce Novas.
Published/Created: New York: Carol
Pub. Group, c1995.
Description: xv, 495 p.: ports.; 26 cm.
ISBN: 0806516518
Notes: "A Citadel Press book." Includes
index.
Subjects: Hispanic Americans. United
States--Civilization--Hispanic influences.
LC Classification: E169.1 .N77 1995
Dewey Class No.: 920/.009268 B 20

Oboler, Suzanne.
Ethnic labels, Latino lives: identity and
the politics of (re)presentation in the
United States / Suzanne Oboler.
Published/Created: Minneapolis:
University of Minnesota Press, c1995.
Description: xxi, 226 p.; 24 cm.
ISBN: 0816622841 0816622868 (pbk.)
Notes: Includes bibliographical
references (p. [203]-217) and index.
Subjects: Hispanic Americans--Ethnic
identity. Hispanic Americans--Name.
LC Classification: E184.S75 O27 1995

Dewey Class No.: 305.868/073 20

Ochoa, George.
Atlas of Hispanic-American history /
George Ochoa.
Published/Created: New York, N.Y.:
Facts on File, 2001.
Description: p. cm.
ISBN: 0816036985 (hardcover: acid free
paper) 0816041296 (pbk.: acid free
paper)
Notes: Includes bibliographical
references and index.
Subjects: Hispanic Americans--History.
Hispanic Americans--History--Maps.
LC Classification: E184.S75 O287 2001
Dewey Class No.: 973/.0468 21

Ochoa, George.
The New York Public Library amazing
Hispanic American history: a book of
answers for kids / George Ochoa.
Published/Created: New York: John
Wiley, c1998.
Description: 192 p.: ill., maps; 23 cm.
ISBN: 047119204X (pbk.: acid-free
paper)
Summary: Consists of questions and
answers about Latinos, revealing the
common history which unites them while
also showing how they differ depending
upon their country of origin.
Notes: "A Stonesong Press book."
Includes bibliographical references (p.
[182]-183) and index.
Subjects: Hispanic Americans--History--
Miscellanea--Juvenile literature.
Children's questions and answers.
Hispanic Americans--Miscellanea.
Questions and answers.
LC Classification: E184.S75 O29 1998
Dewey Class No.: 973/.0468 21

Officer, James E.
Arizona's Hispanic perspective: a
research report / prepared by the

University of Arizona.
Published/Created: [Phoenix, Ariz.] (802
Arizona Title Bldg., Phoenix 85003):
Arizona Academy, 1981.
Related Authors: University of Arizona.
Arizona Academy. Arizona Town Hall
(38th: 1981: Rio Rico, Ariz.)
Description: 235 p.: maps; 28 cm.
Notes: At head of 38th Arizona Town
Hall. Bibliography: p. 223-235.
Subjects: Mexican Americans--Arizona--
Social conditions. Mexican Americans--
Arizona--History. Hispanic Americans--
Arizona--Social conditions. Hispanic
Americans--Arizona--History. Arizona--
Social conditions. Arizona--History.
LC Classification: F820.M5 O35
Dewey Class No.: 305.8/68/0791 19

Officer, James E.
Hispanic Arizona, 1536-1856 / James E.
Officer.
Published/Created: Tucson: University
of Arizona Press, c1987.
Description: xx, 462 p.: ill.; 24 cm.
ISBN: 0816509816 (alk. paper) :
Notes: Maps on lining papers. Includes
index. Bibliography: p. [409]-434.
Subjects: Hispanic Americans--Arizona--
History. Hispanic Americans--Arizona--
Genealogy. Arizona--History. Arizona--
Genealogy.
LC Classification: F820.S75 O33 1987
Dewey Class No.: 979.1/00468 19

Olmos, Edward James.
Americanos: Latino life in the United
States = La vida Latina en los Estados
Unidos / Edward James Olmos, Lea
Ybarra, Manuel Monterrey; preface by
Edward James Olmos; introduction by
Carlos Fuentes.
Edition Information: 1st ed.
Published/Created: Boston: Little,
Brown, c1999.
Related Authors: Ybarra, Lea.

Monterrey, Manuel.
Description: 176 p.: ill. (some col.); 31
cm.
ISBN: 0316649090 (pbk.) 0316649147
(hc)
Notes: Text in English and Spanish.
Subjects: Hispanic Americans--Social
life and customs--Pictorial works.
Hispanic Americans--Social conditions--
Pictorial works. Hispanic Americans--
Social life and customs. Hispanic
Americans--Social conditions.
LC Classification: E184.S75 O48 1999
Dewey Class No.: 305.868/073 21

O'Malley, J. Michael.
Academic growth of high school age
Hispanic students in the United States /
InterAmerica Research Associates; J.
Michael O'Malley; prepared for the
Center for Education Statistics under
contract OE 300-84-0195 with the U.S.
Department of Education.
Published/Created: Washington, D.C.:
U.S. G.P.O., 1987.
Related Authors: InterAmerica Research
Associates. United States. Office of
Educational Research and Improvement.
Center for Education Statistics.
Description: x, 136 p.: ill.; 28 cm.
Notes: S/N 065-000-00285-0 Item 455-
F-1 (microfiche) Distributed to
depository libraries in microfiche.
"March 1987." "CS 87-359c."
Bibliography: p. 51-56.
Subjects: Hispanic Americans--
Education (Secondary) Hispanic
American students. Academic
achievement--United States. High school
students--United States--Statistics.
Series: Contractor report (United States.
Office of Educational Research and
Improvement. Center for Education
Statistics)
LC Classification: LC2670.4 .O46 1987
Dewey Class No.: 373.18/2968073 20

Govt. Doc. No.: ED 1.115:H 62/2

On new ground: contemporary Hispanic-
American plays / edited by M. Elizabeth
Osborn.
Edition Information: 1st ed.
Published/Created: New York: Theatre
Communications Group, 1987.
Related Authors: Osborn, M. Elizabeth.
Description: viii, 280 p.: ports.; 23 cm.
ISBN: 0930452682 (pbk.) :
Contents: The guitarrón / Lynne Alvarez
-- The conduct of life / Maria Irene
Fornes -- White water / John Jesusrun --
Broken eggs / Eduardo Machado -- The
house of Ramon Iglesia / José Rivera --
Roosters / Milcha Sanchez-Scott.
Subjects: American drama--Hispanic
American authors. American drama--
20th century. Hispanic Americans--
Drama.
LC Classification: PS628.H57 O5 1987
Dewey Class No.: 812/.54/0803520368
19

Ortiz, Manuel, 1938-
The Hispanic challenge: opportunities
confronting the church / Manuel Ortiz.
Published/Created: Downers Grove, Ill.:
InterVarsity Press, c1993.
Description: 194 p.: ill.; 23 cm.
ISBN: 0830817735 (alk. paper)
Notes: Includes bibliographical
references (p. [191]-194).
Subjects: Church work with Hispanic
Americans. Hispanic Americans--
Religion.
LC Classification: BV4468.2.H57 O77
1993
Dewey Class No.: 261.8/34868073 20

Orum, Lori S.
The education of Hispanics: selected
statistics / prepared by Lori S. Crum.
Published/Created: Washington, D.C.:
National Council of La Raza, [1985]

Related Authors: National Council of La Raza.
Description: 37 p.: ill.; 28 cm.
Notes: "July 1985." Includes bibliographical references (p. 33-37).
Subjects: Hispanic Americans--Education--Statistics.
LC Classification: LC2669 .O78 1985
Dewey Class No.: 371.97/68/073021 20

Pachon, Harry.
New Americans by choice: political perspectives of Latino immigrants / Harry Pachon and Louis DeSipio; with a foreword by Rodolfo O. de la Garza.
Published/Created: Boulder: Westview Press, 1994.
Related Authors: DeSipio, Louis.
Description: xv, 207 p.: ill.; 22 cm.
ISBN: 0813387949 (softcover: acid-free paper)
Notes: Includes bibliographical references.
Subjects: Hispanic Americans--Politics and government. Hispanic Americans--Social conditions. Immigrants--United States--Political activity. Immigrants--United States--Social conditions. United States--Emigration and immigration.
LC Classification: E184.S75 P334 1994
Dewey Class No.: 323/.042/08968073 20

Padilla, Raymond V.
Debatable diversity: critical dialogues on change in American universities / Raymond V. Padilla and Miguel Montiel.
Published/Created: Lanham, Md.: Rowman and Littlefield Publishers, c1998.
Related Authors: Montiel, Miguel.
Description: xxxix, 276 p.; 25 cm.
ISBN: 0847687309 (cloth: alk. paper) 0847687317 (pbk.: alk. paper)
Notes: Includes bibliographical references (p. [259]-264) and index.

Subjects: Education, Higher--Aims and objectives--United States. Minorities--Education (Higher)--United States. Hispanic Americans--Education (Higher) Universities and colleges--United States--Sociological aspects. Higher education and state--United States. Educational change--United States.
Series: Critical perspectives series
LC Classification: LA227.4 .P33 1998
Dewey Class No.: 378.73 21

Palacios, Argentina.
Standing tall: the stories of ten Hispanic Americans / by Argentina Palacios.
Published/Created: New York: Scholastic, c1994.
Related Titles: Stories of ten Hispanic Americans.
Description: 233 p.: ill.; 19 cm.
ISBN: 0590471406 (pbk.) :
Notes: Includes bibliographical references (p. 218-225) and index.
Subjects: Hispanic Americans--Biography--Juvenile literature. Hispanic Americans.
Series: Scholastic biography
LC Classification: E184.S75 P35 1994
Dewey Class No.: 920/.009268 20

Pannier, Wendy S.
With a Spanish heritage / by Wendy S. Pannier, Joan Thatcher; in consultation with Santiago Soto-Fontanez.
Published/Created: Valley Forge, Pa.: Fund of Renewal, 1975, c1974.
Related Authors: Thatcher, Joan, joint author.
Description: 23 p.; 25 cm.
Notes: Bibliography: p. 22-23.
Subjects: Hispanic Americans. Latin Americans--United States. Latin Americans. Spanish--United States.
LC Classification: E184.S75 P36 1975
Dewey Class No.: 973/.04/68

Pappas, Georgia.
Colorado's Hispanic and non-Hispanic populations: an analysis of change between 1980 and 1990: compiled from U.S. Bureau of the Census data released March, 1991 / prepared by Georgia Pappas.
Published/Created: Denver, Colo.: Latin American Research and Service Agency, c1991.
Description: 31 p.: maps; 28 cm.
Notes: "April 1991"--Cover.
Subjects: Hispanic Americans--Colorado--Census, 1980. Hispanic Americans--Colorado--Census, 1990. Colorado--Census, 1980. Colorado--Census, 1990. United States--Census, 20th, 1980. United States--Census, 21st, 1990.
LC Classification: F785.S75 P37 1991

Perrigo, Lynn Irwin.
Hispanos: historic leaders in New Mexico / by Lynn I. Perrigo.
Edition Information: 1st ed.
Published/Created: Santa Fe, NM: Sunstone Press, 1985.
Description: 94 p.: ill.; 22 cm.
ISBN: 0865340110 (pbk.) :
Notes: Includes index.
Subjects: Hispanic Americans--New Mexico--Biography. New Mexico--Biography.
LC Classification: F805.S75 P47 1985
Dewey Class No.: 978.9/00468 B 19

Perspectivas: Hispanic ministry / [edited by] Allan Figueroa Deck, Yolanda Tarango, Timothy M. Matovina.
Published/Created: Kansas City, MO: Sheed & Ward,c 1995.
Related Authors: Deck, Allan Figueroa, 1945- Tarango, Yolanda. Matovina, Timothy M., 1955-
Description: vi, 152 p.; 22 cm.
ISBN: 1556127707 (pbk.: alk. paper)

Notes: Includes bibliographical references (p. 151-152).
Subjects: Church work with Hispanic Americans. Hispanic American Catholics. Sociology, Christian (Catholic) Christianity and culture--United States.
LC Classification: BV4468.2.H57 M56 1995
Dewey Class No.: 282/.73/08968 20

Perspectives, authentic voices of Latinos / Maureen Devine Sotoohi, editor.
Published/Created: North Billerica, MA.: Curriculum Associates, Inc., 1996.
Related Authors: Sotoohi, Maureen Devine. Curriculum Associates, Inc.
Description: 96 p.: ill.; 28 cm. + teacher guide (29 p.; 28 cm.)
ISBN: 1559158220 (pbk.) 1559158239 (teacher guide)
Subjects: Hispanic Americans--History--Sources. Hispanic Americans--Literary collections. Hispanic American arts. America--Discovery and exploration--Spanish--Sources.
LC Classification: E184.S75 P47 1996
Dewey Class No.: 973/.0468 21

Petrovich, Janice.
Northeast Hispanic needs: a guide for action.
Published/Created: Washington, D.C.: ASPIRA, c1987.
Description: 2 v.: ill.; 22 x 28 cm.
Notes: Bibliography: v. 2, p. 52.
Subjects: Hispanic Americans--Northeastern States--Economic conditions.
LC Classification: F106 .P48 1987
Dewey Class No.: 362.8/46873074 19

Pickle, W. Stewart.
Developing a discipleship model for starting Hispanic congregations in South Florida [microform] / by W. Stewart

Pickle, Sr.
Published/Created: 1996.
Description: vi, 372 leaves: ill.; 29 cm.
Notes: Thesis (D. Min.)--Southwestern
Baptist Theological Seminary, 1996.
Includes bibliographical references.
Microfiche. Portland, Or.: Theological
Research Exchange Network, 1997. 1
microfiche: negative.
Subjects: Discipling (Christianity)
Church work with Hispanic Americans.
Church development, New.
LC Classification: Microfiche 98/207 (B)

Platt, Lyman De.
Hispanic surnames and family history /
Lyman D. Platt.
Published/Created: Baltimore, MD:
Genealogical Publishing Co., 1996.
Description: 349 p.; 23 cm.
ISBN: 080631480X
Notes: Includes bibliographical
references.
Subjects: Names, Personal--Spanish--
Genealogy. Hispanic Americans--
Genealogy--Bibliography. Latin
America--Genealogy--Bibliography.
LC Classification: CS2745 .P55 1996
Dewey Class No.: 929/.4/0946 20

Population by race and Hispanic origin by
age, total housing units, New Jersey,
counties and municipalities, 1990 / State
Data Center.
Published/Created: Trenton, N.J.: The
Center, [1991]
Related Authors: New Jersey State Data
Center.
Description: 163 p.; 28 cm.
Notes: At head of NJSDC 1990 census
publication. "March 1991." Chiefly
tables. "NJSDC-PH90-1."
Subjects: Minorities--New Jersey--
Statistics. Hispanic Americans--New
Jersey--Statistics. New Jersey--
Population--Statistics. United States--

Census, 21st, 1990.
LC Classification: HA521.5 1990a
Dewey Class No.: 304.6/09749/09049 20

Portales, Marco, 1948-
Crowding out Latinos: Mexican
Americans in the public consciousness /
Marco Portales.
Published/Created: Philadelphia: Temple
University Press, 2000.
Description: xiv, 209 p.: ill.; 24 cm.
ISBN: 1566397421 (alk. paper)
156639743X (pbk.: alk. paper)
Notes: Includes bibliographical
references (p. 187-195) and index.
Subjects: Mexican Americans--Public
opinion. Mexican Americans--Education.
Mexican Americans and mass media.
Hispanic Americans--Public opinion.
Hispanic Americans--Education.
Hispanic Americans and mass media.
LC Classification: E184.M5 P67 2000
Dewey Class No.: 305.86872073 21

Privett, Stephen A., 1942-
The U.S. Catholic Church and its
Hispanic members: the pastoral vision of
Archbishop Robert E. Lucey / Stephen
A. Privett.
Published/Created: San Antonio, Tex.:
Trinity University Press, c1988.
Related Titles: United States Catholic
Church and its Hispanic members.
Description: xi, 229 p.; 23 cm.
ISBN: 0939980223
Notes: Errata slip inserted. Includes
index. Bibliography: p. [201]-211.
Subjects: Lucey, Robert Emmet, 1891-
Catholic Church--United States--
Bishops--History--20th century. Church
work with Hispanic Americans--History-
-20th century. Sociology, Christian
(Catholic)--History--20th century.
Series: Trinity University monograph
series in religion; v. 9.
LC Classification: BX4705.L7956 P75

1988
Dewey Class No.: 282/.092/4 B 19

Promis, Patricia.
Habla español?: no, but I can try to help
you: practical Spanish for the reference
desk / Patricia Promis and Maria Segura
Hoopes.
Published/Created: Chicago: Reference
and Adult Services Division, American
Library Association, 1991.
Related Authors: Hoopes, Maria Segura.
Description: iii, 20 p.; 22 cm.
ISBN: 0838975240
Subjects: Spanish language--
Conversation and phrase books (for
library employees) Spanish language--
Conversation and phrase books--English.
Reference services (Libraries)--
Terminology. Hispanic Americans and
libraries--Terminology.
LC Classification: PC4120.L52 P76
1991
Dewey Class No.: 468.3/421/024092 20

Prophets denied honor: an anthology on the
Hispano church of the United States /
Antonio M. Stevens Arroyo.
Published/Created: Maryknoll, N.Y.:
Orbis Books, c1980.
Related Authors: Stevens Arroyo,
Antonio M.
Description: xvi, 379 p.: ill.; 24 cm.
ISBN: 0883443953
Notes: Includes index. Bibliography: p.
364-367.
Subjects: Catholic Church--United
States--Addresses, essays, lectures.
Hispanic Americans--Religion--
Addresses, essays, lectures.
LC Classification: BX1407.H55 P76
Dewey Class No.: 282/.73

Protestantism and Latinos in the United
States / Carlos E. Cortés, editor.
Published/Created: New York: Arno

Press, 1980.
Related Authors: Cortés, Carlos E.
Description: 473 p. in various pagings,
[11] leaves of plates: ill.; 24 cm.
ISBN: 0405131739 :
Contents: Troyer, L.E. The sovereignty
of the Spirit.--Protestant Council of the
City of New York. Dept. of Church
Planning and Research. A report on the
Protestant Spanish community in New
York City.--Haselden, K. Death of a
myth.
Notes: Reprints of 3 works originally
published between 1934 and 1964.
Includes bibliographical references.
Subjects: Hispanic Americans--Religion.
Protestant churches--United States.
Series: Hispanics in the United States
LC Classification: BR563.H57 P76 1980
Dewey Class No.: 280/.4/0896873

Quintana, Frances Leon.
Pobladores: Hispanic Americans of the
Ute frontier / Frances Leon Quintana;
with illustrations gratefully borrowed
from el arte de, the art of Rini
Templeton.
Edition Information: 2nd rev. ed.
Published/Created: Aztec, N.M.: F.L.
Quintana, c1991.
Description: xviii, 267 p.: ill.; 22 cm.
Notes: Revised ed. of: Los primeros
pobladores. Includes bibliographical
references (p.241-253) and index.
Subjects: Hispanic Americans--New
Mexico--History. Ute Indians--History.
New Mexico--History.
LC Classification: F805.S75 Q56 1991
Dewey Class No.: 978.9/00468 20

Quiroga, Jorge, 1950-
Hispanic voices: is the press listening? /
by Jorge Quiroga.
Published/Created: [Cambridge, Mass.]:
Joan Shorenstein Center, Press, Politics,
Public Policy, Harvard University, John

F. Kennedy School of Government, c1995.
Related Authors: Joan Shorenstein Barone Center on the Press, Politics, and Public Policy.
Description: 23 p.; 28 cm.
Notes: Title from cover. Includes bibliographical references (p. 18-21).
Subjects: Hispanic Americans--Press coverage. Hispanic Americans and mass media.
Series: Discussion paper (Joan Shorenstein Barone Center on the Press, Politics, and Public Policy); D-18.
LC Classification: PN4888.H57 Q57 1995

Ramírez, Gonzalo.
Multiethnic children's literature / Gonzalo Ramírez, Jr., Jan L. Ramírez.
Published/Created: Albany, N.Y.: Delmar Publishers, y1994.
Related Authors: Ramírez, Jan L.
Description: xvii, 158 p.: ill.; 23 cm.
ISBN: 0827354339
Notes: Includes index.
Subjects: Minorities--United States--Juvenile literature Bibliography. Hispanic Americans--Juvenile literature--Bibliography. Afro-Americans--Juvenile literature--Bibliography. Asian Americans--Juvenile literature--Bibliography. Indians of North America--Juvenile literature Bibliography.
LC Classification: Z1361.E4 R36 1994 E184.A1
Dewey Class No.: 016.3058/00973 20

Reindorp, Reginald Carl, 1907-
Spanish American customs, culture and personality [by] Reginald C. Reindorp.
Published/Created: Macon, Ga., Dept. of Foreign Languages, Wesleyan College, 1968.
Description: xvi, 344 p. 23 cm.
Notes: Bibliography: p. 337-344.

Subjects: Latin Americans--Psychology. Hispanic Americans--Psychology. Latin Americans--Social life and customs. Latin America--Social life and customs.
LC Classification: F1408 .R4
Dewey Class No.: 918/.03

Rendon, Gabino.
Voting behavior in a tri-ethnic community / by Gabino Rendon, Jr.
Published/Created: San Francisco: R & E Research Associates, 1977.
Description: vii, 102 p.; 28 cm.
ISBN: 0882474642 :
Cancelled ISBN: 0882474643 :
Notes: Bibliography: p. 100-102.
Subjects: Voting--Colorado. Political participation--Colorado. Hispanic Americans--Colorado.
LC Classification: JK7895 .R46
Dewey Class No.: 324/.2

Reyes, Domingo Nick.
Viva: a look at the Hispanic-Americans.
Published/Created: Washington: Distributed by DNR Associates, c1975.
Related Titles: Look at the Hispanic-Americans.
Description: 48 p.: ill.; 18 cm.
Subjects: Hispanic Americans.
LC Classification: E184.S75 R49
Dewey Class No.: 973/.04/68

Reyes, Luis, 1953-
Hispanics in Hollywood: an encyclopedia of 100 years in film and television / Luis Reyes and Peter Rubie.
Published/Created: Hollywood, Calif.: Lone Eagle Pub., 2000.
Related Authors: Rubie, Peter.
Description: xv, 592 p.: ill.; 26 cm.
ISBN: 1580650252 (pbk.)
Notes: Includes bibliographical references (p. 587-588).
Subjects: Hispanic Americans in motion pictures--Encyclopedias. Hispanic

Americans on television--Encyclopedias.
Hispanic American actors--Biography--
Dictionaries.
LC Classification: PN1995.9.H47 R49
2000
Dewey Class No.: 791.43/089/68 21

Reyes, Luis, 1953-
Hispanics in Hollywood: an
encyclopedia of film and television /
Luis Reyes and Peter Rubie.
Published/Created: New York: Garland
Pub., 1994.
Related Authors: Rubie, Peter.
Description: xx, 569 p.: ill.; 29 cm.
ISBN: 0815308272 (acid-free paper)
Notes: Includes index.
Subjects: Hispanic Americans in motion
pictures--Encyclopedias. Hispanic
Americans on television--Encyclopedias.
Hispanic American actors--Biography--
Dictionaries.
Series: Garland reference library of the
humanities; vol. 1761
LC Classification: PN1995.9.H47 R49
1994
Dewey Class No.: 791.43/08968 20

Reyes, Vinicio H.
Bicultural-bilingual education for Latino
students: a continuous progress model /
Vinicio H. Reyes.
Published/Created: New York: Arno
Press, 1978, c1975.
Description: xi, 301 p.; 24 cm.
ISBN: 0405110928 :
Notes: Originally presented as the
author's thesis, Loyola University,
Chicago, 1974. Bibliography: p. 289-
301.
Subjects: Education, Bilingual--United
States. Hispanic Americans--Education.
Latin Americans--Education--United
States.
Series: Bilingual-bicultural education in
the United States

LC Classification: LC3731 .R39 1978
Dewey Class No.: 371.9/7/6873

Rhea, Joseph Tilden.
Race pride and the American identity /
Joseph Tilden Rhea.
Published/Created: Cambridge, Mass.:
Harvard University Press, 1997.
Description: 163 p.; 22 cm.
ISBN: 0674566815 (alk. paper)
Notes: Includes bibliographical
references (p. [129]-157) and index.
Subjects: Minorities--Civil rights--
United States--History--20th century.
Indians of North America--Ethnic
identity. Asian Americans--Ethnic
identity. Hispanic Americans--Ethnic
identity. Afro-Americans--Ethnic
identity. United States--Race relations.
United States--Ethnic relations.
LC Classification: E184.A1 R46 1997
Dewey Class No.: 305.8/00973 21

Richard, Alfred Charles, 1937-
Contemporary Hollywood's negative
Hispanic image: an interpretive
filmography, 1956-1993 / Alfred Charles
Richard, Jr.
Published/Created: Westport, Conn.:
Greenwood Press, 1994.
Description: xlii, 636 p.; 25 cm.
ISBN: 0313288410 (alk. paper)
Notes: Includes indexes.
Subjects: Latin Americans in motion
pictures. Hispanic Americans in motion
pictures. Motion pictures--Catalogs.
Hollywood (Los Angeles, Calif.)--
History.
Series: Bibliographies and indexes in the
performing arts, 0742-6933; no. 16
LC Classification: PN1995.9.L37 R54
1994
Dewey Class No.: 791.43/6520368 20

R'ios-Bustamante, Antonio Jos'e.
Latinos in Hollywood / by Antonio

R'ios-Bustamante.
Published/Created: Encino, CA:
Floricanto Press; 1991.
Description: 190 p.: ill.; 28 cm.
Notes: Bibliography: p. 181-189
Subjects: Hispanic American motion
picture actors and actresses. Latin
Americans in motion pictures. Motion
pictures--United States--History.
LC Classification: ACQUISITIONS IN
PROCESS (COPIED)

Rivera, Ralph.
Latinos in Massachusetts and the 1990
U.S. census: growth and geographical
distribution / Ralph Rivera.
Published/Created: Boston: Mauricio
Gastón Institute, University of
Massachusetts at Boston, 1991.
Related Authors: Mauricio Gastón
Institute for Latino Community
Development and Public Policy.
Description: iv, 17 p.; 28 cm.
Notes: Includes bibliographical
references (p. 16-17).
Subjects: Hispanic Americans--
Massachusetts--Census, 1990.
Massachusetts--Census, 1990. United
States--Census, 21st, 1990.
Series: Publication (Mauricio Gastón
Institute for Latino Community
Development and Public Policy); no. 91-
01.
LC Classification: F75.S75 R58 1991
Dewey Class No.: 929/.3/089680744 20

Robbins, Sandra.
The firefly star: a Hispanic folk tale /
adapted by Sandra Robbins; illustrated
by Iku Oseki.
Published/Created: New York: See-
More's Workshop, c1995.
Related Authors: Oseki, Iku, ill.
Description: 31 p.: col. ill.; 23 cm.
ISBN: 1882601238 (pbk.) :
Subjects: Hispanic Americans--Folklore.

Folklore.
Series: Robbins, Sandra. See-More book.
Robbins, Sandra. See-More's workshop.
LC Classification: PZ8.1.R513 Fi 1995
Dewey Class No.: 398.23/6 E 21

Robertson, Winston.
Employment status of Spanish surnamed
Americans in the San Francisco-Oakland
SMSA / [prepared by Winston
Robertson].
Published/Created: Washington: U.S.
Equal Employment Opportunity
Commission, 1974.
Related Titles: Employment status of
Spanish surnamed Americans ...
Description: iv, 65 p.; 27 cm.
Subjects: Discrimination in employment-
-United States--Statistics. Hispanic
Americans--Employment--California--
San Francisco. Hispanic Americans--
Employment--California--Oakland.
Series: United States. Equal Employment
Opportunity Commission. Office of
Research. Research report; no. 45.
LC Classification: HD4903.5.U58 A33
no. 45
Dewey Class No.: 331.1/33/0973 s
331.1/33

Rodriguez, America.
Making Latino news: race, language,
class / by America Rodriguez.
Published/Created: Thousand Oaks,
Calif: Sage Publications, c1999.
Description: p. cm.
ISBN: 0761915516 (alk. paper)
0761915524 (alk. paper)
Contents: Introduction: what is Latino
news? -- History of U.S. Spanish
language newspapers: 1848-1970 --
History of the Hispanic audience --
Commercial ethnicity: the production
and marketing of the Hispanic audience -
- Nationhood, nationalism and ethnicity
in the making of U.S. Latino news --

Local Latino news: Los Angeles and Miami -- Bilingual and English language media -- The future of Latino news: suggestions for further research -- References.
Notes: Includes bibliographical references (p.) and index.
Subjects: Hispanic Americans--Press coverage--History. Journalism--Social aspects--United States. Hispanic American newspapers--History. Hispanic American mass media--History. Hispanic Americans and mass media. Hispanic American journalists. Ethnic press--United States.
LC Classification: PN4888.H57 R63 1999
Dewey Class No.: 070.4/84 21

Rodriguez, Clara E., 1944-
Changing race: Latinos, the census, and the history of ethnicity in the United States / Clara E. Rodriguez.
Published/Created: New York: New York University Press, c2000.
Description: xv, 283 p.; 24 cm.
ISBN: 0814775462 (cloth: alk. paper) 0814775470 (pbk.: alk. paper)
Notes: Includes bibliographical references (p. 229-263) and index.
Subjects: Hispanic Americans--Census. Hispanic Americans--Race identity. Hispanic Americans--Ethnic identity. Categorization (Psychology) Race--Social aspects--United States. Ethnology--United States. United States--Census. United States--Race relations.
Series: Critical America
LC Classification: E184.S75 R64 2000
Dewey Class No.: 305.8/00973 21

Rodriguez, David.
Latino political coalitions: struggles and challenges / by David Rodriguez.
Published/Created: New York: Routledge, 2001.

Description: p. cm.
ISBN: 0815333714
Notes: Includes bibliographical references (p.) and index.
Subjects: Hispanic Americans--Politics and government. Coalition (Social sciences) Hispanic Americans--Social conditions. United States--Ethnic relations. United States--Politics and government--1989-
Series: Latino communities
LC Classification: E184.S75 R65 2001
Dewey Class No.: 323.1/168073 21

Rodríguez, Eric.
Latinos and jobs: a review of ten states and Puerto Rico / prepared by Eric Rodríguez and Deirdre Martínez.
Published/Created: Washington, D.C.: Poverty Project, Office of Research, Advocacy, and Legislation, National Council of la Raza, c1995.
Related Authors: Martínez, Deirdre.
Description: 67 p.: ill.; 28 cm.
Notes: Includes bibliographical references (p. 65-67).
Subjects: Hispanic Americans--Employment. Hispanic Americans--Employment--Statistics. Hispanic Americans--Economic conditions. Hispanic Americans--Economic conditions--Statistics.
LC Classification: HD8081.H7 R63 1995
Dewey Class No.: 362.85/84/08968073 21

Rodriguez, Joseph.
Spanish Harlem / Joseph Rodriguez.
Published/Created: Washington, D.C.: National Museum of American Art, c1994.
Description: 101 p.: chiefly col. ill.; 24 x 26 cm.
ISBN: 188161624X :
Subjects: Hispanic Americans--New

York (State)--New York--Social life and customs. East Harlem (New York, N.Y.)--Social life and customs. New York (N.Y.)--Social life and customs. Series: American scene (Washington, D.C.); 3.
LC Classification: F128.9.S75 R63 1994
Dewey Class No.: 974.7/100468 20

Ryskamp, George R.
Tracing your Hispanic heritage / by George R. Ryskamp.
Published/Created: Riverside, Calif.: Hispanic Family History Research, 1984.
Description: xx, 954 p.: ill.; 24 cm.
Cancelled ISBN: 09613556000 :
Notes: English and Spanish.
Bibliography: p. [769]-847.
Subjects: Hispanic Americans--Genealogy--Handbooks, manuals, etc. Latin America--Genealogy--Handbooks, manuals, etc. Spain--Genealogy--Handbooks, manuals, etc.
LC Classification: E184.S75 R97 1984
Dewey Class No.: 929/.1/08968 19

Sanchez, Richard, 1954-
The great migration: from farms to cities / Richard Sanchez.
Published/Created: Edina, MN: Abdo & Daughters, c1994.
Description: 32 p.: col. ill.; 26 cm.
ISBN: 1562393359 (lib. bdg.) 1562393855 (pbk.)
Notes: Library bound edition distributed: Minneapolis: Rockbottom Books. Includes bibliographical references (p. 31) and index.
Subjects: Hispanic Americans--Migrations--Juvenile literature. Hispanic Americans--Migrations.
Series: Hispanic heritage (Edina, Minn.); v. 5.
LC Classification: E184.S75 S266 1994
Dewey Class No.: 307.2/4/08968073 20

Sandoval, Moises.
On the move: a history of the Hispanic church in the United States / Moises Sandoval; [foreword by Bishop Ricardo Ramirez].
Published/Created: Maryknoll, N.Y.: Orbis Books, c1990.
Description: xvi, 152 p.; 21 cm.
ISBN: 0883446758
Notes: Includes bibliographical references (p. 147-148) and index.
Subjects: Hispanic Americans--Religion. Hispanic American Catholics--History. United States--Church history.
LC Classification: BR563.H57 S26 1990
Dewey Class No.: 277.3/008968 20

Sandoval-Sánchez, Alberto.
José, can you see?: Latinos on and off Broadway / Alberto Sandoval-Sánchez.
Published/Created: Madison: The University of Wisconsin Press, c1999.
Description: x, 275 p.: ill.; 24 cm.
ISBN: 0299162001 (cloth: alk. paper) 0299162044 (pbk.: alk. paper)
Notes: Includes bibliographical references (233-258) and index.
Subjects: Hispanic American theater. Hispanic Americans in motion pictures. Hispanic Americans in literature.
LC Classification: PN2270.H57 S26 1999
Dewey Class No.: 792/.089/68073 21

Sanjur, Diva.
Hispanic foodways, nutrition, and health / Diva Sanjur.
Published/Created: Boston: Allyn and Bacon, c1995.
Description: xiii, 336 p.: ill.; 24 cm.
ISBN: 013390931X
Notes: Includes bibliographical references and index.
Subjects: Hispanic Americans--Nutrition. Nutrition--Social aspects. Diet--Social aspects. Food habits--Social

aspects. Hispanic Americans--Food.
Diet. Diet Surveys--United States. Food
Habits--United States. Hispanic
Americans. Nutrition.
LC Classification: TX361.H57 S26 1995
Dewey Class No.: 363.8/08968073 20

Santa Ana, Otto, 1954-
Brown tide rising: metaphors of Latinos
in contemporary American public
discourse / Otto Santa Ana.
Edition Information: 1st ed.
Published/Created: Austin, TX:
University of Texas Press, 2002.
Description: p. cm.
ISBN: 0292777663 (alk. paper)
0292777671 (alk. paper)
Notes: Includes bibliographical
references and index.
Subjects: Hispanic Americans--Public
opinion. Hispanic Americans and mass
media. Discourse analysis--United
States--Psychological aspects. Discourse
analysis--Political aspects--United
States. Hispanic Americans--Politics and
government--Public opinion.
Immigrants--United States--Public
opinion. Public opinion--United States.
United States--Ethnic relations--
Psychological aspects. United States--
Race relations--Psychological aspects.
LC Classification: E184.S75 S268 2002
Dewey Class No.: 305.868073 21

Santiago-Rivera, Azara L. (Azara Lourdes),
1952-
Counseling latinos and La Familia: a
practical guide / Azara L. Santiago-
Rivera, Patricia Arrendondo, Ma ritza
Gallardo-Cooper.
Published/Created: Thousand Oaks,
Calif.: Sage Publications, 2002.
Related Authors: Arrendondo, Patricia.
Gallardo-Cooper, Maritza.
Description: p. cm.
ISBN: 0761923292 (c) 0761923306 (p)

Notes: Includes bibliographical
references and index.
Subjects: Hispanic Americans--Mental
health services. Hispanic Americans--
Counseling of. Hispanic American
families--Counseling of. Hispanic
Americans--Family relationships.
Hispanic Americans--Mental health
services.
Series: Multicultural aspects of
counseling series; v. 17.
LC Classification: RC451.5.H57 S28
2002
Dewey Class No.:
362.2/04256/08968073 21

Saunders, Lyle.
Cultural difference and medical care; the
case of the Spanish-speaking people of
the Southwest.
Published/Created: New York, Russell
Sage Foundation, 1954.
Description: 317 p. maps, diagr., tables.
24 cm.
Notes: Bibliographical references
included in "Notes" (p. 247-283)
Subjects: Medical care--Southwest, New.
Hispanic Americans--Southwest, New.
LC Classification: RA563.S7 S3
Dewey Class No.: 610.979

Schmidt, Fred H.
Spanish surnamed American
employment in the Southwest [by] Fred
H. Schmidt.
Published/Created: [Washington, Equal
Employment Opportunity Commission;
for sale by the Supt. of Docs., U.S. Govt.
Print. Off., 1970]
Related Authors: Colorado. Civil Rights
Commission.
Description: v, 247 p. illus. 27 cm.
Notes: Prepared for the Colorado Civil
Rights Commission. Includes
bibliographical references.
Subjects: Discrimination in employment-

-Southwest, New. Hispanic Americans--
Employment--Southwest, New.
LC Classification: HD4903.5.U58 S3
Dewey Class No.: 331.1/13/09791

Schon, Isabel.
A Hispanic heritage, series II: a guide to
juvenile books about Hispanic people
and cultures / Isabel Schon.
Published/Created: Metuchen, N.J.:
Scarecrow Press, 1985.
Related Titles: Hispanic heritage, series
2. Hispanic heritage, series two.
Description: viii, 153 p.; 23 cm.
ISBN: 0810817276
Notes: Includes indexes. Bibliography: p.
119-136.
Subjects: Hispanic Americans--Juvenile
literature--Bibliography. Latin America--
Juvenile literature--Bibliography. Spain--
Juvenile literature--Bibliography.
LC Classification: Z1609.C5 S362 1985
F1408.2
Dewey Class No.: 016.98 19

Schon, Isabel.
A Hispanic heritage, series III: a guide to
juvenile books about Hispanic people
and cultures / Isabel Schon.
Published/Created: Metuchen, N.J.:
Scarecrow Press, 1988.
Related Titles: Hispanic heritage, series
3. Hispanic heritage, series three.
Description: viii, 150 p.; 23 cm.
ISBN: 0810821338
Notes: Includes indexes.
Subjects: Hispanic Americans--Juvenile
literature--Bibliography. Latin America--
Juvenile literature--Bibliography. Spain--
Juvenile literature--Bibliography.
LC Classification: Z1609.C5 S363 1988
F1408
Dewey Class No.: 016.98 19

Schon, Isabel.
A Hispanic heritage, series IV: a guide to
juvenile books about Hispanic people
and cultures / Isabel Schon.
Published/Created: Metuchen, N.J.:
Scarecrow Press, 1991.
Related Titles: Hispanic heritage, series
4. Hispanic heritage, series four.
Description: viii, 165 p.; 23 cm.
ISBN: 0810824620 (alk. paper)
Notes: Includes indexes.
Subjects: Hispanic Americans--Juvenile
literature--Bibliography. Latin America--
Juvenile literature--Bibliography. Spain--
Juvenile literature--Bibliography.
LC Classification: Z1609.C5 S364 1991
F1408
Dewey Class No.: 016.98 20

Schon, Isabel.
A Hispanic heritage: a guide to juvenile
books about Hispanic people and
cultures / Isabel Schon.
Published/Created: Metuchen, N.J.:
Scarecrow Press, 1980.
Description: ix, 168 p.; 23 cm.
ISBN: 0810812908
Notes: Includes indexes.
Subjects: Hispanic Americans--Juvenile
literature--Bibliography. Latin America--
Juvenile literature--Bibliography. Spain--
Juvenile literature--Bibliography.
LC Classification: Z1609.C5 S36
Dewey Class No.: 016.98 19

Schon, Isabel.
A Latino heritage, series V: a guide to
juvenile books about Latino people and
cultures / Isabel Schon.
Published/Created: Lanham, MD:
Scarecrow Press, c1995.
Description: viii, 201 p.; 23 cm.
ISBN: 0810830574 (cloth: alk. paper)
Notes: Includes indexes.
Subjects: Hispanic Americans--Juvenile
literature--Bibliography. Latin America--
Juvenile literature--Bibliography. Spain--
Juvenile literature--Bibliography.

LC Classification: Z1609.C5 S365 1995
F1408
Dewey Class No.: 016.972 20

Spanish-speaking people in the United States.
June Helm, editor. William Madsen,
program chairman.
Published/Created: Seattle, Distributed
by the University of Washington Press
[1969, c1968]
Related Authors: Helm, June, 1924- ed.
Description: vi, 215 p. 28 cm.
Notes: Includes bibliographies.
Subjects: Hispanic Americans--
Congresses.
Series: American Ethnological Society.
Spring Meeting. Proceedings of the ...
Annual Spring Meeting of the American
Ethnological Society; 1968.
LC Classification: E184.S75 A82
Dewey Class No.: 301.44/8

Stylistic analysis of newspaper portrayals of
Hispanic Americans in six western U.S.
communities / Donald G. Ellis ... [et al.].
Published/Created: [East Lansing]: Dept.
of Communication, Michigan State
University, [1981]
Related Authors: Ellis, Donald G.
Michigan State University. Dept. of
Communication.
Description: 18 leaves; 28 cm.
Notes: "April 1981." Bibliography: leaf
18.
Subjects: American newspapers--
Southwest, New. Hispanic Americans--
Press coverage--Southwest, New.
Readability (Literary style)
Series: CASA (Michigan State
University. Dept. of Communication);
report no. 9.
LC Classification: PN4894 .S87 1981
Dewey Class No.: 071/.9 19

Teaching Spanish to the Hispanic bilingual:
issues, aims, and methods / edited by

Guadalupe Valdés, Anthony G. Lozano,
Rodolfo García-Moya.
Published/Created: New York: Teachers
College, Columbia University, 1981.
Related Authors: Valdés, Guadalupe.
Lozano, Anthony G. García-Moya,
Rodolfo.
Description: xiii, 253 p.; 24 cm.
ISBN: 080772629X
Notes: Includes index. Bibliography: p.
235-246.
Subjects: Spanish language--Study and
teaching--United States. Hispanic
Americans--Education. Education,
Bilingual--United States.
LC Classification: PC4068.U5 T28
Dewey Class No.: 460/.4221 19

Teaching the Spanish-speaking child: a
practical guide / Jo Ann Crandall ... [et
al.].
Published/Created: Washington, D.C.:
Center for Applied Linguistics, 1981.
Related Authors: Crandall, Jo Ann.
Description: 74 p.; 23 cm.
ISBN: 0872811514
Subjects: Hispanic American children--
Education--Language arts. Latin
Americans--Education--United States.
English language--Study and teaching--
Spanish speakers.
LC Classification: LC2686.4 .T4
Dewey Class No.: 428.2/461 19

Texas Hispanic.
Published/Created: Houston, Tex.:
Association for the Advancement of
Mexican Americans, [1990-
Related Authors: Association for the
Advancement of Mexican Americans
(Houston, Tex.)
Description: v.: ill.; 28 cm. Vol. 1, no. 1-
Continued by: Texas Hispanic magazine
1086-2722 (DLC)sn 95006672
ISSN: 1055-2944
Cancel/Invalid LCCN: sn 91002664

Notes: Description based on surrogate; title from cover. SERBIB/SERLOC merged record
Subjects: Hispanic Americans--Texas--Periodicals.
LC Classification: F395.S75 T49
Dewey Class No.: 976.4/00468/005 20

The 1985 South Florida Latin market.
Published/Created: [Miami, Fla.]: Strategy Research Corp., c1985.
Related Authors: Strategy Research Corporation.
Description: ii, 82 p.; 28 cm.
Subjects: Hispanic American consumers--Florida--Miami-Dade County. Market surveys--Florida--Miami-Dade County. Household surveys--Florida--Miami-Dade County. Latin Americans--Florida--Miami-Dade County. Consumers' preferences--Florida--Miami-Dade County.
LC Classification: HC107.F62 D512 1985
Dewey Class No.: 658.8/348 19

The anthology of Hispanic literature of the United States / editor, Nicolás Kanellos; co-editors, Kenya Dworkin y Méndez ... [et al.]; coordinator, Alejandra Balestra.
Published/Created: New York; Oxford: Oxford University Press, 2001.
Related Authors: Kanellos, Nicolás. Dworkin y Méndez, Kenya. Balestra, Alejandra.
Description: p. cm.
ISBN: 0195138244
Notes: Includes index.
Subjects: American literature--Hispanic American authors. Hispanic American literature (Spanish)--Translations into English. Hispanic Americans--Literary collections. Hispanic Americans.
LC Classification: PS508.H57 A58 2001
Dewey Class No.: 810.8/0868073 21

The best for our children: critical perspectives on literacy for Latino students / edited by María de la Luz Reyes and John J. Halcón.
Published/Created: New York: Teachers College Press, c2001.
Related Authors: Reyes, María de la Luz. Halcón, John J.
Description: xiii, 258 p.: ill.; 24 cm.
ISBN: 0807740071 (alk. paper) 0807740063 (pbk.: alk. paper)
Notes: Includes bibliographical references and index.
Subjects: Hispanic Americans--Education--Social aspects. Literacy--Social aspects--United States. Language arts--Social aspects--United States. Bilingualism--Social aspects--United States.
Series: Language and literacy series (New York, N.Y.)
LC Classification: LC2672.4 .B48 2001
Dewey Class No.: 370.117/5 21

The Directory of 200: a guide to Hispanic organizations in Houston, Texas: a special edition for the Hispanic Women's Leadership Conference Committee.
Published/Created: Houston,Tex.: Aztlan Development Co., 1990.
Related Authors: Hispanic Women's Leadership Conference Committee.
Related Titles: Directory of two hundred.
Description: 33, [7] leaves; 28 cm.
Notes: Cover title. Includes index.
Subjects: Hispanic Americans--Texas--Houston--Societies, etc. Directories. Houston (Tex.)--Directories.
LC Classification: F394.H89 S753 1990
Dewey Class No.: 976.4/141100468/0025 20

The fire in our souls: quotations of wisdom and inspiration by Latino Americans / [compiled by] Rosie Gonzalez; foreword by Edward James Olmos.

Published/Created: New York: Plume,
c1996.
Related Authors: Gonzalez, Rosie.
Description: xiii, 173 p.; 21 cm.
ISBN: 0452276845
Subjects: Hispanic Americans--
Quotations.
LC Classification: PN6084.H47 F57
1996
Dewey Class No.: 081/.08968 20

The Future of Latino independent media: a
NALIP sourcebook / Chon A. Noriega,
editor.
Published/Created: Los Angeles, CA:
UCLA Chicano Studies Research Center,
2000.
Related Authors: Noriega, Chon A.,
1961-
Description: p. cm.
ISBN: 0895510960 (pbk.)
Notes: Includes bibliographical
references and index.
Subjects: Hispanic Americans and mass
media. Hispanic American mass media.
LC Classification: P94.5.H58 F88 2000
Dewey Class No.: 302.23/089/68 21

The Hispanic almanac.
Published/Created: New York, N.Y.:
Hispanic Policy Development Project,
c1984.
Related Authors: Hispanic Policy
Development Project.
Description: 164 p.: ill. (some col.); 28
cm.
ISBN: 0918911001 (pbk.)
Notes: Bibliography: p. 154.
Subjects: Hispanic Americans--Statistics.
United States--Population--Statistics.
LC Classification: E184.S75 H55 1984
Dewey Class No.: 305.8/68/073021 19

The Hispanic almanac: from Columbus to
corporate America / [edited by] Nicolás
Kanellos; foreword by Luis Valdez.

Published/Created: Detroit: Invisible Ink,
c1994.
Related Authors: Kanellos, Nicolás.
Related Titles: Hispanic-American
almanac.
Description: xxii, 644 p.: ill.; 24 cm.
ISBN: 078760030X
Notes: Abridged ed. of: The Hispanic-
American almanac. 1993. Includes
index.
Subjects: Hispanic Americans.
LC Classification: E184.S75 H557 1994
Dewey Class No.: 973/.0468 21

The Hispanic American almanac: a reference
work on Hispanics in the United States /
Nicolás Kanellos, editor.
Edition Information: 2nd ed.
Published/Created: Detroit: Gale
Research, c1997.
Related Authors: Kanellos, Nicolás.
Description: xxxi, 811 p.: ill.; 29 cm.
ISBN: 0810391651 (acid-free paper)
Notes: Includes bibliographical
references (p. 787-789) and index.
Subjects: Hispanic Americans.
LC Classification: E184.S75 H557 1997
Dewey Class No.: 973/.0468 20

The Hispanic community, the church, and the
Northeast Center for Hispanics: a report.
Edition Information: Bilingual ed., 2nd
ed.
Published/Created: New York: Northeast
Catholic Pastoral Center for Hispanics,
c1982.
Related Authors: Northeast Catholic
Pastoral Center for Hispanics (New
York, N.Y.)
Description: iv, 156 p.; 22 cm.
ISBN: 0939832054 (pbk.)
Notes: Includes bibliographical
references.
Subjects: Northeast Catholic Pastoral
Center for Hispanics (New York, N.Y.)
Hispanic Americans--Atlantic States--

Religion. Hispanic Americans--New England--Religion. Hispanic Americans--Atlantic States. Hispanic Americans--New England.
LC Classification: BX1407.H55 H57 1982
Dewey Class No.: 261.8/34868074 19

The Hispanic experience in the United States: contemporary issues and perspectives / edited by Edna Acosta-Belén and Barbara R. Sjostrom.
Published/Created: New York: Praeger, 1988.
Related Authors: Acosta-Belén, Edna. Sjostrom, Barbara R.
Description: xi, 261 p.: ill.; 24 cm.
ISBN: 0275927407 (alk. paper)
Notes: "Most of the chapters in this volume are drawn from the conference 'The Hispanic Community in the United States,' held at SUNY-Albany in the spring of 1985"--Pref. Includes index.
Bibliography: p. [243]-254.
Subjects: Hispanic Americans--Congresses.
LC Classification: E184.S75 H568 1988
Dewey Class No.: 973/.0468 19

The Hispanic experience in the United States: pastoral reflections using the catechism of the Catholic Church = La experiencia Hispana en los Estados Unidos: reflexiones pastorales con el catecismo de la Iglesia Católica.
Published/Created: Washington, D.C.: United States Catholic Conference, c1996.
Related Authors: United States Catholic Conference. Dept. of Education.
Related Titles: Principles for inculturation of the catechism of the Catholic Church.
Description: 21, 22 p.; 28 cm.
ISBN: 1555867545
Notes: Companion to: Principles for inculturation of the catechism of the Catholic Church. Includes bibliographical references. English and Spanish texts, back to back and inverted.
Subjects: Catholic Church. Catechismus Ecclesiae Catholicae. Church work with Hispanic Americans. Catechetics--Catholic Church.
LC Classification: BX1407.H55 H58 1996
Dewey Class No.: 282/.73/08968 21

The Hispanic literary companion / edited by Nicolás Kanellos.
Published/Created: Detroit: Visible Ink, c1996.
Related Authors: Kanellos, Nicolás.
Description: xxiv, 411 p.: ill.; 23 cm.
ISBN: 0787610143 (alk. paper)
Notes: Includes bibliographical references (p. 407-408) and index.
Subjects: American literature--Hispanic American authors. American literature--Hispanic American authors Bio-bibliography. American literature--20th century--Bio-bibliography. Hispanic Americans in literature--Bibliography. Authors, American--20th century--Biography. Hispanic Americans--Literary collections.
LC Classification: PS508.H57 H566 1996
Dewey Class No.: 810.9/868 B 20

The Hispanic market.
Published/Created: New York, NY: Packaged Facts, [1996]
Related Authors: Packaged Facts (Firm)
Description: xvii, 201, 55, 5 p.: ill.; 201 cm.
ISBN: 1562412272
Notes: "January 1996."
Subjects: Hispanic American consumers--United States. Hispanic Americans--Population. Market surveys--United States. Marketing research--United

States.
LC Classification: HC110.C6 H558 1996

The Hispanic outlook in higher education.
Published/Created: Fairfield, N.J.: Casto Maldonado,
Description: v.: ill.; 28 cm. Began in 1990.
Former Frequency: Monthly, <Nov. 1990-
ISSN: 1054-2337
Notes: Published: Paramus, NJ: The Hispanic Outlook in Higher Education Pub. Co., <July 1992- Description based on: Vol. 1, no. 4 (Nov. 1990); title from caption.
Additional Form Avail.: Also available by subscription via the World Wide Web.
Subjects: Hispanic Americans--Education (Higher)--Periodicals. Hispanic American college students--Periodicals.
LC Classification: LC2670.6 .H59
Dewey Class No.: 378 12

The Hispanic population in the United States.
Published/Created: Washington, D.C.: U.S. Dept. of Commerce, Bureau of the Census: For sale by the Supt. of Docs., U.S. G.P.O.,
Related Authors: United States. Bureau of the Census.
Description: v.: ill.; 28 cm.
Continues: Persons of Spanish origin in the United States (DLC)sn 93035975 (OCoLC)8620352
Notes: Description based on: Mar. 1985. Hispanic population in the United States. Advance report (DLC)sn 87043412 (OCoLC)16783935
Additional Form Avail.: Also available via the Internet from the Census Bureau web site. Address as of 10/30/00: http://www.census.gov/population/www/socdemo/hispanic.ht ml; current access is available via PURL.
Subjects: Mexican Americans--Statistics--Periodicals. Hispanic Americans--Statistics--Periodicals. Puerto Ricans--United States--Statistics--Periodicals.
Series: Current population reports. Series P-20, Population characteristics.
Govt. Doc. No.: C 3.186/14-2: C 3.186/14:992

The Hispanic presence, challenge, and commitment: a pastoral letter on Hispanic ministry, December 12, 1983 / National Conference of Catholic Bishops.
Published/Created: Washington, D.C. (1312 Massachusetts Ave., N.W., Washington 20005): United States Catholic Conference, c1984.
Description: 73 p.; 22 cm.
Notes: English and Spanish. "Publication no. 891"--P. 4 of cover. Includes bibliographical references.
Subjects: Catholic Church--Pastoral letters and charges. Hispanic Americans--Missions.
LC Classification: BV2788.H56 C37 1984
Dewey Class No.: 282/.73/08968 19

The Hispanic vote: Chicago mayoral general election, April 7, 1987.
Published/Created: Columbus, Ohio: Midwest Voter Registration Education Project, [1987]
Related Authors: Midwest Voter Registration Education Project (U.S.)
Related Titles: Chicago mayoral general election, April 7, 1987.
Description: iii, 31 leaves; 28 cm.
Subjects: Voting--Illinois--Chicago--Statistics. Hispanic Americans--Illinois--Chicago--Politics and government--Statistics. Hispanic Americans--Illinois--Chicago--Statistics. Mayors--Illinois--Chicago--Election--Statistics.

LC Classification: JS718.5 .H57 1987

The Hispanic-American almanac: a reference
work on Hispanics in the United States /
Nicolás Kanellos [editor].
Published/Created: Detroit: Gale
Research, c1993.
Related Authors: Kanellos, Nicolás.
Description: xxix, 780 p.: ill., map; 29
cm.
ISBN: 0810379449 (alk. paper)
Notes: Includes bibliographical
references (p. 753-754) and index.
Subjects: Hispanic Americans.
LC Classification: E184.S75 H557 1993
Dewey Class No.: 973/.0468 20

The Hispanic-American experience
[computer file].
Published/Created: Woodbridge, CT:
Primary Source Media, c1995.
Related Authors: De Varona, Frank.
Primary Source Media (Firm)
Description: 1 computer laser optical
disc; 4 3/4 in.
ISBN: 0892351640
Computer File Info.: Computer data and
program.
Notes: Title from disc label. "General
editors: Frank De Varona ... [et al.]"--
Jewel case insert. System requirements:
PC; CD-ROM drive. LC copy missing
documentation.
Subjects: Hispanic Americans--History.
Series: Research Publications' American
journey
LC Classification: E185.S75
Dewey Class No.: 973 12

The Hispanics, a missing link in public
policy: the official conference report of
the Spanish Speaking Peoples
Commission of Iowa, State Capitol, Des
Moines, Iowa / editors, Virginia Correa-
Jones, Alfredo Benavides, Miguel A.
Terán.

Published/Created: Des Moines, Iowa:
The Commission, [1979]
Related Authors: Correa-Jones, Virginia.
Benavides, Alfredo. Terán, Miguel A.
Spanish Speaking Peoples Commission
of Iowa.
Description: 107, [33] p.; 28 cm.
Notes: Held in Des Moines, Iowa,
October 12-13, 1979. Includes
bibliographical references.
Subjects: Hispanic Americans--Iowa--
Social conditions--Congresses. Iowa--
Social conditions--Congresses.
LC Classification: F630.S75 H57 1979
Dewey Class No.: 353.7770084/84 19

The Latino encyclopedia / editors, Richard
Chabrán and Rafael Chabrán.
Published/Created: New York: Marshall
Cavendish, c1996.
Related Authors: Chabrán, Richard.
Chabrán, Rafael.
Description: 6 v. (1821 p.): ill.; 26 cm.
ISBN: 0761401253 (set) 0761401261
(vol. 1) 076140127X (vol. 2)
0761401288 (vol. 3) 0761401296 (vol.
4) 076140130X (vol. 5) 0761401318
(vol. 6)
Notes: Includes bibliographical
references and index.
Subjects: Hispanic Americans--
Encyclopedias.
LC Classification: E184.S75 L357 1996
Dewey Class No.: 973/.0468/003 20

The Latino review of books / University at
Albany, SUNY, CELAC, Center for
Latino, Latin American, and Caribbean
Studies.
Latin Review of Books
Published/Created: Albany, NY:
CELAC, 1995-1998.
Related Authors: State University of
New York at Albany. Center for Latino,
Latin American, and Caribbean Studies.
Description: 3 v.: ill.; 28 cm. Vol. 1, no.

1 (spring 1995)-v. 3, no. 3 (winter 1998).
Former Frequency: Quarterly, 1995
Continued by: Latino(a) research review
(DLC) 00240644 (OCoLC)43794181
ISSN: 1088-3851
Cancel/Invalid LCCN: sn 95036105
Notes: Title from cover. Chiefly English,
with some articles in Spanish.
SERBIB/SERLOC merged record
Subjects: Hispanic Americans--Book
reviews--Periodicals. Latin Americans--
Book reviews--Periodicals. Caribbean
Americans--Book reviews--Periodicals.
LC Classification: E184.S75 L363
Dewey Class No.: 305.868073 20

The Latino studies reader: culture, economy,
and society / edited by Antonia Darder
and Rodolfo D. Torres.
Published/Created: Malden, Mass.:
Blackwell Publishers, 1998.
Related Authors: Darder, Antonia.
Torres, Rodolfo D., 1949-
Description: xii, 308 p.; 26 cm.
ISBN: 1557869863 (alk. paper)
1557869871 (pbk.: alk. paper)
Notes: Includes bibliographical
references and index.
Subjects: Hispanic Americans.
LC Classification: E184.S75 L3627 1998
Dewey Class No.: 305.868073 21

The multicultural Southwest: a reader / edited
by A. Gabriel Meléndez ... [et al.].
Published/Created: Tucson: University
of Arizona Press, 2001.
Related Authors: Meléndez, A. Gabriel
(Anthony Gabriel)
Description: p. cm.
ISBN: 0816522170 (alk. paper)
0816522162 (pbk.: alk. paper)
Contents: The Southwest: a definition /
D. W. Meinig -- The golden key to
wonderland / Charles Lummis -- The
Chicano homeland / John Chávez -- Dry
root in a wash / Simon Ortiz -- Sky

looms: texts of transformation and sacred
worlds / Marta Weigle and Peter White -
- Hopi Indian ceremonies / Emory
Sekaquaptewa -- Seeing with the native
eye: how many sheep will it hold? /
Barre Toelken -- Romancing Mora /
Eduardo Paz-Martinez -- You don't know
cows like I do: twentieth-century New
Mexico ranch culture / Steve Cormier --
Am / Joy Harjo -- Raisin eyes / Luci
Tapahonso -- Remembering Tewa
Pueblo houses and spaces / Rina
Swentzell -- And then I went to school:
memories of a Pueblo childhood / Joe
Suina -- Ode to the land: the Diné
perspective / Luci Tapahonso -- We're
not extinct / David Pego -- Milo maizes /
Fabiola Cabeza de Baca -- Lent in El
Paso, Texas / Alicia Gaspar de Alba --
Sunday Mass / María Herrera-Sobek --
Sombras de la jicarita / Gabriel
Meléndez -- Mexamerica / Joel Garreau -
- Mexican children get hard lesson: new
laws cut them from N.M. schools / Steve
Fainaru -- To live in the Borderlands
means you / Gloria Anzaldía -- Baroque
principles of organization in
contemporary Mexican American
Arizona / James S. Griffith -- Interview,
Jesus Martínez and Ricardo Murillo /
Denis Lynn Daly Heyck -- Legal alien /
Pat Mora -- Raising hell as well as
wheat: Papago Indians burying the
borderline / Gary Paul Nabhan --
Albuquerque learns it really is a desert
town / Bruce Selcraig -- In the belly of
the beast / Barbara Kingsolver -- The
box that broke the barrier: the swamp
cooler comes to southern Arizona / Bob
Cunningham -- Urbanization drains
reverence for water / Ted Jojola -- The
Navajos and national sacrifice / Donald
Grinde and Bruce Johansen -- Make-
believe and graffiti: envisioning New
Mexico families / Virginia Scharff --
Creating a tradition: the great American

duck race / Patricia Moore and M. Jane Young -- Roads to heaven: pilgrimage in the Southwest / Steve Fox -- Sedona and the new (age) frontier / Barbara A. Campbell -- Queen of two cultures / Leslie Linthicum -- Mythical dimensions/political reality / Rudolfo Anaya -- Jefe, todavía no saben / Jimmy Santiago Baca.
Subjects: Pluralism (Social sciences)--Southwest, New. Indians of North America--Southwest, New--Social conditions. Hispanic Americans--Southwest, New--Social conditions. Human geography--Southwest, New. Ethnicity--Southwest, New. Southwest, New--Ethnic relations. Southwest, New--Social conditions. Southwest, New--History.
LC Classification: F790.A1 M85 2001
Dewey Class No.: 979/.033 21

The New Mexican.
Published/Created: Santa Fe, N.M.: C.P. Clever, -1868.
Description: v. Began in 1863. -v. 6, no. 38 (Oct. 20, 1868).
Continues: Nuevo Mejicano (DLC)sn 96083000
Continued by: Weekly New Mexican (Santa Fe, N.M.: 1868) (DLC)sn 84020633
Notes: Section in Spanish: Novo-mejicano [sic], 1863-May 21, 1864. Section in Spanish: Nuevo-mejicano, May 27, 1864-1868. Description based on: Vol. 1, no. 32 (Aug. 8, 1863). Daily ed: Daily New Mexican (Santa Fe, N.M.: 1868), 1868.
Additional Form Avail.: Also on microfilm: Salt Lake City, Utah: Genealogical Society of Utah.
Subjects: Hispanic Americans--New Mexico--Newspapers. Santa Fe (N.M.)--Newspapers. Santa Fe County (N.M.)--Newspapers. United States New Mexico Santa Fe Santa Fe.
LC Classification: Newspaper 8813-X
Geographic Class No.: 4323 S5

The New Mexico directory of Hispanic culture / compiled and edited by Mary Montaño Army, Carol Guzmán, Juanita Wolff.
Edition Information: 1st ed.
Published/Created: Albuquerque, New Mexico: Hispanic Culture Foundation, c1990.
Related Authors: Montaño, Mary Caroline. Guzman, Carol. Wolff, Juanita.
Description: x, 111 p.: ill.; 28 cm.
ISBN: 0944725015 :
Subjects: Hispanic Americans--New Mexico--Directories. Hispanic American arts--New Mexico--Directories.
LC Classification: F805.S75 N49 1990
Dewey Class No.: 978.9/00468/0025 20

The Prentice Hall anthology of Latino literature / [edited by] Eduardo del Rio.
Edition Information: 1st ed.
Published/Created: Upper Saddle River, NJ: Prentice Hall, 2001.
Related Authors: Rio, Eduardo del, 1960-
Description: p. cm.
ISBN: 0130266876
Notes: Includes bibliographical references and index.
Subjects: American literature--Hispanic American authors. Hispanic Americans--Literary collections. Mexican Americans--Literary collections. Cuban Americans--Literary collections. Puerto Ricans--Literary collections.
LC Classification: PS508.H57 P74 2001
Dewey Class No.: 810.8/0868073 21

The quality of life for Hispanics in Michigan: a report of hearings conducted by the Michigan Commission on Spanish Speaking Affairs, July 10-August 7,

1990.
Published/Created: Lansing: Michigan
Dept. of Civil Rights, 1992.
Related Authors: Michigan. Commission
on Spanish Speaking Affairs. Michigan.
Dept. of Civil Rights.
Description: [7], 60, A-1; 28 cm.
Notes: Includes bibliographical
references (p. 59-60).
Subjects: Hispanic Americans--
Michigan--Social conditions. Hispanic
Americans--Serivces for--Michigan.
Quality of life--Michigan.
LC Classification: E184.S75 Q3 1992
Dewey Class No.: 305.8680774 21

The Spanish-American population of Denver:
an exploratory survey / conducted by the
Denver Area Welfare Council, Inc.
Published/Created: [Denver]: The
Council, [1950]
Description: v, 112 leaves; 28 cm.
Notes: "July, 1950."
Subjects: Hispanic Americans--
Colorado--Denver--Social conditions.
Hispanic Americans--Colorado--Denver-
-Economic conditions. Denver (Colo.)--
Social conditions. Denver (Colo.)--
Economic conditions.
LC Classification: F784.D49 S753 1950

The state of Hispanic girls.
Published/Created: Washington, DC:
COSSMHO Press, c1999.
Related Authors: National Coalition of
Hispanic Health and Human Services
Organizations (U.S.)
Description: iii, 70, [1] p.: ill.; 26 cm.
ISBN: 093308403X
Contents: Hispanic girls: nationwide
snapshots -- Resiliency and risky
behaviors by Hispanic girls -- Voices of
Hispanic girls, families and communities
-- Recommendations.
Notes: Includes bibliographical
references (p. 61-[71]).

Subjects: Hispanic American teenage
girls--Social conditions. Hispanic
American teenage girls--Health risk
assessment. Hispanic American teenage
girls--Mental health. Adolescent
Behavior. Health Education--methods.
Hispanic Americans. Social
Environment. Women.
LC Classification: HQ798 .S73 1999
Dewey Class No.: 305.235 21

The voice of Hispanic higher education.
Published/Created: San Antonio, TX:
HACU,
Related Authors: Hispanic Association
of Colleges and Universities.
Description: v.: ill.; 28 cm.
Continues: HACU 1089-8999 (DLC)sn
96036219 (OCoLC)32957319
ISSN: 1096-2301
Cancel/Invalid LCCN: sn 97036730
Notes: Description based on: Vol. 6, no.
1 (Jan. 1997); title from cover.
SERBIB/SERLOC merged record
Subjects: Hispanic Association of
Colleges and Universities Periodicals.
Hispanic Americans--Education
(Higher)--Periodicals.
LC Classification: LC2670.6 .V65
Dewey Class No.: 378 13

Training hispanics: implications for the JTPA
system: special report.
Published/Created: Washington, D.C.:
National Commission for Employment
Policy, [1990]
Related Titles: Implications for JTPA
system, special report.
Description: [4], 89 p.: ill.; 28 cm.
Notes: Shipping list no.: 90-116-P. Item
1089-H "January 1990." Includes
bibliographical references.
Subjects: Occupational training--United
States. Hispanic Americans--
Employment.
Series: United States. National

Commission for Employment Policy.
Report; no. 27.
LC Classification: HD5715.2 .U55 1990
Govt. Doc. No.: Y 3.Em 7/3:9/27

Trends in segregation of Hispanic students in
major school districts having large
Hispanic enrollment: final report.
Published/Created: [New York]: Aspira
of America, 1979-<1980
Related Authors: Noboa, Abdín.
Description: v. <1-2, 4-5 >; 28 cm.
Incomplete Contents: v. 1. Desegregation
and the Hispano in America -- v. 2.
Ethnographic case studies -- v. 4. Sample
III -- v. 5. Bibliography, general and
legal.
Notes: Cover title. Vols. <2, 4-5 >:
Project director, Abdín Noboa.
Subjects: Hispanic Americans--
Education. Latin Americans--Education-
-United States.
LC Classification: LC2670 .A85 1979
Dewey Class No.: 370/.8968/073 19

Twenty-five years of Hispanic literature in
the United States, 1965-1990: an exhibit,
with accompanying text / curated by
Roberta Fernández; produced and
installed by Patricia Bozeman.
Published/Created: [Houston, Tex.]:
M.D. Anderson Library, University of
Houston, [1992]
Related Authors: Fernández, Roberta.
Bozeman, Pat. University of Houston.
Libraries.
Description: 58 p.; 22 cm.
Notes: Includes bibliographical
references and indexes.
Subjects: American literature--Hispanic
American authors--History and criticism-
-Exhibitions. American literature--20th
century--History and criticism
Exhibitions. Hispanic Americans--
Intellectual life--Exhibitions.
LC Classification: PS153.H56 T88 1992

Dewey Class No.: 810.9/868 20

U.S. Hispanic perspectives: a four state
survey / [project directors, Rodolfo O. de
la Garza, Gary Freeman, Harry Pachon].
Published/Created: Claremont, CA:
Tomás Rivera Center, c1996.
Related Authors: De la Garza, Rodolfo
O. Freeman, Gary P. Pachon, Harry.
Tomás Rivera Center.
Description: 14 p.: ill.; 28 cm.
Notes: "A Tomás Rivera Center survey"-
-Cover.
Subjects: Hispanic Americans--
Attitudes. Public opinion--United States.
LC Classification: E184.S75 U2 1996

U.S. Latino literature: a critical guide for
students and teachers / edited by Harold
Augenbraum and Margarite Fernández
Olmos under the auspices of the
Mercantile Library of New York.
Published/Created: Westport, Conn.:
Greenwood Press, 2000.
Related Authors: Augenbraum, Harold.
Fernández Olmos, Margarite. Mercantile
Library Association of the City of New-
York.
Description: xv, 215 p.; 24 cm.
ISBN: 0313311374 (alk. paper)
Notes: Includes bibliographical
references and index.
Subjects: American literature--Hispanic
American authors--History and criticism-
-Handbooks, manuals, etc. Hispanic
Americans in literature--Handbooks,
manuals, etc.
LC Classification: PS153.H56 U7 2000
Dewey Class No.: 810.9/868 21

U.S. Latino literatures and cultures:
transnational perspectives / Francisco A.
Lomelí, Karin Ikas, editors.
Published/Created: Heidelberg: C.
Winter, c2000.
Related Authors: Lomelí, Francisco A.

Ikas, Karin.
Description: xxi, 333 p.: ill.; 25 cm.
ISBN: 3825310655
Notes: "Chicano Literature: 1995 and
Beyond: a Bibliography": p. [297]-315.
Includes bibliographical references.
English and Spanish contributions.
Subjects: American literature--Hispanic
American authors--History and criticism.
Hispanic Americans in literature.
Hispanic Americans--Civilization.
Series: Anglistische Forschungen; Heft
290.
LC Classification: PS153.H56 U75 2000
Dewey Class No.: 810.9/868073 21

United States Hispanic population by county,
1980.
Published/Created: [S.l.]: Market
Growth, c1982.
Description: 1 map: col.; 39 x 57 cm.
Scale Information: Scale not given.
Notes: Base map copyright by: American
Map Company, Inc. Includes insets of
Alaska and Hawaii.
Subjects: Hispanic Americans--Maps.
LC Classification: G3701.E1 1980 .M3
MLC
Geographic Class No.: 3701

Valdés, Dennis Nodín.
Barrios norteños: St. Paul and
midwestern Mexican communities in the
twentieth century / Dionicio Nodín
Valdés.
Edition Information: 1st ed.
Published/Created: Austin: University of
Texas Press, 2000.
Description: viii, 380 p.; 24 cm.
ISBN: 029278743X (cloth: alk. paper)
0292787448 (pbk.: alk. paper)
Notes: Includes bibliographical
references (p. [313]-360) and index.
Subjects: Mexican Americans--
Minnesota--Saint Paul--History--20th
century. Mexican Americans--

Minnesota--Saint Paul--Social
conditions--20th century. Hispanic
American neighborhoods--Middle West-
-Case studies. Saint Paul (Minn.)--Social
conditions--20th century.
LC Classification: F614.S4 V35 2000
Dewey Class No.: 977.6/5810046872073
21

Valdés, Dennis Nodin.
Materials on the history of Latinos in
Michigan and the Midwest: an annotated
bibliography / Dennis Nodin Valdés.
Published/Created: [S.l.]: D.N. Valdés;
Detroit, Mich: Additional copies, Wayne
State University, College of Education,
c1982.
Description: 34 p.; 23 cm.
Subjects: Hispanic Americans--
Michigan--History--Bibliography.
Hispanic Americans--Middle West--
History--Bibliography. Michigan--
Middle West--History--Bibliography.
LC Classification: Z1297 .V34 1982
F575.S75
Dewey Class No.: 016.9774/00468073
19

Valdivieso, Rafael.
U.S. Hispanics: challenging issues for
the 1990s / by Rafael Valdivieso and
Cary Davis.
Published/Created: Washington, DC
(777 14th St., NW, Washington 20005):
Population Reference Bureau, c1988.
Related Authors: Davis, Cary B.
Related Titles: US Hispanics.
Description: 16 p.: ill.; 26 cm.
Notes: Includes bibliographical
references (p. 16).
Subjects: Hispanic Americans--
Population. Hispanic Americans--
History--20th century. Hispanic
Americans--Social conditions.
Series: Population trends and public
policy; no. 17.

LC Classification: E184.S75 V34 1988
Dewey Class No.: 973/.0468 20

Valencia, Humberto.
The U.S. Hispanic market.
Published/Created: New York, N.Y.:
Find/SVP, [1984]
Related Authors: Find/SVP (Firm)
Description: 1 v. (various foliations): ill.;
29 cm.
ISBN: 0931634482 (pbk.)
Notes: "November 1984."
Subjects: Hispanic American consumers.
Hispanic Americans--Economic
conditions.
Series: A Business information report
LC Classification: HC110.C6 V35 1984
Dewey Class No.: 658.8/348 19

Valle, Victor M.
Latino metropolis / Victor M. Valle and
Rodolfo D. Torres.
Published/Created: Minneapolis:
University of Minnesota Press, c2000.
Related Authors: Torres, Rodolfo D.,
1949-
Description: xvi, 249 p.: ill., maps; 24
cm.
ISBN: 0816630291 (alk. paper)
0816630305 (pbk.: alk. paper)
Notes: Includes bibliographical
references (p. 221-233) and index.
Subjects: Hispanic Americans--
California--Los Angeles--Politics and
government. Hispanic Americans--
California--Los Angeles--Economic
conditions. Hispanic Americans--Race
identity--California--Los Angeles. Los
Angeles (Calif.)--Race relations. Los
Angeles (Calif.)--Politics and
government. Los Angeles (Calif.)--
Economic conditions.
Series: Globalization and community; v.
7
LC Classification: F869.L89 S757 2000

Dewey Class No.: 320.9794/94/08968 21

Van Ness, John R.
Hispanos in northern New Mexico:
development of corporate community
and multicommunity / John R. Van Ness.
Published/Created: New York, N.Y.:
AMS Press, c1991.
Description: ix, 300 p.; 24 cm.
ISBN: 0404194869 (alk. paper)
Notes: Includes bibliographical
references (p. 267-294) and index.
Subjects: Hispanic Americans--New
Mexico--Santa Fe Region--Social
conditions. Social structure--New
Mexico--Santa Fe Region. Santa Fe
Region (N.M.)--Social conditions.
Series: Immigrant communities & ethnic
minorities in the United States &
Canada; 76.
LC Classification: F804.S29 S758 1991
Dewey Class No.: 978.9/5600468 20

Veltman, Calvin J.
The future of the Spanish language in the
United States / by Calvin Veltman.
Published/Created: New York City (250
Park Ave. S., Suite 5000A, New York
10003): Hispanic Policy Development
Project, 1988.
Description: xviii, 133 p.: ill.; 28 cm.
Notes: Bibliography: p. 133.
Subjects: Spanish language--United
States. Bilingualism--United States.
English language--Acquisition. Spanish
language--Acquisition. Hispanic
Americans--Languages.
LC Classification: PC4826 .V45 1988
Dewey Class No.: 420/.4261/0973 19

Veltman, Calvin J.
The role of language characteristics in
the socioeconomic attainment process of
Hispanic origin men and women / Calvin
J. Veltman; Department of Sociology,
The State University of New York at

Plattsburgh, and Rassemblement en études urbaines, Université du Québec à Montréal.
Published/Created: [Washington, D.C.?]: The Center: For sale by the Supt. of Docs., U.S. G.P.O., 1980.
Related Authors: United States. Dept. of Education. State University of New York College at Plattsburgh. Dept. of Sociology. Université du Québec à Montréal. Rassemblement en études urbaines. National Center for Education Statistics.
Description: iv, 103 p.; 28 cm.
Notes: "Prepared for the National Center for Education Statistics under contract OE-300-78-0503 with the U.S. Department of Education." Contract report"--Cover. "June, 1980." "NCES 81-103." S/N 065-000-00067-9
Bibliography: p. 102-103.
Subjects: Hispanic Americans--Economic conditions. Hispanic Americans--Social conditions.
LC Classification: E184.S75 V44
Dewey Class No.: 305.8/68073 19
Govt. Doc. No.: ED 1.115:L26

Vernez, Georges.
Goal: to double the rate of Hispanics earning a bachelor's degree / Georges Vernez, Lee Mizell.
Published/Created: Santa Monica, CA: Rand Education, Center for Research on Immigration Policy, 2001.
Related Authors: Mizell, Lee. Rand Education (Institute). Program for Research on Immigration Policy (U.S.). Hispanic Scholarship Fund.
Description: xi, 48 p.; 28 cm.
ISBN: 0833030256
Notes: "Prepared for the Hispanic Scholarship Fund" -- t.p. "DB-350-HSF" -- back cover. Includes bibliographical references.
Subjects: Hispanic American college students--United States. Hispanic Americans--Education (Higher)--United States.
LC Classification: LC2670.6 .V47 2001
Dewey Class No.: 378.1/9829/68073 21

Vetter, Betty M.
Status of Hispanics in science & engineering in the United States / prepared by Betty M. Vetter; under contract with American Association for the Advancement of Science, Science Linkages in the Community Initiative.
Published/Created: Washington, D.C.: American Association for the Advancement of Science, c1995.
Related Authors: American Association for the Advancement of Science.
Description: vi, 10 p.: ill.; 28 cm.
ISBN: 0871685655
Notes: Includes bibliographical references (p. 10).
Subjects: Science--Study and teaching (Higher)--United States. Engineering--Study and teaching (Higher)--United States. Hispanic Americans--Education (Higher)
Series: AAAS publication; 95-11S
LC Classification: Q181.A1 A68 no. 95-11s Q183.3
Dewey Class No.: 500 s 508.968/073/021 21

Vigil, Angel.
Teatro!: Hispanic plays for young people / Angel Vigil.
Published/Created: Englewood, Colo: Teacher Ideas Press, 1996.
Description: xviii, 167 p.: ill.; 28 cm.
ISBN: 156308371X
Summary: Consists of fourteen scripts for classroom use based upon Hispanic culture and traditions of the American Southwest.
Notes: Includes bibliographical references.

Subjects: Hispanic Americans--Juvenile drama. Children's plays, American. Hispanic Americans--Drama. Plays.
LC Classification: PS3572.I338 T43 1996
Dewey Class No.: 812/.54 20

Vigil, Maurilio E., 1941-
Hispanics in American politics: the search for political power / Maurilio E. Vigil.
Published/Created: Lanham, MD: University Press of America, c1987.
Description: x, 147 p.; 24 cm.
ISBN: 0819161187 (alk. paper): 0819161195 (pbk.: alk. paper) :
Notes: Bibliography: p. 137-146.
Subjects: Hispanic Americans--Politics and government.
LC Classification: E184.S75 V54 1987
Dewey Class No.: 324.973/008968 19

Vigil, Maurilio E., 1941-
Hispanics in Congress: a historical and political survey / Maurilio E. Vigil.
Published/Created: Lanham, Md.: University Press of America, c1996.
Description: ix, 127 p.; 23 cm.
ISBN: 0761804749 (cloth: alk. paper) 0761804757 (pbk.: alk. paper)
Notes: Includes bibliographical references and index.
Subjects: United States. Congress--History. Hispanic Americans--Politics and government. Hispanic American legislators--History.
LC Classification: E184.S75 V543 1996
Dewey Class No.: 324/.089/68073 20

Vigil, Maurilio E., 1941-
Los patrones: profiles of Hispanic political leaders in New Mexico history / Maurilio E. Vigil.
Published/Created: Washington, D.C.: University Press of America, c1980.
Description: x, 169 p.; 22 cm.

ISBN: 0819109622: 0819109630 (pbk.) :
Notes: Includes bibliographical references.
Subjects: Hispanic Americans--New Mexico--Biography. Hispanic Americans--New Mexico--Politics and government. Politicians--New Mexico--Biography. New Mexico--Politics and government.
LC Classification: F805.S75 V53
Dewey Class No.: 920/.0092680789

Vigil, Maurilio E., 1941-
The Hispanics of New Mexico: essays on history and culture / Maurilio E. Vigil.
Published/Created: Bristol, Ind., U.S.A.: Wyndham Hall Press, c1985.
Description: iv, 113 p.; 22 cm.
ISBN: 093226901X (pbk.)
Notes: "Originally published by the Foundations Press of Notre Dame in the Scholastic monograph series"--T.p verso. Includes bibliographies.
Subjects: Hispanic Americans--New Mexico--History. Hispanic Americans--New Mexico--Social life and customs. New Mexico--History. New Mexico--Social life and customs.
LC Classification: F805.S75 V52 1985
Dewey Class No.: 978.9/00468 19

Villafañe, Eldin, 1940-
The liberating Spirit: toward an Hispanic American Pentecostal social ethic / Eldin Villafañe.
Published/Created: Grand Rapids, Mich.: W.B. Eerdmans, 1993.
Description: xiii, 257 p.; 23 cm.
ISBN: 0802807283 (pbk.: alk. paper)
Notes: Includes bibliographical references (p. [223]-257).
Subjects: Sociology, Christian. Holy Spirit. Christian ethics--Pentecostal authors. Social ethics--United States. Hispanic Americans--Religion. Hispanic American Pentecostals--Religious life.

Pentecostal churches--United States--
Doctrines.
LC Classification: BJ1251 .V55 1993
Dewey Class No.: 241/.04994/08968073
20

Villafañe, Eldin, 1940-
The liberating Spirit: toward an Hispanic
American Pentecostal social ethic / Eldin
Villafañe.
Published/Created: Lanham, Md.:
University Press of America, c1992.
Description: xi, 257 p.: ill.; 23 cm.
ISBN: 0819185329 (alk. paper)
0819185337 (pbk.: alk. paper)
Notes: Includes bibliographical
references (p. [223]-257).
Subjects: Sociology, Christian. Holy
Spirit. Christian ethics--Pentecostal
authors. Social ethics--United States.
Hispanic Americans--Religion. Hispanic
American Pentecostals--Religious life.
Pentecostal churches--United States--
Doctrines.
LC Classification: BJ1251 .V55 1992
Dewey Class No.: 241/.04994/08968073
20

Wade, Linda R.
Careers in law and politics / Linda R.
Wade.
Published/Created: Bear, Del.: Mitchell
Lane Publishers, c2002.
Description: p. cm.
ISBN: 1584150807
Summary: Examines careers in law and
politics from a Latino perspective,
focusing on the experience of Hispanic
Americans through interviews with
successful Latinos in the field.
Notes: Includes bibliographical
references and index.
Subjects: Law--Vocational guidance--
United States--Juvenile literature.
Hispanic American lawyers--Juvenile
literature. Hispanic American politicians-

-Juvenile literature. Law--Vocational
guidance. Politics, Practical--Vocational
guidance. Vocational guidance. Hispanic
Americans.
Series: Latinos at work
LC Classification: KF297.Z9 W29 2002
Dewey Class No.: 340/.023/73 21

Warren, Nancy Hunter.
Villages of Hispanic New Mexico / text
and photographs by Nancy Hunter
Warren.
Edition Information: 1st ed.
Published/Created: Santa Fe, N.M.:
School of American Research Press,
c1987.
Description: xiv, 111 p.: ill.; 29 cm.
ISBN: 0933452195: 0933452209 (pbk.) :
Notes: Bibliography: p. 109-111.
Subjects: Hispanic Americans--New
Mexico--Social life and customs.
Villages--New Mexico--Pictorial works.
New Mexico--Social life and customs.
New Mexico--Pictorial works.
LC Classification: F805.S75 W37 1987
Dewey Class No.: 978.9/00468073 19

Weigle, Marta.
Hispanic villages of northern New
Mexico / by Marta Weigle. Part II.
Bibliography.
Published/Created: Santa Fe, N.M.:
Lightning Tree, [1975?]
Related Authors: United States. Indian
Land Research Unit. Hispanic villages of
northern New Mexico.
Description: 40 p.: map; 23 cm.
ISBN: 0890160325
Notes: Originally published in the
complete text of Hispanic villages of
northern New Mexico by Indian Land
Research Unit.
Subjects: Hispanic Americans--New
Mexico--Bibliography. New Mexico--
Ethnic relations--Bibliography.
LC Classification: Z1315 .W34

F805.S75
Dewey Class No.: 016.9789/500468 19

Weigle, Marta.
The lore of New Mexico / Marta Weigle
and Peter White.
Edition Information: 1st ed.
Published/Created: Albuquerque:
University of New Mexico Press, c1988.
Related Authors: White, Peter, 1947-
Description: xiv, 523 p.: ill.; 29 cm.
ISBN: 0826309917: 0826310478 (pbk.) :
Notes: Includes indexes. Bibliography: p.
435-499.
Subjects: Folklore--New Mexico.
Hispanic Americans--Folklore. Indians
of North America--New Mexico--
Folklore. New Mexico--Social life and
customs.
Series: Publications of the American
Folklore Society. New series
(Unnumbered)
LC Classification: GR110.N6 W45 1988
Dewey Class No.: 398/.09789 19

Wheelock, Anne.
The status of Latino students in
Massachusetts public schools: directions
for policy research in the 1990s / Anne
E. Wheelock.
Published/Created: [Boston, Mass.]:
Mauricio Gastón Institute for Latino
Community Development and Public
Policy, [1990]
Description: 43 p.; 28 cm.
Notes: "October 1990"--T.p. verso.
Includes bibliographical references (p.
29-31).
Subjects: Hispanic Americans--
Education--Massachusetts. Hispanic
Americans--Education--Massachusetts--
Statistics.
Series: Publication (Mauricio Gastón
Institute for Latino Community
Development and Public Policy); no. 90-
01.

LC Classification: LC2674.M4 W47
1990

Who's who among Hispanic Americans.
Published/Created: Detroit, MI: Gale
Research, c1991-c1994.
Related Authors: Gale Research Inc.
Description: 3 v.; 29 cm. 1st ed. (1991-
92)-3rd ed. (1994-95).
ISSN: 1052-7354
Cancel/Invalid LCCN: sn 90000451
Notes: SERBIB/SERLOC merged record
Subjects: Hispanic Americans--
Biography--Directories. Hispanic
Americans--biography. Hispanic
Americans--directories.
LC Classification: E184.S75 W53
E184.S75 W36
Dewey Class No.: 920/.009268 20

Who's who in Florida's Latin community:
biographical dictionary of the Hispanics
in Florida.
Published/Created: Washington, DC:
Worldwide Reference Publications,
1986.
Related Authors: Worldwide Reference
Publications, Inc.
Description: xvi, 311 p.: ill.; 29 cm.
ISBN: 0921261004
Notes: Includes indexes.
Subjects: Cuban Americans--Florida--
Biography--Dictionaries. Hispanic
Americans--Florida--Biography--
Dictionaries. Florida--Biography--
Dictionaries.
LC Classification: E184.C97 W48 1986
Dewey Class No.: 920/.00926872910759
19

Who's who in Hispanic America for ...
Published/Created: Woodside, NY: Saito
Pub. Co., c1993-
Description: v.: ill.; 29 cm. 1993-
ISSN: 1076-5115
Notes: SERBIB/SERLOC merged record

Subjects: Hispanic Americans--
Biography--Dictionaries.
LC Classification: E184.S75 W54
Dewey Class No.: 920/.009268073 B 20

Winchester, Faith.
Hispanic holidays / by Faith Winchester.
Published/Created: Mankato, Minn.:
Bridgestone Books, c1996.
Description: 24 p.: col. ill.; 21 x 22 cm.
ISBN: 1560654570
Summary: Briefly introduces Hispanic
Americans and discusses nine Hispanic
holidays. Includes instructions for
making a piñata.
Notes: Includes bibliographical
references (p. 24) and index.
Subjects: Holidays--Latin America--
Juvenile literature. Latin Americans--
Social life and customs--Juvenile
literature. Hispanic Americans--Social
life and customs--Juvenile literature.
Holidays--Latin America. Hispanic
Americans--Social life and customs.
Series: Read-and-discover ethnic
holidays
LC Classification: GT4813.5.A2 W55
1996
Dewey Class No.: 394.2/698 20

Winter, Jonah.
Béisbol!: Latino baseball pioneers and
legends / by Jonah Winter; introduction
by Bruce Markusen Rodróguez.
Edition Information: 1st ed.
Published/Created: New York: Lee &
Low Books, c2001.
Description: 1 v. (unpaged): col. ill.; 29
cm.
ISBN: 1584300124 (hardcover)
Summary: Presents profiles of fourteen
Latino baseball players who, from 1900
through the 1960s, were pioneers of the
sport in their home countries and the
United States.
Subjects: Baseball players--Latin

America--Biography--Juvenile literature.
Baseball players--United States--
Biography--Juvenile literature. Baseball
players. Latin Americans--Biography.
Hispanic Americans--Biography.
LC Classification: GV865.A1 W555
2001
Dewey Class No.: 796.357/092/368 B 21

Zannos, Susan.
Latino entrepreneurs / Susan Zannos.
Published/Created: Bear, DE: Mitchell
Lane Publishers, 2001.
Description: p. cm.
ISBN: 1584150890
Summary: Describes what it takes to be a
successful entrepreneur, whether starting
from scratch or buying an existing
business, focusing on the unique
experiences of Hispanic Americans
through profiles of Latino business
owners.
Notes: Includes bibliographical
references and index.
Subjects: New business enterprises--
Vocational guidance--United States--
Juvenile literature. Hispanic American
youth--Vocational guidance--Juvenile
literature. Success in business--
Vocational guidance--United States
Juvenile literature. Entrepreneurship--
United States--Juvenile literature.
Hispanic American business enterprises-
-Juvenile literature. Hispanic American
businesspeople--Juvenile literature.
Business enterprises. Entrepreneurship.
Hispanic Americans. Businesspeople.
Business--Vocational guidance.
Vocational guidance.
Series: Latinos at work
LC Classification: HD62.5 .Z36 2001
Dewey Class No.: 338/.04/0896073 21

Zimmerman, Marc.
U.S. Latino literature: an essay and
annotated bibliography / Marc

Zimmerman.
Published/Created: Chicago, Ill.:
MARCH/Abrazo Press, c1992.
Related Titles: US Latino literature.
Description: 156 p.; 22 cm.
ISBN: 1877636010 :
Notes: "Revised, expanded and corrected
second edition of U.S. Latino literature:
the creative expression of a people,
commissioned and published by the
Chicago Public Library in 1990"--T.p.
verso.
Subjects: American literature--Hispanic
American authors Bibliography.
Hispanic American literature (Spanish)--
Bibliography. Hispanic Americans in
literature--Bibliography.
LC Classification: Z1229.H57 Z55 1992
PS153.H56
Dewey Class No.: 016.8108/0868 20

Zimmerman, Marc.
   U.S. Latino literature: the creative
   expression of a people: an essay and
   annotated bibliography / Marc
   Zimmerman.
   Published/Created: Chicago, Ill.:
   Chicago Public Library:, MARCH
   [Distributor], [c1989]
   Related Titles: US Latino literature.
   United States Latino literature.

Description: 90 p.; 28 cm.
ISBN: 1877636010
Subjects: American literature--Hispanic
American authors Bibliography.
Hispanic American literature (Spanish)--
Bibliography. Hispanic Americans in
literature--Bibliography.
LC Classification: Z1229.H57 Z55 1989
PS153.H56
Dewey Class No.: 016.8108/0868 20

Zuiker, Virginia Solis, 1960-
   Hispanic self-employment in the
   Southwest: rising above the threshold of
   powerty / Virginia Solis Zuiker.
   Published/Created: New York: Garland
   Publishing, 1998.
   Description: xvi, 135 p.; 23 cm.
   ISBN: 0815331983 (alk. paper)
   Notes: Includes bibliographical
   references (p. 125-131) and index.
   Subjects: Self-employed--Southwest,
   New. Hispanic Americans--Southwest,
   New--Economic conditions. Hispanic
   American business enterprises--
   Southwest, New.
   Series: Garland studies in the history of
   American labor
   LC Classification: HD8037.U5 Z85 1998
   Dewey Class No.: 331.6/368079 21

Author Index

Title Index

C

D

E

F

I

J

L

M

N

SUBJECT INDEX

W

Washington, 8, 10, 14, 18, 22, 26-28, 30, 39, 44, 46,
    47, 49, 51, 56, 58-60
Washington Region, 96
Washington, D.C., 9, 80
welfare, 18, 19, 20
whites, 5, 10, 11, 13, 16-19, 21, 23, 30, 31, 35, 66
Wisconsin, 70, 74, 75, 113, 135, 149
women, 10, 35, 49, 117, 153, 160
women authors, 117
women authors, American, 117
work ethic, 10, 18
workforce, 10, 11, 18, 30
world records, 116
World War II, 4, 57
Wyoming, 4, 42

Y

young adult literature, American, 83
young adult poetry, American, 119